UCD WOMEN'S

UNLEASHING

critiquing
Lesbian Sadomasochism
in the
Gay Nineties

FEMINISM

Pat Parker, Kathy Miriam, Anna Livia
Jamie Lee Evans, Irene Reti,
Sharon Lim-Hing, D.A. Clarke

Printed in the United States of America by McNaughton and Gunn. ISBN: 0-939821-04-4.

"Bar Conversation" by Pat Parker was included in *Jonestown and other madness* published by Firebrand Books, Ithaca, New York, in 1985, and is reprinted with permission of the publisher.

"Remember the Fire: Lesbian Sadomasochism in a Post Nazi Holocaust World" was previously published in pamphlet form by HerBooks in 1986.

Acknowledgements:
The editor would like to specially thank Julia Chapin (once again) for her invaluable editing and proofreading (some of these essays really were "beasts"); Kathy Miriam and D. A. Clarke for their intrepid editorial assistance, moral support and good humor, without which this book would not have been possible; Jamie Lee Evans for her courage in pushing me towards diversifying this anthology, and for challenging me to think about how HerBooks can continue to work towards truly multicultural feminism in the future; Shoney Sien for her support, brilliant insights, and persistence all these years; Valerie Chase, for her fine common sense and fierce opinions; and finally, all feminists who fight violence against women, everywhere.

CONTENTS

Introduction

Why another anthology critiquing lesbian sadomasochism? In an era where so many issues of dire importance to our very survival demand our attention and action, does it make sense to focus on an "internal" debate? After all, wasn't this position already articulated over ten years ago in *Against Sadomasochism*? The debate over sadomasochism seems to have stalemated into three camps—"for," "against," and a vast number of women who don't think it's worth all the fuss one way or the other.

As Kathy Miriam points out, ten years ago when *Against Sadomasochism* was written, lesbian sadomasochists were demanding inclusion as feminists. But "today they seem to be disassociating lesbianism from feminism altogether, claiming that feminist lesbianism is an unrealistic and outdated concept." In the Gay Nineties, lesbian sadomasochism has been reframed as a rebellion against feminism itself. Miriam analyzes this revisionism, and then goes much further by putting forth an internal critique of lesbian-feminism, and suggesting that "lesbian sadomasochism has moved into a space voided by political inertia (not sexual repression): a space where lesbian values have become abstracted from their historical *movement* in women's liberation struggles."

While Kathy Miriam's essay calls for a revitalization and repoliticization of feminism, D. A. Clarke places lesbian sadomasochism in the larger context of capitalism and "shrewd, calculating, manipulative commercialism." She sees the dividing line not so much as between straight and gay as between two ethics for living: "One is the 'tough-guy' laissez-faire or consumer-oriented philosophy which American industry would like us all to pursue; the other is a nascent, often inconsistent, 'Green' outlook: an awkward mix of ecological and feminist concern, anti-racist intentions, and a striving away from excess and towards responsibility and moderation." Clarke calls for the interpolation of ecological ethics into a feminism dedicated to a "concrete and political commitment to the well-being of all women and children."

Writing from the immediacy of current events, Jamie Lee Evans shows how the Rodney King beating was fueled and justified by sadomasochistic ideology. The jury "said their verdict was based on the belief that *Mr. King* was the party in control the entire time he was being beaten. They said that *Mr. King* determined how long and how severe his beating would be and that *he* was in control of the situation." Evans writes as an urban woman of color, an Asian dyke, a survivor of ritual abuse, who struggles daily to "feel good, vibrant, alive."

My own piece, "Remember the Fire," was first published in 1986 as a pamphlet. This book began when I decided it might be a good idea to reprint "Remember the Fire," not as a pamphlet, but as a small book with a couple of more up-to-date essays. For many years I have been engaged in conversations with Kathy Miriam and D. A. Clarke about lesbian sadomasochism; and since I knew they had a lot to say, I invited them to write companion pieces. Thus this book began as a collection of three essays. Through friendship networks and inspirational encounters it grew to include seven writers. The smallness and intimacy of this project lends the book a refreshing intensity and depth, but it also creates and embodies a problem endemic to lesbian publishing projects of this kind. While the final book that you hold in your hands is certainly not culturally homogenous, the collection didn't begin as a multicultural endeavor. The process by which it grew to be more diverse was sometimes painful, and I had to do a lot of thinking about racism in publishing, and tokenization of contributors. I realized that the original lack of diversity in the book was partially a result of the informal process of soliciting contributions through lesbian friendship networks which often reflect the segregation in US society. We need as a movement to think about how to subvert this defacto segregation in aspects of our communities. I continue to learn from the complex challenges of being a Jewish lesbian running a very small, marginal feminist publishing house

This small collection is a "jumping off point." There is so much more to be said. We live in a time of increasingly virulent racial and sexual violence—in Los Angeles, California, in Somalia, Bosnia, in Germany—all over the world. In what ways has this sexualized violence permeated the lesbian community? While my essay delves in-depth into an exploration of the ways that sadomasochism fueled the Holocaust, and the anti-Semitic insult sadomasochism is to Jewish women, much could be written about the racist content of sadomasochism. How does playing with slavery and torture trivialize the experience of Black women under slavery; the whipping and shackling of California Indian women in the Mission system, the torture of Latin American women in El Salvador? To what extent does sadomasochism itself power this racism, or vice versa? Some of the contributors have begun to address these questions.

I like the variety of form in this book. Kathy Miriam's and D. A. Clarke's extensive essays live side-by-side with Anna Livia's dry satirical story, "Look on the Bright Side," and Sharon Lim-Hing's "The Rules of Love," a dystopian, haunting account of two Asian lesbians trying to have an egalitarian romance in a world in which sadomasochism is mandatory. While this collection is complex and challenging, it is not an academic and detached treatise. All seven of these writers brought their passion, wit, and intelligence to their work. I hope there is something for everyone here.

In *Almanac of the Dead,* her brilliant epic novel about Indigenous resistance in the Americas, Leslie Marmon Silko (Laguna Pueblo) writes about the Destroyers—both Aztecs and Europeans—"attracted to and excited by death and the sight of blood and suffering." [Silko, p. 475] In her essay, Kathy Miriam quotes sadomasochist Jan Brown: "We dream of someone's blood on our hands, of laughing at cries for mercy." If this is our dream, of blood on our hands and no mercy, then we are surely lost. We are living in the time of the Destroyers and it seems to me we have to make a critical choice, as lesbians living in a time of such enormous change and uncertainty. As D. A. Clarke writes, "You cannot simultaneously oppose and worship violence . . . The symbols of slavery, imprisonment, torture and death have no place in the hearts of women who plan to fight for less glamorous things like dignity, life and justice."

Unleashing Feminism is ultimately presented in the spirit of hope, as an earnest plea for a revitalized, powerful feminism—in an era where earnestness is caricatured more and more as old-fashioned and silly, uncool, uptight. But in times like these I believe despair is deadly. We do not have the luxury of cynicism. We do not have the luxury of retreat. If there is any possibility of turning this polluted, woman-hating planet around toward some ecological, socially just future, time is perilously short. And despite all my frustration with the lesbian community, I still believe in the potential of lesbian-feminism to change the world. And that is why I published this book.

—*Irene Reti, March 1993*

Pat Parker

Bar Conversation

Three women were arrested for
assault recently after they beat up
a woman who put a swastika
on another woman's shoulder during
an S&M encounter.

It's something you should write about.
If you talk about it
then women will listen
and know it's ok.
Now, envision one poet sitting in a bar
not cruising
observing the interactions
and then sitting face to face
with a young woman
who wants a spokesperson for
sado-masochism
among lesbians.
The first impulse is to dismiss
the entire conversation as more
ramblings of a *SWG*

> (read Silly White Girl:
> derogatory
> characterization
> used by minorities for
> certain members of the
> caucasian race.)

The second is to run rapidly
in another direction.
Polite poets do not run,
throw up, or strike
the other person in a conversation.
What we do is let our minds ramble.

So nodding in the appropriate places
I left the bar
traveled
first to the sixties
back to the cramped living rooms
activist dykes
consciousness-raising sessions
I polled the women there
one by one
Is this what it was all about?
Did we brave the wrath of threatened bar owners
so women could wear handkerchiefs in their pockets?
One by one I asked.
Their faces faded
furrows of frowns on their brows.
I went to the halls
where we sat hours upon hours
arguing with Gay men
trying to build a united movement
I polled the people there
one by one

Is this why we did it?
Did we grapple with our own who hated us
so women could use whips and chains?
The faces faded
puzzled faces drift out of vision.
I returned to the jails
where women sat bruised and beaten
singing songs of liberation
through puffed lips
I polled the women there
one by one
Is this why we did it?
Did we take to the streets

so women can carve swastikas on their bodies?

Hundreds and hundreds of women
pass by
no, march by
chant, sing, cry
I return to the voice
the young voice in the bar
and I am angry
the vision of women playing
as Nazis, policemen, rapists
taunts me
mocks me
words drift through

it's always by consent
we are oppressed by other dykes
who don't understand
and I am back in the bar
furious
the poll is complete
no, no no no
this is not why we did it
this is not why we continue to do.

We need not play at being victim
we need not practice pain
we need not encourage helplessness
they lurk outside our doors
follow us through the streets
and claim our lives daily.
We must not offer haven
for fascists and pigs
be it real or fantasy
the line is too unclear.

Kathy Miriam

From Rage to All the Rage:
Lesbian-Feminism, Sadomasochism,
and the Politics of Memory

"What is a Lesbian?"
　　　　—Radicalesbians,"Woman-Identified-Woman"

Introduction

Any Woman Can be a Lesbian

In the early seventies a specter was haunting U.S. women's liberation feminism—the specter of lesbianism. In the 1970 manifesto, *The Woman-Identified-Woman*, the Radicalesbians wrote, "A lesbian is the rage of all women condensed to the point of explosion." "The terrible child of the women's revolution is still being born," wrote Lucia Valeska in 1975. At the juncture of women's liberation and gay/lesbian liberation movements, lesbianism emerged as a new political identity. Previously the word "dyke" had been used to scare women away from feminism:

> Lesbian is the word, the label, the condition that holds women in line. When a woman hears this word tossed her way, she knows she is stepping out of line. She knows she has crossed the terrible boundary of her sex role.[1]

But against the prevailing cultural (male) definition of lesbianism as evil, perverse and sick, *feminists* (including lesbians who came out before and during the movement) declared that women *should* step out of line and defy the boundary of their sex role. Feminists *reclaimed* lesbianism as *woman loving* and redefined woman loving as a

---

[1]Radicalesbians, "The Woman-Identified-Woman," Koedt et. al. eds., *Radical Feminism* (New York: Quadrangle, 1973).

political love inciting outraged resistance against a woman-hating culture. The tables had turned: the threat was now a promise. *Any woman can be a lesbian*, as Alix Dobkin sang.[2] The threat of this love and new political identity "spreading" was either infuriating or intoxicating, sometimes both, depending upon one's perspective. Within women's liberation movement contexts lesbian-feminism became the site of furious debate and infighting, as well as vision.

In 1993, some twenty years after the *lavender menace*—as lesbians within the movement came to be known—stirred the imagination and ire of a generation of feminists, lesbian-feminist politics has taken a decisive turn away from its women's liberationist beginnings. A notion of lesbian identity as *the rage of all women*, once celebrated as the embodiment of women's resistance to male supremacy, has given way to a new era of "hot dykes": of "sex rebels." The "sex rebel" image not only gives us the light without the heat of rebellion, but reverses the political meaning of lesbian-feminism as women loving. Sadomasochism has replaced woman loving as the most visible (public and publicized) emblem of lesbian identity.

"Real" Lesbians Today

Lesbian sadomasochism is much more than what women do in bed, it is a widespread *ideology* concerning what lesbian identity means (or doesn't mean). Lesbian sadomasochism is a cultural fantasy of what "real lesbians do and not just what the sex police or censors say we ought to do. You've never seen a lesbian nation like this one before," as one writer exudes on the back blurb of Susie "Sexpert" Bright's sex manual.[3] This dose of "realism" in the nineties looks awfully like fantasy to me, traditional male fantasy. Yet it is typically contrasted to the supposedly old-fashioned and "unrealistic" world-view of lesbian-feminists of the seventies generation discussed above (AKA the censors and sex police). Indeed, even mainstream media such as the *San Francisco Chronicle/Examiner* have jumped on the bandwagon, heralding the arrival of a new generation of lesbians who "are more adventurous . . . than their older sisters," as one writer puts it in a Nov. 1992 story about the opening of a new lesbian sex club, The Ecstacy Lounge.[4] Similar stories about this adventuresome lesbian generation have appeared in the *Chronicle/Examiner* over the past 2-5 years.[5] These mainstream publications join a trend established by at least a decade of alternative and queer media propagating what I would call the *good girl/bad girl story* of rifts between contemporary lesbians.[6]

---

[2]Alix Dobkin, *Lavender Jane Loves Women* (New York: Women's Wax Works, 1975).

[3]Susie Bright, *Susie Sexpert's Lesbian Sex World* (San Francisco: Cleis Press, 1990).

[4]Lisa M. Krieger, "Embracing a New She-donism: Sugar, Spice, Variations on 'Nice' at Lesbian Clubs," *San Francisco Chronicle*, November 8, 1992, p. d-1.

[5]See for example, Patricia Yollin, "Painting the Town Lavender," S*an Francisco Examiner Image Magazine*, March 10, 1991. 18:1.

[6]This story in the more popular media—*Out/Look, Village-Voice*, the defunct *Out/Week* etc.—both takes its cue from and gives its own credentials (of flash and hipness) to academia, where the conception of eighties debates as a battle between good girls and bad girls pretty much originated.
(Footnote Continued on Next Page)

It is not uncommon for this story to be presented as a *generational* divide between lesbians. This is how *Village Voice* writer Alisa Solomon packages the tale, in a piece headlined *Dykotomies* which juxtaposes the hedonism of today's "young" lesbians with an "older" generation's leanings towards a crusty political correctness.[7] "We've been screaming 'women's liberation' long enough. Let's do something for fun," as a dancer at a new lesbian strip joint puts it—she is quoted in a *Washington Post* article entitled, "Lesbo-A-Go-Go: Where women treat women as sex objects."[8] Liberation is out. Objectification is in. And the straight media are licking their chops over this one. Thus the *Examiner* writer of the feature on the Ecstacy Lounge is licensed to glide into the kind of adventuresome prose once "censored" by the "older" generation as objectification; she lards her piece with such descriptions as "bosomy coatcheck girl," "leggy hostesses," "feisty black woman with a 'Demand It!' T-Shirt," and "an aging Latina with giant breasts squeezed into a sequined red dress." Then, along with the "hard, coiled bodies" of "macho" dykes are patrons "impossibly young and slender . . . . a pornographer's dream." Real lesbians must be a dream come true to men lately: *a pornographer's dream*, lesbians who *are tired of screaming women's liberation*.

The story emerged as a sex-liberal response to the anti-porn movement and feminist critique of lesbian sadomasochism. For an academic sampling see: Chris Bearchell, "Why I am a gay liberationist: thoughts on sex, freedom, the family and the state," *Resources for Feminist Research/documentation sur la recherché féministe* 12:1 (March/Mars 1983), pp. 57-60; Judith Butler, "The Force of Fantasy: Feminism, Mapplethorpe, and Discursive Excess," *differences: A Journal of Feminist Cultural Studies* 2.2 (1990), pp. 105-124; Wendy Clark, "The Dyke, the Feminist and the Devil," in *Sexuality: A Reader*, ed. *Feminist Review* (London: Virago, 1987), pp. 201-215; Alice Echols, *Daring to be Bad: Radical Feminism in America 1967-1975* (Minneapolis: U of Minnesota Press, 1989), "The New Feminism of Yin and Yang," *Powers of Desire: The Politics of Sexuality*. Ed. Ann Snitow, Christine Stansell, and Sharon Thompson, (New York: Monthly Review Press, 1983), pp. 439-458, "The Taming of the Id: Feminist Sexual Politics, 1968-83," *Pleasure and Danger: Exploring Female Sexuality*. Ed. Carole S. Vance, (Boston: Routledge, Kegan and Paul, 1984), pp. 50-72; Kate Ellis, "Stories without Endings: Deconstructive Theory and Political Practice," *Socialist Review*; 1989. Shane Phelan, *Identity Politics: Lesbian-Feminism and the Limits of Community*. (Philadelphia: Temple University Press, 1989); Ann Snitow, "Pages from a Gender Diary," *Dissent* (Spring 1989); Arlene Stein, "New Social Movement Trajectories: The Decentering of Lesbian Feminism," [Lecture], *Social Movements and Cultural Politics Conference;* University of California, Santa Cruz, March 22-24, 1991.

[7] Alisa Solomon, "Dykotomies," *Village Voice* June 26, 1990, p. 39.

[8] Laura Blumenfeld, *Washington Post*, August 11, 1991, reprinted from Sunday Punch section of San Francisco Examiner. p. 2.

And Now for Something Completely Different:
Any Woman Can be a Lesbian[9]

In sharp divergence from their "older" sisters—the radical lesbians of the seventies who rose up in confrontation with men, today's lesbians seem overcome by a mood of reconciliation. Everywhere the message is the same: any woman can be a lesbian, even if she fucks men. The logic, honed gradually in the eighties with a resurgent sex liberation agenda, reaches its conclusion in the queer melting pot politics that rule the day. Lesbian nation has given way to queer nation, where anything goes. Thus Scott Tucker exults in a recent issue of *Social Text*: "It's an open secret that men and women active in ACT UP . . . and Queer Nation are having sex together in unpredictable patterns . . . Splendid: this is hedonism with a conscience, and one practical prefiguration of utopia."[10] But *whose* utopia is this? For *whom* is it splendid? Three guesses. Under a new sexual pluralism an old sexual dualism is thinly veiled: heterosexuality. Today heterosexuality is advanced under the rubric of a kind of polymorphous sexuality, more liberatory of course than the rigid, old fashioned, lesbian-feminism.

Thus former lesbian-feminist Jan Clausen's account of taking a male lover in a 1989 feature of the queer national glossy, *OUT/LOOK*:

> At this moment in the dialectic heterosexuality ironically represents for me the anarchic power of the erotic, in contrast to the bourgeois respectability of a stable lesbian family unit.[11]

But to which "dialectic" is Clausen referring? Surely she cannot be implying that heterosexuality has become less dangerous for women? Far from having evolved into a benign, erotic choice, the heterosexual institution remains an ever-reliable source of the major forms of violence against women today.[12] The construction of a "bourgeois lesbianism" contrasted to a "anarchic" heterosexuality is a breathtaking reversal of social reality, and indeed conveniently glosses over the *history* of lesbian-feminism as critique and opposition, and an attempt to really create something different from institutionalized heterosexuality.

---

[9]My insight into this new 1990s meaning for "any woman can be a lesbian" was inspired by Linda Hooper, who distributed an extremely witty protest pamphlet entitled "Lesbians Do Not Exist," at the Santa Cruz, California 1992 Gay/Lesbian/Bisexual Pride Day March satirizing the new inclusiveness of "lesbian" identity today.

[10]Scott Tucker, "Gender, Fucking, and Utopia: An Essay in Response to John Stoltenberg's *Refusing to Be a Man*," *Social Text* 27 (1991): pp. 3-34.

[11]Jan Clausen, "My Interesting Condition," *OUT/LOOK* 7 (Winter 1990), p. 15.

[12] According to FBI homicide data, 34% of all female homicide victims were killed by husbands or boyfriends between 1976 and 1987. A 1988 study concluded that domestic violence is the largest cause of injury to women in the U.S., greater than rape, car accidents and mugging *combined*. (Flitcraft & Hasselt. "Violence among Intimates: Epidemiological Review,") *Handbook of Family Violence* (New York: Plenum Press pub. corp., 1988) pp. 293-318). Another study reports that "more than 1,000 women per year, or 4 per day" are killed by husbands or male partners. Black Women's Health Project, *Vital Signs*. no. 3 (Oct. 1991).

Any woman can be a lesbian: originally a threat to heterosexuality, the idea has been reversed to signify its political/ethical opposite, namely, that any "woman," whether bisexual, even heterosexual, and yes, even male (witness the advent of *transgender nation!*), can be a lesbian. What is queer? Queer is the identity of all lesbians confused to the point of dilution.

Clausen's tale is no aberration from the good girl/bad girl story of lesbian debates over pornography and sadomasochism. Lesbian sadomasochism and the myth of the *sex rebel* dyke are primary catalysts of the trend in which lesbian-feminism is figured as the conservative older relation of her "younger," more adventuresome sisters. It sets the scene, so to speak, for the kind of fantasy indulged by Clausen, the fantasy of heterosexuality as liberation from (radical) lesbianism.

I'm Not Your Mother

The so-called generation gap between old and new lesbians is an explanation of a political struggle which glosses over the complexity of debates among lesbians and feminists over the issue of sadomasochism and pornography, and the relation of sexual violence to the institution of heterosexuality. Casting lesbian-feminism in the role of "mother," this story is not only revisionist (in that it revises the real terms of the debate), but pernicious. Thus another "queer" writer with a "lesbian past" joins the chorus and invokes her defection as follows:

> Privately, I like to ram feminism—it's disappointed me . . . . Feminism is sort of like your mother: you can't get rid of it, but how do you get beyond its limitations?[13]

The two dominant motifs of lesbian sadomasochist fantasy are displayed here, one being feminism as Mother, the other being how "mother" might be treated in a pornographer's dream: "ram her." Bellamy's choice of words, I'd argue, is not accidental but goes with the rhetorical flow made so "hip" with the help of queer publications such as *OUT/LOOK*, and merely reflects the prevailing climate of sexualized violence. How adventuresome. As Jamie Lee Evans puts it, "I think the older sisters were more adventuresome. They tried to change the world."[14] But changing the world is less and less an option in these contexts; in the "realist" frame of sadomasochist fantasy, patriarchy is increasingly assumed to be an unshakable given. The only remaining adventure is the oldest patriarchal feat in the book: ramming "the mother"—rebelling *against feminism.*

---

[13]Dodie Bellamy, "Mrs. America at the Congress of Dreams," (from a presentation given at the "Queer Perspectives" panel at OutWrite '91, the second National Lesbian and Gay Writers Conference), *OUT/LOOK* summer 1991.

[14]Conversation, Nov. 1992.

O.K., You Consent, So What?

Radical feminists continue to argue that pornography is a system of sexual violence which destroys women's lives.[15] Lesbian sadomasochists (most of whom are also pro-pornography) claim that there is a clear line between sadomasochist sexual practices, based on *consent,* and sexual violence. They claim that consent makes all the difference. Agreed. But the question, as I see it, is not whether sadomasochist sexual practices are based on consent. For me the question is, what is lesbian sadomasochism consenting to? Does lesbian sadomasochism itself constitute consent to a culture of sexual violence? The issue then becomes, how do we activate a culture of *dissent* to rape culture?

I agree that there is a difference between sexual violence and sadomasochism. Sadomasochism is not rape. But a parallel point, rarely accepted by lesbian sadomasochists, is also true: there is a clear line between thinking critically about lesbian sadomasochism on the one hand, and censorship on the other. I agree that sadomasochism (unlike pornography and other systems of sexual violence) should not be legally regulated. Lesbian sadomasochists, however, tend to blur this line and squelch critical thinking by screaming "censorship" and "sex police" whenever feminists attempt to articulate a *connection* between sadomasochist sexuality and rape culture. The implications of redefining radical critique/debate as censorship are scary. Who is now being censored? Who is speaking? Take, for example, the publication of this book and how unusual it is in contrast to the regular publication and promotion of lesbian sadomasochism—in academic conferences, mainstream media and alternative media, as well as in the social events and discourses of contemporary lesbian/gay communities.

Despite what I would call a *suppression* of radical/lesbian-feminist thought and practice in a wide range of U.S. lesbian-feminist contexts, advocates of lesbian sadomasochism see radical feminism as hegemonic: as the orthodox, dominant form of feminism that needs to be rebelled against. Within the frame of this fantasy, radical/lesbian-feminism has no content *except* as a repressive "political correctness": real political differences are seen as little more than divisive tactics. Even feminists attempting to take a so-called "middle ground" subscribe to this fantasy when the focus of discussion becomes "divisions" between feminists rather than the issue of pornography and sadomasochism. While these divisions *are* immobilizing to feminism today, and that *is* sad, I have more grief over what divides us: the reality of sexual violence. The popularity of lesbian sadomasochism far exceeds the power of any attempt to critique, let alone suppress it. The real problem is not "divisions between feminists" but the triumph of an ideology which has popularized sadomasochism and *marginalized radical/lesbian-feminism.*

---

[15]And we have to argue this against the insistence that porn is "just" ideology, comparable to other violent "representations" of women in the media. But porn is a multi-billion dollar industry based on men's trafficking in women which uses the women who are "represented," and produces specific kinds of images for a specific type of consumer and consumption. No other product in the world is made exclusively for men, and exclusively for men to jack off to.

Changing the Scene

My purpose in writing the present essay is to voice dissent to the going story of the lesbian sadomasochist debate. It is an attempt to re-appropriate the terms of the debate, which are currently framed within the scene of the lesbian sadomasochist fantasy itself: the good girls vs. the bad. I feel that feminist lesbianism has been demeaned: robbed of its meaning. The task, as I see it, is to regain that meaning, specifically the historical meaning of resistance in lesbian-feminist contexts. In 1978 Adrienne Rich observed that, "We are now for the first time at a point of fusing lesbianism and feminism. And this is precisely the thing that patriarchy has most to dread, and will do all in its power to keep us from grasping."[16] To me the popularity of lesbian sadomasochism is a sign of some success in this patriarchal venture. Lesbian sadomasochism is about, above all else, a radical cleavage between feminism and lesbianism. Not only does lesbian sadomasochism represent a split between lesbian and feminist identity, but its fantasy of the old guard vs. the new establishes a redefinition of *lesbianism* as a *rebellion against feminism*. This, of course, is a reversal not only of recent seventies lesbian history but of the original lesbian sadomasochists' strategy: to claim inclusion as feminists. This was the crux of the debate in, for example, the anthology *Against Sadomasochism*: were sadomasochist lesbians feminist or not?[17] At that point they demanded recognition; but today they seem to be dissociating lesbianism from feminism altogether, claiming that feminist lesbianism is an unrealistic and outdated concept. This historical shift—and the way it is (mis)represented by advocates of lesbian sadomasochism—is what impels me to write a critique of lesbian sadomasochism at a time when most lesbian radical feminists would rather get on with the task of organized political resistance. But resistance is the point of this essay. In my view, the debate over sadomasochism must be located in a deeper struggle, the struggle to clarify and re-invigorate lesbian-feminism.

Lesbian sadomasochism cannot be understood except in the context of an ongoing contest over the meaning of lesbian identity. There has never been, of course, any monolithic, seamless entity identifiable as Lesbian Feminism or The Lesbian Community. Lesbian-feminism has *always* been a contested identity—and hopefully it always will be. As a political identity lesbian-feminism is dynamic and shifting, the product of both political dialogue among dykes and the cultural spaces and practices we are still in the process of collectively shaping. Nevertheless, to say that an identity should be dynamic is not to say that it ought to remain open to *any* and *every* challenge or change whatsoever.

Even in the debates in the seventies, a common thread of agreement was sustained throughout the fractious disagreements, a factor which sharply differentiates those debates from the sadomasochism debates of the eighties and nineties. What was being debated in the seventies was the political meaning of lesbian identity *in relation to what was widely regarded as a common task:* overthrowing male supremacy. Within this broadly conceived but (to my mind) still crucial goal, there was a diversity of opinion

---

[16] "The Meaning of Our Love for Women is What We Have Constantly to Expand," *On Lies, Secrets, and Silence: Selected Prose 1966-1978* (New York: Norton, 1979), p. 226.

[17] See Linden et. al. eds., *Against Sadomasochism: A Radical Feminist Analysis* (East Palo Alto, CA: Frog in the Well Press, 1982).

about the best possible strategy and the question of how, if at all, lesbianism played a part.

Critique as Self-Reflexive

The approach I take in the present essay is *self-reflexive* critique, by which I mean that my argument against lesbian sadomasochism includes reflection upon the position from which I'm arguing it, namely lesbian-feminist ideology. I advocate here an approach which does not take lesbian-feminism as a timeless identity but as a historical project, not yet fully realized. A self-reflexive critique, in my opinion, is crucial to reinvigorating lesbian-feminist ideology, to rethink it in order to extend it but at the same moment to confront its internal stumbling blocks to radical vision.

The difficulty of attempting a reflexive and internal critique is, of course, the difficulty of critiquing a position which is already so marginalized. Surrounded by external hostile forces everywhere, it seems justifiable to remain silent about our internal weaknesses. We are not slow to critique *individual* lesbian/radical feminists, but typically do so in the name of a position that remains fairly rigid, unquestioned. But I think it is possible and desirable to remain righteous and still debate the meaning and worth of various lesbian/radical feminist ideologies, practices and political stances, thereby strengthening and clarifying the grounds of a radical lesbian-feminist strategy for women's liberation.

This essay will be divided into two sections: Part I, "What's so bad about lesbian sadomasochism," presents what I'm calling the revisionist paradigm of lesbian-feminist ideology, the "good girl/bad girl story." What is "bad" about lesbian sadomasochism, I argue, is that it demeans radical lesbian-feminism and does so in such a way that it absorbs everything into the frame of its fantasy, including the debate itself. Within this frame there is no outside to the culture of sadomasochism.

Part II, "What's so good about lesbian-feminism," opens up a self-critical dialogue with respect to the meaning of lesbian-feminism. I want to argue that lesbian-feminism is a historically unique attempt to create something outside the patriarchal "realism" which lesbian sadomasochism consents to as inevitable. At stake is the meaning of resistance. Thus the focus of my critique will be to question the extent to which, in aspiring to create a new reality, lesbian-feminists have embraced "idealism."[18] Furthermore I will argue that idealist notions of change have limited our vision, confining us to an individualist perspective on social transformation. I will advocate a *collective* practice of personal transformation as a strategy for decolonizing our psyches in a sadomasochist culture.

---

[18] I will be invoking two senses of idealism in these pages. On the one hand there is the positive aspiration towards creating an elsewhere to patriarchal reality: idealism as in having visionary ideals. On the other hand there is a tendency among some radical feminists/lesbians to subscribe to an idealism which is a *product* of patriarchal (western, capitalist) ideologies, namely the individualist world view that all change is rooted in *the way people think*, in contrast to changing *structures of power*. This idealism makes it extremely hard to achieve our ideals—for example, our ideals about lesbian sexuality.

What's So "Bad" About Lesbian Sadomasochism?

The Good Girl/Bad Girl Story
of the Sadomasochism Debate

The debate between feminists over sadomasochism erupted in the context of the anti-pornography movement as the latter gained critical mass by the late seventies.[19] Key events included political skirmishes between groups in the Bay area of Northern California, notably between WAVPAM[20] (one of the first feminist groups to organize against pornography) and Samois, (one of the first groups to hyphenate the term *lesbian-sadomasochist* and vindicate the new identity as feminist).[21] From the first it was clear that the crux of the debate was the meaning of lesbian-feminism.

Lesbian sadomasochists, then as now, have framed the debate as a challenge to the ideological rigidity of lesbian-feminism. At first, they demanded inclusion. "We are lesbian-feminists too," was their battle cry. It would not be long, however, before they moved beyond a position of demand for *tolerance* (for what they defined as a different sexual preference) to a *celebration* of sadomasochism as the pinnacle of *liberation*—in contrast to the sexual repressiveness of lesbian-feminism. These new *sex radicals,* as they now called themselves, advanced beyond their early representation of radical/lesbian-feminists as prudish—as, for example, "vanilla" in their sexual practices—and fully committed themselves to a characterization of radical/lesbian-feminism as both *product and perpetrator of sexual repression.*

Thus begins the good girl/bad girl story of the pornography and sadomasochism debates. According to this story the debate is an argument about Desire. Whereas once women's rage was seen as the force of political movement, today all that has changed. First repressed now expressed, Desire not only explains how it is that feminists/lesbians came apart over porn but how the very history of lesbian-feminism ought to be told. In a short story, Anna Livia satirizes this as the *new orthodoxy* account of lesbian-feminism:

> The New Orthodoxy dictated that in the bad old days lesbians had not talked about sex, thereby creating sadomasochism, but that all this had changed now that a few brave women were saying loudly and clearly that they liked to fuck and, what's more, so had their mothers.[22]

One of the more irritating characteristics of this account is that it not only explains the outbreak of sadomasochism as *daring to be bad* (after years of being so-called good girl lesbians/feminists) but tells us—and tells us and tells us—that it is lesbian/radical

---

[19] For a sense of the scope and focus of the anti-pornography movement in this period, see Lederer ed., *Take Back the Night* (New York: William, Morrow & Company, 1980).

[20] *Women against Violence in Pornography and Media* .

[21] See *Against Sadomasochism*; and Samois, eds., *Coming To Power: Writings and Graphics on Lesbian S/M.* 2nd ed. (Boston: Alyson Publications, 1982).

[22] Anna Livia, "Lust and the Other Half," *Incidents Involving Mirth (Short Stories)* (Portland, Oregon: The Eighth Mountain Press, 1990) p. 26.

feminist ideology which is responsible for generating the good girl/bad girl scene in the first place. Thus, in the anthology *Coming to Power* (the second major lesbian-sadomasochist tract) Gayle Rubin writes,

> S/M appears to be the mirror opposite [of the 'happy healthy lesbian']. It is dark and polarized, extreme and ritualized, and above all it celebrates difference and power. If S/M is understood as the dark opposite of the happy and healthy lesbian, accepting that happy and healthy lesbians also do S/M would threaten the logic of the belief system out of which this opposition was generated.[23]

But to *whom* does sadomasochism appear in this way? According to *whom* is sadomasochism understood as the "dark opposite" of "happy and healthy" lesbians? Who generates the logic that Rubin refers to? Although she places the onus squarely on radical/lesbian-feminist critics of sadomasochism, it is sadomasochism, in fact, which depends upon caricaturing radical/lesbian-feminism as the Moral Majority for its story as outlaw to fly. The good-girl/bad-girl story is itself a sadomasochist *fantasy*, a fantasy of lesbian-sadomasochism as myth-breaking in the face of lesbian-feminist conservatism.

The sadomasochist plot depends on a re-vamped (as it were) virgin-whore dualism, with radical lesbian-feminists cast in the role of uptight virgin. According to this script, lesbian-feminists oppose sadomasochism in a conservative, moralistic defense of our *virginity*, the *virginity* of the category *lesbian*, in order to protect the purity of our (egalitarian) sexuality. In the introduction to her collection of short stories, *Macho Sluts*, Pat Califia contrasts her own rebelliousness with the aspirations to virginity held by most other women:

> Most women remain identified with the virgin, the woman who looks on and suffers, who refrains from action, who always forgives, who heals wounds and gives birth[24]

At the same time, it is Califia's imagination which provides such scenarios as the following:

> The assembled dominatrices fed on her pain . . . . They were nourished and awed by the sight of her. Her helplessness was so voluptuous that it infuriated them. She trembled for herself, victim-without-end.[25]

Yet Califia claims that it is the anti-pornography movement which invokes the suffering virgin archetype. "[T]he anti-porn movement," she asserts, "has done at least as much as 'the male system' to make 'whores' seem vile in the popular imagination."[26] (Are the scare quotes set around "male system" and "whores" intended to unsettle our

---

[23]Gayle Rubin, "The Leather Menace: Comments on Politics and S/M," *Coming to Power.* p. 213.

[24] "Introduction," *Macho Sluts.* (Boston: Alyson Publications, 1988), p. 19.

[25] "The Calyx of Isis," *Macho Sluts,* p. 150.

[26] "Introduction," *Macho Sluts,* p. 18.

misplaced belief that these things actually exist—outside of the constructions of the radical feminist movement?) Historian Alice Echols concurs, claiming that "[anti-porn feminists] indict pornography for eroding the traditional boundary between virgin and whore."[27] Radical feminists, according to this logic, oppose pornography in order to preserve the traditional boundary, to keep Woman virginal and pure. This rhetoric iconifies the radical/lesbian-feminist as super-nanny, creating a pseudo-opposition between the violence of sadomasochism and the (supposed) passive femininity of lesbian-feminists. As pro-sadomasochist Carol LeMasters puts it:

> . . . At a time when more and more feminists were entering the peace movement [sadomasochism] was an exposure of all the myths about women being gentle healers . . . sadomasochism has proven to be a massive rupture in our collective identity as women and as lesbians. Our separatist enclosures can no longer protect us. The enemy is within.[28]

Note the sleight of hand which supports the dualism between the healthy happy girl and the bad girl. Lesbian sadomasochism is contrasted with feminist entry into the peace movement. Yet female entry into a traditionally male-led, leftist movement is identified with lesbian separatism. Whereas the historical record tells us that conflicts over sadomasochism erupted during the anti-pornography debate, the anti-pornography position against sadomasochism has now been revised by LeMasters into a peace movement ideology of woman-as-gentle-healer.

But few were bigger critics of the peace-movement ideology that attracted so many feminists into its ranks during the (mostly early) eighties than separatists and radical/lesbian-feminists.[29] LeMasters' binary opposition of the sadomasochist vs. the peace movement dyke depends upon obscuring the more historically accurate opposition between the *dyke as ball-busting bitch* and the caretaker role of women in male dominated peace movement groups. Given the rep that the radical-feminist-separatist-dyke has for being a man-hating bitch (and rightly earned at that) it seems likely that the separatist dyke as earth mother is little but a prop for the sadomasochist scene. Without which the show does not go on. But the show is given away when one considers the real disruptive effect of lesbian sadomasochism upon lesbian-feminist identity. It is somewhat true that lesbian sadomasochism jars romanticized notions of lesbianism as essentially gentle. But, in my opinion, lesbian sadomasochism represents a deeper political threat. *S/M has proven to be a massive rupture in our collective identity as **man-hating dykes***. We can indeed read the emergence of sadomasochism as a "rupture" in lesbian

---

[27]Alice Echols, "The Taming of the Id: Feminist Sexual Politics, 1968-1983," *Pleasure and Danger*: p. 82.

[28]"S/M and the Violence of Desire," *Trivia* 15 (Fall 1989) p. 15.

[29] I'm referring to the ideology, promoted for example by Helen Caldicott, that women are the caretakers of the planet. For a radical lesbian-feminist critique of this ideology see *Breaching the Peace: A Collection of Radical Feminist Papers* (London: Onlywomen Press, 1983), a pamphlet written by revolutionary feminists in Britain which critiques the ideology of the Greenham Common Women's Peace Camp.

identity—a rupture in the political, feminist definition of lesbian as rebel against heterosexuality.

What's Taboo about Sadomasochism?

Another term for the conservatism of lesbian-feminism allegedly exposed by sadomasochism is "political correctness." In the name of subverting "p.c.ness" not only does "anything go" but proclaiming that anything goes is seen as an act of courage. Thus we have porn columnist Susie Bright (renowned for her tell-it-like-it-is "sexpertise," Bright represents the entrepreneurial faction of the new lesbian sex industry) praising sadomasochist writers like Artemis Oakgrove for their "guts" when they invent fictional scenarios like the following (provided in synopsis by Bright):

[in Oakgrove's NightHawk,] . . . a ditzy voluptuous blonde finds herself stranded in a rough ghetto billiard room where she is unceremoniously stripped by the meanest black butch in the place, and gang banged by the rest.[30]

Bright elevates Oakgrove—who "has guts" but writes "plain dreadful prose"—above those writers "who won't risk their precious literary reputations" to write porn. (88, 89) The low/high culture opposition is strikingly disingenuous given the long tradition of "high culture" porn in Western literature. (Hasn't Bright been reading her Bataille lately? How about Miller, D. M. Thomas or Mailer?)[31] But Bright cashes in on it anyway, serving up Oakgrove's low literary merit as one more credential for pornography, (along with its political incorrectness), as if the anti-pornography position was little more than cultural elitism. Bright admits that Oakgrove's sadomasochist scene "has no careful intellect, no political sensitivity, no historic basis." (89) She's got it right on the first two counts anyway. The fact that she sees no *historic basis* for pornographic representations of race and rape such as this one is astounding—but par for the sadomasochist course.

Bright continues, "I wish someone *would* write about rape fantasies, gang bangs and inter-racial sexual confrontations with social insight *and* salaciousness." (89) The bracketed regret that Oakgrove lacks social insight belies Bright's main point, which is to praise Oakgrove for having the "guts" to exploit racial and sexual myth. As Bright has just made obvious, this pornographic plot is like most pornography: it turns on (its turn-on *is*) the exploitation of racial and sexual stereotypes. It's difficult to see how the addition of "social insight" would increase its value as "one handed reading" (Bright's lingo), or achieve the same desired effect.

---

[30] *Susie Sexpert's Lesbian Sex World*, p. 89. (Future references given in text). Oakgrove's passage reads as follows: "Lori froze. She knew what a big stick like that could do if she fought against it—it could rip her wide open. She knew only too well. Lori was twenty-one years old but she had already lost her uterus because Cloud had gone crazy one night and wouldn't listen when she begged her to stop."

[31] See Andrea Dworkin, *Pornography: Men Possessing Women* (New York: Perigee, 1981), and Susanne Kappeler *The Pornography of Representation* (Minneapolis: University of Minneapolis Press, 1986) for lucid critiques of these high culture pornographers and the tradition of avant garde literary/leftist apologism for porn in the West in general.

Bright is suggesting that Oakgrove's modest reputation affords her the freedom to tell it like it is. Bright is grossly conflating racism and poor writing: but is it really writerly risk-taking that Bright applauds, or the racism itself? Indeed, what *else* in this passage would require the "guts" Bright attributes to Oakgrove if not her "honest" racism and misogyny? It is hardly hack writing that generates race and sex stereotypes: it is, rather, the production of pornography that *depends on* these stereotypes, completely irrespective of its "literary merit."[32]

In the name of the kind of gutsy truth-telling which defies political correctness, the pornography of sexual and racial representation becomes not only permissible; it becomes desirable. Political analysis and resistance to oppression are portrayed as politically correct forces of elitism which forbid the enjoyment of this desire. Racist, misogynist myth is "taboo breaking" with respect only to feminist and anti-racist principles, i.e. it is not taboo-breaking at all.

"Do we desire what is forbidden?" writes Amber Hollibaugh: "If the forbidden is connected to taboo, how can we resist oppression without destroying our means to excitement?" [33] Thus the dilemma is summed up. What will the earnest feminist choose? Will it be our excitement, or our resistance to oppression? Hollibaugh's suggestion that the "excitement" of women's oppression is *taboo* echoes Bright's praise for the "guts" of Oakgrove's racist pornography. But the race and sex oppression of women is hardly taboo; it is enacted daily.

Hollibaugh's real question: If "taboo" is what is "forbidden" *by feminism* how can we resist oppression without destroying our means to excitement? But are *all* means of sexual excitement also the means of our oppression? There is nothing new about the patriarchal imperative that women's *oppression* must be the only means to women's excitement. The question regarding sadomasochism is not, Do we desire what is *forbidden*, but, Do we desire what is *prescribed*? And is it only that which we desire? Don't we also already desire what is wild and outside this prescription? Writer Gillian Hanscombe suggests that eroticized domination and subordination is hardly the only lust known by lesbians:

> Sex as outlined by enthusiasts for sadomasochism (empty-headed, wrong-headed, disreputable, disrespectful, decadent), or as recommended by exponents of half-baked therapies, is not what most of us ever went to the barricades for; is not why we came out; is not the source of our strength in

---

[32] I am not contesting Bright's assumption that racial/misogynist myth is erotically charged as taboo. What I am critiquing is her implicit erasure of those feminist and anti-racist analyses which have blasted the definition of "taboo" as "forbidden." Such radical critiques have long shown that "taboo" means *access: groups with more social power get access to groups with less*. Incest is not taboo, for example—it is not actually forbidden. Incest is the word masking men's access to girls, most typically fathers to daughters. (Although it is also true that women sometimes sexually abuse daughters and that both parents, or adult relatives, abuse boys and girls). In the case of racial/sexual ideology, the "taboo" of inter-racial sex has masked the reality of white men's rape of black women, and white men's control of white women and black men through the myth of the former's sexual purity and the latter's innate and animal sexuality.

[33] "Desire for the Future: Radical Hope in Passion and Pleasure," in Vance, p. 402.

resistance to the patriarchy; is not the hope for development and renewal we offer to all women everywhere.[34]

Rebels Against a Cause

The sadomasochist lesbian's rebellion is a *rebellion against history,* which re-writes second wave lesbian-feminism—the story of why we came out and what gives us strength as lesbians—reductively through the grid of good girl/bad girl logic. This revisionist tale accounts for sadomasochism as an inevitable return of repressed (by feminism) sexuality. "What is most evident about anti-S/M feminists is their fear of the unconscious," asserts Carol LeMasters, "as though the unconscious were a dangerously overpowering force which, if unleashed, could 'take over' one's rational life."[35] In a similar vein, Alice Echols retells the history of lesbian-feminism as an aversion to sexuality:

> The elusive quest for egalitarian relationships and politically correct sex has encouraged lesbian cultural feminists to deemphasize sex on ideological grounds. This flight from ambivalence inevitably leads to repression because sexuality is too conflict-laden to ever pass a political litmus test.[36]

Evidently lesbian-feminism is not too conflict-laden to be reduced by Echols' own litmus test of sex, reduced to a one-dimensional history of the collective feminist libido, a story of true lust lost, or averted. But what remains unargued is the assumption that the effort to enact egalitarian sexual relationships *inevitably* leads to repression. Why must it do so? Elaborating somewhat on this claim, Echols writes that lesbian-feminists' "insistence that lesbianism is an issue of 'radical female friendship' rather than sexual preference reflects an unwillingness to accept that within the larger culture lesbianism is viewed as 'perversion' "[37] The formula here is that emphasizing female friendship is equivalent to cleaning up the image of lesbianism and that this in turn is equivalent to repressing lesbian desire. It is certainly true that seventies lesbian-feminism redefined lesbian relationships in terms of "radical female friendship," sustained bonds of intimacy and community. While this ethical and political re-definition of lesbianism has had all kinds of implications for how lesbians have represented our sexuality, the claim that it inevitably boils down to this single implication, repression of sexual perversion, is itself a perversion of history and cultural meaning.[38] It can be argued that Echols is unwilling to grasp the

---

[34]"In Among the Market Forces?" Judith Barrington ed., *An Intimate Wilderness: Lesbian Writers on Sexuality* (Portland, Oregon: The Eighth Mountain Press, 1991), p. 218.

[35]LeMasters, p. 20.

[36]"The New Feminism of Yin and Yang," *Powers of Desire,* pp. 452-3.

[37] *Powers of Desire*, p. 452.

[38] Echols' dichotomy of "radical feminist" and "sex preference" lesbians reflects concrete struggles of definition, of course. Echols' categorization, however, abstracts lesbian identity from the historical complexity of those struggles, charting a one-dimensional plot of "pro-sex" vs. "anti-sex" elements in lesbian communities. The meaning of lesbian identity has always been in process, a site of political contest. What tends to be overlooked by Echols and others is the historical
(Footnote Continued on Next Page)

political implications of lesbian "perversity." Is it lesbian sex in itself that is so threatening to the fabric of civilization? What does lesbian sex represent? What does it *mean* when women in the military are jailed for lesbianism, or killed for it, or beaten up in bar rooms? *Is* it the right to *fuck*? *"We're built on richer things,"* Hanscombe asserts, *"and they're things that can't be bought, sold, bribed, or bartered."* [39] What is contested here is what's "perverse" about lesbianism. Which is really more threatening: "liking to fuck" or the possibility that women create our lives together, apart from men, in ways that last (and let women last longer)?

Repressive Tenderness and Imaginary Evil

> We jerk off to the rapist, the Hell's angel, to the Nazi, to the cop and to all the other images that have nothing to do with the kind of lesbian sex that entails murmurs of endearment, stroking of breasts and long slow tongue work.[40]

Thus boasts Jan Brown in a 1990 *OUT/LOOK* article entitled, "Sex, Lies and Penetration, a Butch Finally 'fesses Up." The terribly repressive orthodoxy of woman-loving-woman sex has been overturned, ushering in revolutionary new forms of sexuality:

> We wear the uniform and the gun . . . we haul our cocks out of our pants to drive into a struggling body. (31)

---

significance of the contest, namely the historical significance of claiming lesbian identity in the context of a women's liberation movement critique of sexual liberation ideology. As Margot Farnham addresses this tendency, ". . . [S]eventies feminism emerged with a spontaneous articulation of the banality, the poverty of heterosexual sex as many women experienced it and centred by the end of the decade on sexual violence. What came to be heavily emphasized was the political meanings of sexuality, one of the stormiest debates of the decade concerning political lesbianism. In the course of time, women who stressed and campaigned against sexual violence were criticized for neglecting 'pleasure'. What seems to be overlooked today is that seventies feminism emerged in a climate of supposed 'pleasure': the sexual revolution. Our analysis was shaped by our disaffection with the sexual revolution, was formed partly in reaction to its mindlessness in terms of women's experience." What Farnham is pointing out is that the political meaning of lesbianism was and remains the stormy center of debate over sexuality, and that this political meaning cannot be reduced to neatly bifurcated categorizations of "pro-sex" vs. "anti-sex" political forces in lesbian-feminist communities. The good girl /bad girl binary in Echols' story, the opposition between radical female friendship and sexual lesbianism, glosses over the meaning of lesbian-feminism as contested history, contested identity, settling the matter once and for all that lesbianism *is* sexual preference. A feminist lesbianism posed against this settled account can only be read as hypocrisy, as ideology masking true desire. Readings like Echols' are a flight from memory, reducing the complexity of the story to a single line of plot: a flight from sex. Such simplification supports an interpretation of contemporary debates that not only favors but aggrandizes the role of lesbian sadomasochism. See Margot Farnham, "The Body Remembers," *Trouble & Strife* 17 (Winter 1989) pp. 22-3.

[39](Italics mine.) Gillian Hanscombe, *An Intimate Wilderness*, p. 214.

[40]Jan Brown, "Sex, Lies, and Penetration: A Butch Finally 'Fesses Up," *OUT/LOOK* 7 (Winter 1990) p. 31. (Further references in text)

In here we find the "robustness" hankered after by the opponents of the anti-pornography civil rights ordinance, the FACT women who wanted to "appropriate for themselves the robustness of what has traditionally been male language."[41] Similarly Pat Califia expresses her desire:

> to be the brazen hussy, the woman who travels, who wants to go where men go and see what they see, who wears their clothes and appropriates their pleasures and mannerisms, who carries a razor . . . [42]

The need and desire to take men's mannerisms is an act of survival or of sheer wanton defiance for many lesbians. But the real perversion here is not the desire to be "robust," but the association of "gutsiness" with the sadomasochism of pornography. "And yes, we also dream of the taking," confesses Jan Brown. "We dream of someone's blood on our hands, of laughing at cries for mercy." (31) Big dream, that. This "dream" is set up against what is categorized as "vanilla" sex and associated with a supposed "dogma of tenderness." The phrase is drawn from a novel co-written by Kim Chernin and Renate Stendhal. The message is that feminism is responsible for taking the fun out of sex. Their character, Alma, says:

> Feminism taught me to suspect any power that would drive others to their knees. It taught me to keep my own knees straight. No more submission! Beware of domination![43]

But at what point was it decided that domination and submission was the only form of sexual power? In a favorable review of this book, former *Trivia* editor Lise Weil upholds this view, writing, "Feminism itself . . . held [Alma's] virginity in place . . . . " and Weil describes this "virginity" as "lesbian smugness":

> a virginity that insists it knows all that needs to be known about sex, that refuses to acknowledge the presence of power in relationships between women. What Alma calls 'the dogma of tenderness'.[44]

It is true that lesbian-feminists have sometimes been smug in our assurances about the nature (e.g. inherently equal) of lesbian sex. We need a more complex picture of sexuality, one that indeed "acknowledges" power in relationships. But why must we *choose* between such an acknowledgment and tenderness? The acceptance of this choice impoverishes rather than expands our understanding of lesbian sexuality. What I

---

[41] Brief *Amici Curiae* of Feminist Anti-Censorship Task Force, et. al. 31, Hudnut v. American Booksellers, 771 F.2d 323 (7th cir. 1985).

[42] Califia, "Introduction," *Macho Sluts*, p.19.

[43] quoted in Lise Weil, "Lowering the Case: An After-Reading of *Sex and Other Sacred Games*," *An Intimate Wilderness*, p. 244.

[44] Weil, p. 244.

object to in Weil's comment is not the call to push ourselves to reflect further on power in sexuality, but the good-girl/bad-girl story which re-hashes a mind-deadening dualism between some virgin/feminist caricature and—what's the other side? the alternative? Domination and submission as the expression of sexual freedom?

"Sex that is gentle, passive, egalitarian and bloodless does not move us," Brown boasts. (31) Note the unqualified heaping up of adjectives: gentle = passive = egalitarian = bloodless. He-man stuff, this: egalitarian (conceived as passive) is opposed to strong (conceived as violent, cruel, and merciless).

Like a machine, the good girl/bad girl concept keeps on keeping on its automated reproduction of binary oppositions in lesbian culture, of tenderness vs. power in lesbian sexuality. A good example of the latter manufacture is the categorization of "good girl" erotica and "bad girl" pornography according to Jan Zita Grover in *The Women's Review of Books*. Departing not at all from type, Grover associates lesbian-feminism with erotica, which she describes as follows:

> Erotica celebrates the pleasure and security of sex between women, and to that extent it's good-girl writing.[45]

In contrast is "lesbian porn" in which, Grover writes, "sexual gratification is something women actively devise or negotiate." (21) Already the dichotomy is specious—as if pleasure and especially security, were not *typically* negotiated in lesbian sex. But in Grover's framework, "Lesbian porn celebrates the dangers of sex, and to that extent it's bad-girl writing."(21) The false opposition between pleasure and security on the one hand and "danger," on the other, pits tenderness against risk, equating a truer, more "robust" lust with "danger." As if sexual tenderness did not involve risk and fear, or the ritualized sex games of sadomasochism offer a specific security.

Grover juxtaposes the conventionally romantic imagery of erotica with that of lesbian pornography. The satire in her descriptions is admittedly on target as she invokes the lesbian-feminist erotica writer's predilection for outdoor scenes and ecofeminist love:

> They are earnest. They enact their passion in rustic cabins, in nature, in beds. They want to see (themselves in) Her again . . . (21)

And perhaps even better:

> The only toys entering into most lesbian erotica are feathers, steaming mugs of coffee (afterwards), candles . . . and music . . . . [A]ll it takes to pass the wet test is a strong (other) woman in denim, a beach at sunset or a forest floor at dawn, and the protagonist (and presumably the reader) gets off. (21)

But Grover's wit knows predictable bounds; her satire is spent on the "good girls" alone. About the bad girls and the "porn body" Grover waxes rhapsodic, invoking:

---

[45]"Words to Lust By," *The Women's Review of Books* Vol. VIII, No. 2 (November 1990), p. 21. (Further references will be given in text.)

a terrain that can be traveled in many ways; surfaces and fissures that erotica usually ignores are its chosen *terra cognita*. (21)

"We haul our cocks out of our pants to drive into a struggling body," wrote Jan Brown. *Surfaces and fissures, terra cognita, a terrain traveled in many ways?* While the earnestness of so-called "vanilla" passion reaps the scorn of pundits like Grover, these same writers appear to be oblivious to their own earnest pursuit of florid lit-crit tropes with which to clothe the hackneyed conventions of porn. But the emperor wears no (new) clothes.

Simone Weil once wrote something very relevant here:

Imaginary evil is romantic, fanciful, varied; real evil is dreary, monotonous, barren and tedious. Imaginary good is tedious; real good is always fresh, marvelous and intoxicating.[46]

Karen Davis, who brought the Weil quote to my attention, comments,

By way of comparison, I would say that the fantasy of sadomasochism is 'romantic, fanciful, varied' while the fantasy of equality is 'tedious'. The inverse formulation would of course hold that the reality of sadomasochism is 'dreary, monotonous, barren and tedious', while the reality of sexual equality is 'fresh, marvelous, intoxicating'.[47]

Indeed, what is lost under all the rhetorical "excess" of "bad girl" stylists is the kind of power of lesbian touch so simply expressed in a line—yet again from Rich—that has haunted me as I write these pages—*without tenderness, we are in hell.* [48]

Idealizing *Sex*—or *Banality*?

Of course power dynamics, including those of domination and submission, are *erotically charged* for many lesbians. But are the only alternatives to celebrate or deny/repress these dynamics? As Margot Farnham addresses this issue (in her critique of Joan Nestle's *celebration* of power dynamics in butch-femme role play) we might be more imaginative:

Other feminists may recognize the kind of sex she [Nestle] writes about but place them in a wholly different history [than Nestle]: one which recognizes women's struggles to love their bodies in a culture which hates them or

---

[46] *Notebooks of Simone Weil*, trans. Arthur Wills, (London: Routledge & Kegan Paul, 1956) Vol. 1, pp. 143-144.

[47] Personal Communication, Nov. 1991.

[48] "Twenty-One Love Poems," *The Dream of a Common Language* (New York: Norton, 1978), p. 30.

objectifies them; one which recognizes that other dramas over personal power and self-esteem, love and neglect may be enacted in sex.[49]

The "wholly different history" here, I think, is a history of feminism as a struggle for *women's freedom*: what is overlooked by current sadomasochist discourse is the *ecstasy*, sexual and otherwise, as well as the power struggles that were unleashed in this context. Seventies lesbian-feminist identity didn't *only* emerge in *opposition* to men's sexual objectification of women. As Farnham writes, "Within lesbian political circles it was also a time of affirmation of lesbian sexual pleasure, an affirmation which today may seem naive, but which at the time inspired quite a few women to become lesbians."[50] In the context of a history of reclaiming lesbian pleasure from the banal scripts of heterosexual unfreedom, why not invent a way to transform the dynamic of submission and domination that many women find "pleasurable"? In my opinion we need to do so without shame, without self-hatred.

While for some women this may take the shape of celibacy and/or of stopping one's fantasies, most of us will continue to stumble along through a terrain that is as marked by bad memories, canned fantasies and the bitter residue of our own nasty mistakes as it is by Adrienne Rich's "Twenty One Love Poems." Moments of grace are often more than matched by those moments in which we succeed in realizing *only* the tawdriest of our hopes. In light of the "new orthodoxy" stories that have been rewriting our history and collective self-conception, the task of naming the reality of lesbian sex in both its mundane and lofty manifestations takes on a new significance.

We need an account of sexuality that encompasses a dynamic of change. Are we capable of sustaining our (worthy) ideals while shame-lessly (meaning both *without sexual shame* and *brazenly*) evaluating our experience with a loving as well as critical eye? We need a more complex story of sexuality. But the neat polarity of boring sexual tenderness vs. exciting sexual "danger" shrinks sexuality to a single narrative: power over, power under, master/slave, top/bottom. This either/or plot glosses over the realm of possibility, the ferocity of tender sex, the kind of risk-taking that can require extraordinary gentleness, the "danger" of allowing full presence of self in intimacy and the challenge of facing that presence in the other. The fiction of power in sadomasochism requires a simplified up and down story, the topping by sadomasochist sex of a bottom, vanilla genre of sex.

Much of the hype surrounding sadomasochist excitement requires downgrading the lesbian-feminist ideal of an egalitarian lesbian sexuality. But lesbian sadomasochism offers nothing so much as its own idealized banality:[51] that lesbianism is sex, and that the truth of sex is domination and submission.

---

[49]Farnham, p. 25.
[50]Farnham, p. 23.
[51]Thanks to Julia Chapin for this insight.

"Liberty is the right not to lie," Camus's phrase, is the epigraph that Pat Califia chose for the introduction to her collection of sadomasochist stories, *Macho Sluts*. Starting from the first sadomasochist lesbian publication, in which the writers named themselves The Ministry of Truth ("the truth hurts"), "truth" has been a key buzz word of the lesbian sadomasochist text. For Jan Brown, for example, "truth" becomes one more sex toy—or weapon. Brown aims to disarm her reader with truth, she likes the "smell of truth," (34) a "dick as hard as truth between [her] legs." (31) The goal of her "confession" is to come out sadomasochist in a way that surpasses the best/worst of sadomasochist fantasies. Whereas even the baddest bad girls, such as Pat Califia, had always insisted on a critical boundary between fantasy and real life, Brown breaks the final boundary, writing:

> Remember when we all agonized over our fantasies? . . . . We emphasized the simple difference between fantasy and reality . . . . Well, we lied. The power is not in the ability to control the violent image. It is in the lust we have to see how close we can get to the edge. It is in the lust to be overpowered, forced, used, objectified. (31)

It is not sadomasochist illusions that Brown aims to bash, however, but the feminist "lies," or rather the feminist hypocrites who made Brown and others like her "lie" for their own survival. The theme was introduced in the first Samois writings. Thus Pat Califia describes coming out sadomasochist: "Despite my vigorous participation in the women's movement, my S/M fantasies had not been 'cured' . . . It was possible to do it and survive."[52]

This has become a prominent theme of "pro-sex" defenses of pornography and sadomasochism. The urgency of sex has been extrapolated into *self-preservation,* with the accompanying construction of anti-sadomasochist and anti-pornography feminism as a threat to survival itself. In recent years the anti-AIDS activist agenda has unfortunately provided a new rubric (of safe sex) for this polemic. "Since the AIDS pandemic," as gay writer Earl Jackson argues:

> porn has taken on a new urgency, in its role of as [sic] a provider of clear safer sex information and as a conduit through which the body and its actions can be re-eroticized to create healthy and fulfilling sex lives that do not contribute to the spread of the disease.[53]

While Jackson's "the body" dangles gender-neutral, we know whose "healthy and fulfilling sex lives" matter the most—not women's. Indeed the "urgency" that pornography takes on is emphasized through Jackson's anecdote of a friend for whom "pornography had a direct role in a partial recovery of his stolen sexuality." (31) The old adage that

---

[52]Califia, *Coming to Power*, p. 245.

[53]Earl Jackson Jr., "The Politics of Ecstasy," *Lavender Reader* (Fall 1991), p. 34. (Further references given in text)

pornography is *therapeutic* (cathartic) is here given a new spin under the rubric of safe sex and gay liberation. While "pro-sex" ideologues have always defined the anti-pornography position as a danger to their pleasure, their erotica, they now define it as a threat to their lives. Addressing himself, in part, to "those anti-pornography feminists who promote the physical destruction and legal suppression of sexually explicit materials," Jackson says, ". . . it is clear that in the current crisis to restrict access to explicit sexual information, images, and forms of fantasy concretization is tantamount to manslaughter, if not homocide[sic]." (34) It is "clear" that limiting fantasy concretization is tantamount to manslaughter, but what is not clear to Jackson is the woman-slaughter that is central to fantasies concretized in pornography and prostitution. Jackson, of course, differentiates "gay/lesbian pornography" from "heteropatriarchal pornography." Jackson's distinction is arguable. However, whether gay porn is different from heterosexual porn or not, this distinction begs the question, namely, is the protection of *any* erotica worth protecting the multi-billion dollar pornography industry? Whose body counts in the pornography debate to which Jackson is addressing himself here, and whose *body count* matters?

Women, as concretely embodied, strangely disappear in the rhetoric of "the body" so cherished by apologists for porn like Jackson. The mysterious case of the missing population—women used (bought and sold, consumed) in pornography and prostitution—in arguments such as Jackson's, is surely related to the fact that the so-called sex industry *dehumanizes* women. Indeed, sometimes even when women are missing in the literal sense (as in dead, murdered) this very absence is missed: why are there "no humans involved" when prostitutes are killed, in police jargon?[54] If there is any remaining confusion as to the answer to these questions, a recent debate at an Out/Write conference (1990) on the subject of "censorship" will clear up the matter. Lesbian porn magazine editor Amy Hoffman recounts an incident at the conference in which Black poet Ayofemi Folayan "criticiz[ed] an 'end censorship' position as 'simplistic'." Hoffman writes:

> Concerned about how violence is perpetrated against black women and other women of color in greater proportion than in the rest of the population, she cited the recent unsolved murders of 24 black women in south central LA (most identified in the media as prostitutes). 'I celebrate myself, celebrate erotica,' Folayan concluded, 'but I'm real nervous about the other shit that's going on'.[55]

Hoffman remarks, "her comment was emotional and angry," and describes the ensuing exchange,

> 'But what gives you the right to decide?' a woman from the audience yelled [at Folayan]

---

[54]The jargon is from San Diego, CA. where there have been 45 uninvestigated murders of prostitutes since 1985. A coalition of feminists and artists organized a response to this atrocity with a number of public education and arts projects. These included a campaign in which photographed faces of the missing women were placed on city billboards with the caption, "NHI: No Humans Involved," (*Ms.* Sept./Oct. 1992, p. 69).

[55]*Sojourner*, (Cambridge, Ma. June, 1990. p-2.)

[Folayan responded:] 'It's killing us!'
[the audience member:] 'You're not dead yet!'
[Folayan:] 'Someone has to speak for them. They are already dead!'

It is the "gay nineties," the era of "queer," how do you spell nonchalance? *You're not dead yet.* Institutionalized nonchalance is certainly one way of looking at racism and misogyny in the nineties. Furthermore, Hoffman seems complicit with racist ideology when she invokes the angry Black woman stereotype to discredit Black women's calls for justice. Instead of addressing the specific toll that men's war against women takes on African-American women and other women of color, Hoffman expresses her irritation with Folayan for speaking out:

> as Folayan started to speak, I felt suddenly exhausted and annoyed, and I sensed some of the same exhaustion and annoyance from the rest of the audience. We had heard arguments like hers before. We didn't want to deal with this fight anymore. I believed I knew what assumptions she would make about the relationship between representations and behavior, and I'd already decided these were themselves 'simplistic'.

But feminists are also tired of this argument; we are tired of arguing that there *is* a connection between the pornographic "fantasy" in which women=sex=trash and the "concretization of fantasy" in murder, the murder of prostitutes in San Diego for example, or the Black women in L.A. that Folayan was talking about: "throw away women."[56] Hoffman's flip dismissal of Folayan and the issue she raised is particularly pernicious in light of attempts by lesbian sadomasochists to identify with communities of color as an oppressed group. (See below)

It is the nineties, and these are the terms of the fight. This is about responsibility (to our dead, for one) the *ability to respond* in an era in which it has become less and less possible to express outrage: *It's killing us. They're already dead. Someone has to speak for them.* When this voice registers at all, it registers as "emotional and angry," as "shrill." Alarmist. Meanwhile, "porn takes on a new urgency," and anti-pornography activism is "tantamount to manslaughter if not homocide [sic]." The degree of nonchalance about women's deaths is matched only by the deadly seriousness with which men's right to "healthy and fulfilling sex lives" is defended.

Many lesbians, such as Hoffman, have adopted this male-defined agenda. On the band-wagon of gay-male dominated issues, lesbians are taken seriously as activists for dying men. It is surely irresistible to be taken seriously for once, on a national scale, to be taken seriously at last. We can be bad girls and caretakers too, we *can* have it both ways. We can be "transgressive" users of porn, supposedly defying the status quo, while "providing food for the hungry" (as Susie Bright has described her service as porn-provider).[57] We can have it both ways, deriding lesbian-feminists for "sanitizing" sexuality

---

[56] In *Female Sexual Slavery* Kathleen Barry condemned the treatment of prostitutes as "throw away women." (Englewood Cliffs, N.J.: Prentice-Hall, 1979).

[57] Talk given at Amherst College, Amherst, Ma., Oct. 29, 1990.

in the seventies, while promoting "bad girl" sex as ideal sex hygiene in the age of AIDS. What needs to be asked here is whose interests are really being represented by an agenda that prioritizes "concretizing fantasies" over trying to end men's war on women?

The triumph of sadomasochism as a cultural credo is that it shrinks feminists' capacity to express outrage at atrocities against women. Lesbian sadomasochism shrinks feminist response to a single variable of an unchanging sequence—a variable of the sadomasochistic formula which precludes any alternative to the options of "good" getting off or "bad" repressiveness. Thus lesbian sadomasochism does more than accept, it *affirms* the limits of the pornographic imagination, restoring to these limits an inevitability that, historically, feminist critics and activists have aimed to unsettle. This affirmation, furthermore, is its "consent" to patriarchal, pornographic logic and mores.

What's so Bad about an Attitude?

Writing about pornography, Susanne Kappeler clarifies the meaning of this "consent":

> The options are strictly defined within the one imperative that it [sexual violence] will happen to her; [the victim] can [only] choose an attitude.[58]

Choosing an attitude indeed defines the sadomasochist posture, the position advanced by its most fervent advocates. Hence "bad attitude," the title of the magazine edited by Hoffman, becomes the only possible option for rebellion. However, this "bad attitude" misnames "*consent*" as "*defiance*." The "bad attitude" is the attitude that enjoins and enjoys sexual violence—sadism or masochism is presupposed, inevitable. ". . . She [the victim] makes herself a victim because she chooses to scream." This is the avant garde male apologist for pornography speaking, (Roland Barthes, whose words, cited by Kappeler, strangely articulate the lesbian sadomasochist credo):

> If under the same vexation she were to ejaculate [sic], she would cease to be a victim, would be transformed into a libertine: to scream/discharge, this paradigm is the beginning of choice, i.e. Sadian meaning.[59]

Similarly Carol LeMasters informs her reader, "It is in our power to turn even pain into pleasure and terror into pure delight."[60] The inversion of feminist critique, specifically the critique of pornography, is startling; feminists have always claimed, of course, that pornography turns women's pain into (men's) pleasure, making female terror a source of (men's) entertainment, of "pure delight." What can be made of this reversal in which the feminist *critique,* that pornography is the source of men's pleasure, is recast as *affirmation,* that pornography is the source of *our* pleasure? That lesbian sadomasochism *affirms* that pornography/sadomasochism converts female pain into female pleasure?

---

[58]Kappeler, p. 90.

[59]Kappeler, pp. 90-91. (parenthetical "sic" is Kappeler's)

[60]LeMasters, p. 29.

That it is in our *power* to do so; it is in *our* power? That we agree to convert pain into pleasure, that we consent, that therefore we have the power to do so? But the power of consent presupposes the power of refusal, a power women do not have with respect to sex in heteropatriarchy.

Kappeler writes, (referring to the Barthes passage above):

> Note how suddenly the passive female sufferer becomes an apparently active agent; *she makes herself* a victim because she *chooses* to scream. Note how 'the same vexation' she is under is beyond any choice, beyond alteration. The text, the scenario, is given, 'she' can choose to mark it.[61]

Sadomasochist ideologues assume the posture of defiance as restricted by this pornographic scene; the act of defiance, for women, becomes the "choice" to "ejaculate" rather than "scream." But this posture of "defiance" is in fact consent to a very limited notion of rebellion: "lie back and enjoy it," as there is no other option for change than changing attitude, within the unquestioned boundaries of the pornographic scene.

Sadomasochism as an ideology corroborates what Susan Sontag discussed as the "totalizing imperative" of the pornographic imagination.

> The universe proposed by the pornographic imagination is a total universe. It has the power to ingest and metamorphosize and translate all concerns that are fed into it, reducing everything into the one negotiable currency of the erotic imperative.[62]

Indeed, in pornography everything and anything in and of the world can be converted into a variable of its logic—an erotic variable of its scenes. Everything and anything can be erotic currency, exchanged, that is, according to the gold standard of the pornographic subject's (the male subject's) ejaculation: the (female) victim's "ejaculation" is subsumed under that imperative.

"Conventional" pornography is a negotiation between men, and the item of barter is female flesh. In the bargain the male, erotic imperative spreads farther and farther into the world of ordinary objects: nothing is immune from the victimizer's use as a site and/or instrument of/for the (female) victim's violation.[63] Everything can be ingested by the scene, including the scene. That is, there is no "outside" to the scene, no possibility of "escape" into a critical vantage point that might grasp the meaning of the production of

---

[61]Kappeler, p. 91.

[62] "The Pornographic Imagination," *Styles of Radical Will.* (New York: Dell Publishing, 1970), p. 66.

[63]Andrea Dworkin's reflections on her experience writing about pornography inform this point: "The photographs I had to study changed my whole relationship to the physical world in which I live . . . . I saw so many photographs of common household objects being used as sexual weapons against women that I despaired of ever returning to my once simple ideas of function. I developed a new visual vocabulary, one that few women have at all, one that consumers of pornography carry with them all the time: any mundane object an be turned into an eroticized object—an object that can be used to hurt women in a sexual context with a sexual purpose and a sexual meaning." *Letters from a War Zone: Writings 1976-1989* (New York: E.P Dutton, 1989) p. 34.

pornography as a systematic investment in/of male power. Even such an "escape," i.e. a possible resistance to the scene, becomes one more of its erotic variables—something to "get off" on. Feminism, lesbian-feminism, can be converted into a function of pornography; sadomasochist lesbianism signifies this conversion.[64] And that is what is bad about lesbian sadomasochism.

What's So "Good" about Lesbian-Feminism?

The Lesbian Feminist Critique of Sadomasochism:
Sadomasochism and the Straight Mind

Lesbian sadomasochism is not merely about what women do in bed, although it is that. What is so bad about lesbian sadomasochism is that it reverses[65] the terms in which feminists, historically, have defined the meaning of a struggle for women's liberation. Pro-sadomasochist Jan Brown sums it up:

---

[64]This idea first began to crystallize in my Feminist Militancy Study Group in Northampton, Ma., July, 1989. The absorption of lesbian-feminists into the porn/sadomasochist imagination is concretely played out in those lesbian sadomasochist porn writings which include as a central or minor plot element the humiliation of lesbian-feminist/anti-porn feminist characters. Feminist characters have long been a staple of *male* pornography. *Hustler* has an "Asshole of the month" that has featured both Andrea Dworkin and anti-pornography activist, Dorchen Leicholdt. The same magazine has had a cartoon series depicting Gloria Steinem. *Penthouse* has featured an account by a fictional ex-boyfriend of Susan Brownmiller's that details—what else?—Brownmiller's "rape fantasies." Dworkin discusses, at length the depiction of "liberated women" in pornography (1981, pp. 30-36; pp. 208-209). For examples of the lesbian equivalent of this pornographing of feminists, see Califia, *Macho Sluts*. For a striking example see Alexander, "Passion Play" (Samois, *Coming to Power*). In this story a "top" creates a scene explicitly tailored for her high-powered academic feminist lover: "Carole knew that frills would almost always break Meg's tight composure and get to her in a way that explicit pain would not." (p. 233) So Carole collars, leashes and paints Meg, etc. Converting the public feminist into a submissive poodle is just what she, the high-powered feminist needs.

[65] Lesbian sadomasochists flaunted their affinity with Orwellian *newspeak* in one of the earliest lesbian sadomasochist publications, *What Color is your Handkerchief? A Lesbian/S/M Sexuality Reader* (ed. Samois, Berkeley, Ca. 1979) in which The Ministry of Truth was credited as a source. In Orwell's *1984*, the Ministry of Truth, a ministry of the totalitarian state in Orwell's dystopia, manufactures lies. The particular character of the lies produced by Orwell's fictional government bureau is that they are *reversals* of reality: war is peace, hate is love, are the slogans produced by the ministry. "The truth hurts," the members of Samois quipped. But the joke escapes me. In using Orwell's fiction to name themselves, lesbian sadomasochists called themselves, oddly enough, by the one name that was not a reversal of what they were. Reversals are lies that work to confuse and block thought by calling things the opposite of what they really are. "Reversal" is a central term in the radical feminist philosophy of Mary Daly and her method of demystifying reversals is a major source of inspiration for this essay. See especially *Beyond God the Father* (Boston: Beacon Press, 1973) and *Gyn/Ecology* (Boston: Beacon Press, 1978).

*Sometimes we need, to have a dick hard as truth between our legs, to have the
freedom to ignore 'no' or have our own 'no' ignored.* [66]

Lesbian sadomasochism not only redefines *freedom*: it re-works the language in
which it is possible to speak of freedom meaningfully and distorts the historical context
(women's liberation struggles) in which women found this speech. Ignoring "no" or having
our own "no's" ignored is not the freedom that, as Gillian Hanscombe might have said,
women "went to the barricades for." Many women originally went to the barricades, in the
second wave momentum of feminism, to repudiate the male left's "sexual liberation" as
what these feminists came to name *liberation for men to gain greater sexual access to
women.*[67] Lesbian sadomasochism abstracts sex from the social and historical context of
male entitlement and thus from the historical context of feminist struggle. Given a scene
in which freedom is re-scripted as an abstract *consent*, radical lesbian-feminism becomes
redefined as a *constriction* of *freedom*, rather than a liberation of women from compulsory
heterosexuality.

But the sound of the word "no" is still a bass-note of women's freedom—as the
erosion (or nonexistence) of basic civil rights for women with respect to rape, sexual
harassment and pornography[68] should make clear. There is no meaningful "Yes" to sex if
there is no meaningful "No." By robbing "no" of its meaning, lesbian sadomasochism also
loses the "yes" that is implicit in radical dissent, a *visionary* yes that affirms the possibility
of an outside to the sadomasochist scene. In contrast, lesbian sadomasochism confirms
the boundaries of the "straight mind,"[69] insisting that there is no alternative to sexualized
subordination and domination, irrespective of gender—that lesbianism is no such
alternative. Within this heterosexual mind-set the only possible alternatives are "pro-sex"
vs. "anti-sex," good girls vs. bad, in bed with the left, in bed with the right. Given the
gridlock of this sadomasochist imagination some true "escape artists" might be called
for.[70]

It takes a "qualitative leap"[71] of imagination to get outside of the straight mind and
conceive of (radical) lesbianism. Such leaps are necessarily inconceivable to the mind-

---

[66]Brown, p. 31.

[67]See, for example, the anthologies *Radical Feminism* Koedt et. al., especially Densmore,
"Independence From the Sexual Revolution," and Ed. Robin Morgan, *Sisterhood is Powerful:
Anthology of Writings from the Women's Liberation Movement,* (New York: Random House, 1970).

[68]See Dworkin and MacKinnon, *Pornography and Civil Rights: A New Day for Women's Equality*
(Minneapolis, Minnesota: Organizing Against Pornography, 1988), for a discussion of pornography
as a violation of women's civil rights.

[69]Monique Wittig, *The Straight Mind.* (Boston: Beacon Press, 1992).

[70] I draw this term "escape artists" from an inspiring group of radical dykes in the British Isles who
published a small zine, *Doodling Dykes*, invoking escape artists as (my description) lesbians
committed to using all their wits—as in humor and creativity—to "escape" patriarchal constructions
of reality.

[71]Daly, *Beyond God the Father.*

set that "beds" women down in the couplings of the heterosexual social order.[72] According to the heterosexual logic of the straight mind "there is no category of the woman-identified-woman . . ."[73] Lesbianism, defined politically as a *new social relation*, is invisible: i.e. outside the scope of vision only capable of entertaining the kind of *lesbian men can see*,[74] à la lesbo-agogo and Susie Bright. I'm not advocating lesbian invisibility, of course, but to "be and be seen" on our own terms. We, meaning lesbian-feminists, hinge perilously at times between the invisible no-place of utopian idealism (ou-*not* topia-*place*, a word meaning *no place*) and the visible projections of male fantasy.

Shadow Boxing

Lesbian sadomasochists and their apologists typically suggest they are exposing lesbian-feminist ideals as the utopian face of a repressive and aggressive power-play. Lesbian-feminists as we are portrayed, for example, in Alice Echols' version of the good girl/bad girl story, have "viciously attacked S/M lesbian-feminists because they seem to undermine the former's belief in an ideal lesbian sexuality."[75] There is a kernel of truth in the allegation that lesbian-feminists have idealized lesbian sexuality. However, I take issue with the assumption that, having recognized this, what ought to follow is an abandonment of the ideals, rather than an attempt to rethink (and revitalize) them. Radical lesbianism in this view is utopian as in hopelessly out of touch with the real world—nowhere, in other words. This view of lesbianism only makes sense if we presuppose that sadomasochism is everywhere. Given the unspoken assumption that sadomasochism is everywhere, it follows that any *criticism* of lesbian sadomasochism must be revised in the cynical terms of sadomasochism itself. Lesbian value seems to evaporate into a mirage.

One gets the feeling of shadow boxing: I find myself, indeed, as many do, in a futile pursuit of credibility as each player in this debate is unmasked by her "opponent" and charged with being the opposite of what she claims to be. The strategy follows a certain formula: defeat your opponent by demonstrating that what she claims to belong most to her—what is most one's own, essential to who one is, in this case what we believe lesbian-feminism to be—has been most taken away, i.e. is a product of the patriarchy.[76]

---

[72] As Elise Ficarra puts it, the accusation that radical feminists are in bed with the right is based on the notion that women are always in bed with someone. This model, based upon domination and subordination omits *liberation*: what Ficarra calls the "jump out of the paradigm."

[73] Sarah Hoagland, quoted in "To Be and Be Seen: The Politics of Reality," an essay by Marilyn Frye on the subject of lesbian visibility with respect to patriarchal metaphysics, i.e. constructions of reality. Frye, *The Politics of Reality: Essays in Feminist Theory* (Trumansburg, N.Y.: Crossing Press, 1983), p. 152.

[74] Allusion here is to SF writer James Tiptree's (a woman) protypically feminist story, "The Women Men Don't See," *Warm Worlds and Otherwise* (New York: Ballantine, 1977).

[75] Echols, "The New Feminism of Yin and Yang," p. 453.

[76] This is a play on Catharine MacKinnon's analogy between the exploitation of women's sexuality and the Marxist concept of alienation: in each case what is most one's own is most taken away, sexuality in the first case, work in the second. In my spin on MacKinnon's point: what seems to be most one's own is called an illusion by the political opponent who says what is really the case: that
(Footnote Continued on Next Page)

This has sometimes been called the "Idiot Woman" argument and attributed to radical feminists, who presumably claim to know what's best for all other women: "What are you saying, that I'm a 'pawn of the patriarchy'? That I don't know what's good for me?" Yet lesbian sadomasochists have their own insidious version of the strategy they ascribe to lesbian-feminists: "You don't know what you want (baby), you don't know *your desire.*"

The sadomasochist's attack on lesbian-feminism (egalitarianism is a mask for good-girl patriarchal morality) is a symmetrical rebuttal of the feminist critique of sadomasochism as a product of conditioning. Another way of describing this game is that each player strikes at what is most "utopian" in the other's position, namely what the opponent claims not only belongs to them, but places them most *outside* the mainstream. "You say you are visionary revolutionaries, we say you are the same old story," goes the attack on both sides. Your utopianism is, in fact, mainstream ideology re-baked. This can take the form of humiliation, an act of unmasking that (in the case of sadomasochist discourse) becomes more like disrobing:

> Most dominants are fond of confronting their victims with their response to punishment and insult. There is no defense and no denial possible when one tastes the liquid evidence of lust that is flowing unhampered between one's legs.[77]

The text of the "debate" begins to resemble the sadomasochist scene as our attempts to name the social meaning of sadomasochism are stripped down, as it were, by sadomasochists to the raw essence of desire—repressed desire that is. The utopian impulse of lesbian-feminism is construed as a lie. *"Liar," screams the whip (*152)—to cull another fragment from Califia. The "truth" becomes reduced to the single question, What is your desire? Any and everything else merely masks that question. Egalitarian dreams wrap a veneer of hypocrisy around a tyranny of sexual repression: lesbian-feminists know, but deny the truth of, desire. The reality of sadomasochist desires in women is "liquid evidence" that feminism lies, the truth of the body, of sex trapped beneath the veneer of lofty (feminist) ideals. The argument has a distinctly pornographic ring: underneath their feminism women want it, no matter what else we say and do, we "want it."

---

this natural woman feeling is the sign of social conditioning. Of course this kind of analysis can be a radical strategy for *demystifying* social conditioning. It can also be further *mystifying,* as I'm arguing that the lesbian sadomasochist position is with respect to the charge that lesbian-feminism masks patriarchal moralism. In the case of lesbian-feminist ideals of equality the question becomes, *is* the desire for eroticized equality the sign of patriarchal moralism that lesbian sadomasochists claim it to be? We have the tools of historical analysis, with respect to both the meaning of feminism and the meaning of patriarchal moralism with which we *can* answer this question. See MacKinnon, *Toward a Feminist Theory of the State* (Cambridge: Harvard University Press, 1989).

[77]Califia, *Macho Sluts*, p. 152. (Further references in text)

'You lied to me before,' he said, flicking one of her nipples. 'Remember? You told me you didn't like it. But you do. I'm your worst fear and your best fantasy' (227).

Or as the blurb on the book from which this quote is taken claims: "This collection of erotic fiction is a bad girl's wet dream and a WAP (Women Against Pornography) woman's nightmare." Worst fear; best fantasy. Wet dream; nightmare. What hurts "good girls" turns the "bad girls" on. It's all a matter of attitude—whatever turns you on. But it's not. The difference between lesbians over sadomasochism is not whether one gets off and the other doesn't, it's what value we place on getting off to begin with. Perhaps the question is not so much, What are our desires? but, Which desires do we value and why? And secondly, how are we to reappropriate à language of dissent from a "debate" which casts our very resistance to "sexual liberation ideology" into the terms of its own sexual fantasy? Since a pornographic culture has ensured that most women's "best" fantasies, as in most sexually arousing, are also our nightmares and vice versa, getting off is hardly the criterion that distinguishes one from the other. As Sheila Jeffreys puts it, "This is a problem which feminists fighting porn have already recognized and understood. It feels humiliating and paralyzing to be turned on by the very degradation of women that you wish to challenge."[78] It is this very humiliation which is grist for the lesbian sadomasochist mill, that makes feminists' sexual response (real or attributed) to pornography justify the pornographic assertion: *You told me you didn't like it. But you do.* But what this scene excludes is the possibility that not all "desires" are of equal value, and that not all values are equally "desirable."

Desire, Desired Therefore Desirable?

Within the lesbian sadomasochist scene lesbian-feminist values hold no value outside their function as a mask upon sexual repression. The only real value that remains is getting off. Within this logic any attempt by lesbian-feminists to place sexual pleasure in a context of *other* values is equivalent to denying the truth (that women have sadomasochist fantasies).

I began to realize that I had been lied to [by the feminist movement]. *S/M was a part of women's sexuality. It was possible to do it, and survive.*[79] So goes Califia's "coming out" story as sadomasochist in the early eighties. Borrowing from the rhetoric of coming out *lesbian*, coming out *sadomasochist* becomes self-preservation, becomes "truth."[80]

---

[78]"Sado-Masochism: The Erotic Cult of Fascism," *Lesbian Ethics*, vol. 2 no. 1, Spring 1986, p. 73.

[79]*Coming to Power*, p. 245.

[80] This is a topic that demands much more discussion. Whereas in the present context I am critiquing lesbian sadomasochists, the need to be validated by one's political/cultural community has deep and legitimate dimensions and is hardly unique to sadomasochists. Surely the intensity with which women, and lesbians in particular, seek authenticity through recognition accounts partly for the psychological mire of the lesbian sadomasochist debate, especially when such a search for recognition is connected to expressions of sexuality, so shame-laden in our culture. This psychological aspect is important but does not, however, exhaust the meaning of the political conflicts at stake. What I'm trying to look at here is how, in fact, the psychologization of feminism
(Footnote Continued on Next Page)

Anticipating the attack on "homocidal" anti-porn feminists in years to come, Califia suggests that a feminism which excludes sadomasochism is a threat to women's very survival. One gets the sense that feminism is supposed to function, not as a political movement, but as some kind of "sugar momma"[81]—a way to protect every woman's desires.

The "truth" here, that "sadomasochism *was* a part of women's sexuality," is juxtaposed with the "lie": the feminist assertion that there is a likely connection between the real life subordination and sexual abuse of women, and the cultural enjoyment of domination and subordination (i.e. sadomasochism): that women are socialized to respond sexually to sadomasochism. But saying that sadomasochism is a product of social conditioning is not the same as saying that sadomasochist desires do not exist. A political analysis of sadomasochism *presupposes* rather than denies the existence of sadomasochist desires.

The issue named as "what is your desire?" begs the question: what is the relation between our desires and the goals of women's liberation? The *fact* that people desire something begs the question of what people *ought* to desire, while presupposing it at the same moment. Madison Ave. prescribes desires, legitimizing any and all products according to the same rule: people want them. Sound familiar? Sure we want them, but *ought* we to want all things Madison Ave. says that we want? Real women, for example, ought to want douches, diets, deodorants etc. Women *buy* them don't they?

In traditional ethics the claim that such and such a thing is desired, therefore this thing is desirable, is called the "ought-is fallacy," the distortion of logic that leads people to claim that because such and such a thing is *desired, desirable*, therefore it is *good*. Saying what something *is* does not address what it *ought* to be, although saying what a desire *is* often *masks* a buried social "ought," i.e. a dominant social *norm*. Like Madison Ave., lesbian sadomasochism doesn't merely describe, it prescribes desire. Three major selling concepts are shared between the two: "new," "free," "sexy." Enough has been said on the subject of how sadomasochism is neither new or free in a rape culture. Its admitted sex appeal (or what D. A. Clarke calls "sexism appeal") is as much the result of a marketing strategy as the "desire" for scented toilet paper. What appears to be free choice is in fact manipulated: why else would so much effort be exerted to "sell" these desires? But I am not saying that lesbian sadomasochism *the ideology and social fashion of the day* is truly *compulsory*. On the contrary, its *rhetoric* of compulsory, urgent sexuality masks its social prescription: to do sadomasochism on a grand, fully elaborated and increasingly profitable scale. Lesbian sadomasochism is increasingly a business venture. Its styles and tools and toys are literally on sale everywhere; its pundits are equally on sale in mainstream media venues—note Susie Bright's appearance in the *San Francisco Chronicle* as occasional columnist.

Lesbian sadomasochism is not a neutral description of what some women and lesbians desire, but a resounding call to go out and "do it." As has become blatantly clear in the "gay nineties," lesbian sadomasochism is a culture, a style of politics and speech.

(i.e. as "mother") is a political myth that works to de-politicize lesbian-feminist ideology and the argument against lesbian sadomasochism. Lesbian feminists, of course, have our own versions of playing and rebelling against Mother, but this is no reason to therefore "adopt" sadomasochism.

[81] Conversation with Elise Ficarra. October, 1992.

When feminists say that lesbian sadomasochism is not *feminist* we typically mean that lesbian sadomasochism and lesbian-feminist ideology are two different *and incompatible* ethical, cultural and political practices, not that there are two different species of woman or lesbian: those who have such and such a sexual desire, and those who do not. Yet the conflict between the two is typically described as a conflict between *What lesbians really do* and, *What the sex police and censors say we ought to do.* This drama, of course, is confined within the terms of the fantasy of feminism-as-Mother described above. Within this fantasy of feminism, any prescriptive content to feminist ideals—what a group or individual *ought* to do according to feminist principles—registers as repressive.

Every social movement and political ideology, however, has a prescriptive content, radical feminism as well as any other. Politics would not be politics without opinions about how the world *ought* to be and judgments about what actions should be taken to create that world. Political movements always *prescribe*, they are practical and focused on the question, *What is to be done?* The anti-judgment stance pushed by lesbian sadomasochism (and sappy liberalism in general) not only denies its own prescriptiveness but depoliticizes feminism and lesbianism with its assumption that "anything goes" as long as it's "desirable," that "is" equals "ought."[82]

Having said this, I also want to say that lesbian-feminists commit an inversion of the same "ought-is" fallacy. We tend to take our ideals about the kind of lesbian community we *ought* to live in (one based upon equality) as description rather than ideal, and are devastated by the ensuing failure of lesbians to live up to this description. Lesbian sadomasochism prescribes sexual norms—it prescribes what sex *should* be—under the rubric of telling it like it *is*. Lesbian-feminism tends to evade the complexity of what lesbian desire really *is* under an ideal of how this desire *ought* to be. But moving from *ought* to *is* is not so simple. In *Against Sadomasochism*, contributor Karen Rian makes the following argument:

> While the pro-sadomasochism arguments often suffer from psychological determinism (the belief that our behavior is the result of fixed inner psychological influences over which we have no control), the anti-sadomasochism arguments usually suffer from utopian idealism. That is, they have mistakenly assumed that our desires and behaviors can be changed automatically by mentally accepting the 'correct' political ideas.[83]

In other words, from the ideal that lesbian-feminists *ought* to find equality and nothing else erotic, we often tacitly assume that therefore, lesbian-feminists *are* the kind of people who have egalitarian relationships and egalitarian desires. Or we tend to assume that change follows automatically from idea(l)s.

So there is in fact some substance to the sadomasochist's allegation that lesbian-feminists deny the existence of sadomasochist desire in lesbians—check out some of the

---

[82] As D. A. Clarke points out, this liberalism does pay "lip service" to human rights: thus far it does not justify criminal assault or murder. (Personal communication, 1993)

[83] Karen Rian, "Sado-masochism and the Social Construction of Desire," *Against Sadomasochism*, p. 46.

(pre-debate) literature in the seventies (for example, the sourcebook, *The Joy of Lesbian Sex*).[84] To be sure, once the debate broke out, most radical feminist critics of sadomasochism *took it for granted* that most women (and that means lesbians too) *have* sadomasochist desires in a pornographic society. However, our near-silence on the topic of sexuality, particularly a radical feminist discussion of our own desires (including sadomasochist desires) can give the impression that lesbian-feminists do not believe we have these desires. This impression is given by the leap we take from *ought* to *is*, in other words by our *lack of a collective practice* of constructing a new subject of desire.[85] And I would argue that transformation of desire[86] *is* a critical part of the liberation process. As Sheila Jeffreys writes:

> The construction of SM sexuality is a mighty clever ploy for the oppressor. Our resistance is undermined in our very guts if our response to the torture of others or to the trappings of militarism is erotic rather than politically indignant. It is very hard to fight what turns you on.[87]

Decolonizing our bodies and psyches in a sadomasochist culture has the urgency of survival in terms set *outside* the prescriptions of sadomasochism, its equation of survival with getting off. *It is very hard to fight what turns you on.* The value of re-claiming those desires already outside the means of our oppression is the value of fighting back—of dissent. By doing so we might re-figure a lesbian identity that is indigestible to the patriarchal dream factory which makes the source of women's fears into the "best" fantasies.

The Radical Feminist Critique of Sadomasochism

In my view, the lesbian-feminist tendency to assume that change in desires and/or behavior (in this case sexual desires and/or behavior) is just a matter of transforming ideas is due, in part, to flaws in the radical feminist critique of sadomasochism. The section that follows is an attempt to *extend* that critique, not jettison it.

The logic of lesbian sadomasochism is: you have the feelings, therefore "do it," act it out. A central, powerful insight and argument in the radical feminist critique of

---

[84]Bertha Harris and Emily L. Sisley, *The Joy of Lesbian Sex: a tender and liberated guide to the pleasures and problems of a lesbian lifestyle* (New York: Crown Publishing, 1977).

[85]Conversation with Ellen Scott, July, 1992.

[86] Since I think that there are, in fact, *competing* desires (see below) rather than one desire (sadomasochism) vs. the (presumably asexual) ideals of lesbian feminism, I admit that the term "transformation" can be misleading, i.e. as if women had only one desire (sadomasochist) which needed to be transformed. I admit that I am stumped as to how to talk about the process of looking at our desires and moving towards what Margot Farnham calls "sexual integrity," or Andrea Dworkin has called "sexual intelligence," ("The Politics of Intelligence," *Right Wing Women*. (New York: Perigee, 1983), p. 61. There is transformation involved, but not from one singular desire into another singular desire. What I am certain about is my desire to open up dialogue among radical/lesbian-feminists with respect to these questions.

[87]Jeffreys, p. 73.

sadomasochism is that there is a more subtle relationship between desire and action (or behavior), that what is desired may not necessarily be desirable. Whereas lesbian sadomasochists interpret this argument to mean that real lesbians/feminists don't believe that they *have* sadomasochist desires, in fact, the radical feminist argument depends upon the assumption that most women *are* conditioned to respond sexually to sadomasochism. The question that follows for radical feminists is, given that many women have these desires, must we *act* upon them? Typically this question is construed as presupposing a scenario in which immense will power is wielded against sexual urges: hence the moralizing momma figure of radical feminism. However, the binary construction of a sadomasochist compulsory sexuality vs. a radical feminist will power is belied by the reality that lesbian sadomasochism is a matter of no small amount of willful deliberation, in or out of the bedroom. On a cultural, collective level, the entrepreneurial and political propagandist aspects of lesbian sadomasochism are an operation of political planning and will.

The lesbian-feminist as will power vs. the lesbian sadomasochist as natural, compulsive sexuality depends upon the ideological gridlock discussed above, in which every dissent to sadomasochism is defined as a willful repression of sexuality. This framing of the issue generates a scenario in which all sex is domination and submission. As Elise Ficarra perceptively puts it, if sex *is* sadomasochism, all that is left, within this frame of definition, is will power, the drive to overcome sexual impulses.[88] It is assumed by this scenario that lesbian-feminism and a sexuality based on feminist values are wholly a matter of translating political will into sexual wants and acts, rather than one of emphasizing *different* desires.

Yet in all forms of *truly consensual* sex (and here I am including lesbian sadomasochist practices) there is an element of choice with respect to the enactment of desires—limited of course, within a (social, psychological) framework in which options seem (or, indeed are) limited or expansive. Acting, or not acting, on sadomasochist sexuality is not inevitably an exertion of sheer will power vs. the expression of desire. The will vs. desire opposition implies that any ideal sexuality is a product of will power artificially imposing the utopian not-yet onto the now. What is excluded (precluded) by this scenario is the possibility of a sexual dynamic that is not based upon a conflict between will power and sexual desires, but between different sorts of desires, and that sexual values may encompass what is already part of our experience as well as what has not yet taken shape.

As Sheila Jeffreys writes:

There is every ground for optimism. Some lesbians and gay men are very little affected by SM, and are able to practice a different kind of sexuality. Even those of us who do know the extent of SM influence in our lives usually have experienced moments of unusual sexual intensity and pleasure which have not involved fantasized dominance and submission to any degree. In all of us are

---

[88] Conversation, September, 1992. I am grateful to Bonnie Mann and Ger Moane, as well as Ficarra, for discussion which helped me formulate the ideas in this section.

the seeds of change. We can seek to maximise positive sexuality instead of maximising the negative sexuality of SM.[89]

Indeed, as Jeffreys also points out, the insight that sexuality is socially shaped is a key to radical cultural transformation. Yet, having said all this, what I am not clear about at present is what it means (*what is to be done*) to "maximize" a positive sexuality, and to engender such transformation. And furthermore, why is it that dialogue on this subject has been so minimal (if it happens at all) within radical lesbian-feminist contexts? If there are *competing* desires rather than a *singular* desire defined as sadomasochist, what does it mean to *choose* between them? When we're talking about sex we're in a realm where choices and intentions have specific meanings, not assimilable, in my opinion, to the kinds of choices made in other areas of our lives. If it sometimes *feels as if,* on an individual level of sexual interactions, refusing to enact sadomasochist fantasies is a matter of sheer will-power opposed to sexual urge,[90] this may be partly due to a lack of radical feminist dialogue on the matter, and thus lack of a language in which to discuss and imagine the particulars of lesbian sexuality.

Jeffreys is right when she suggests, "we are not to blame for the way our sexuality is constructed, though we have a total responsibility for how we choose to act on it," but this responsibility is not merely individual.[91] If radical lesbian-feminists lack a language for a process of creating what Andrea Dworkin calls "sexual intelligence,"[92] this may be partly due to our tendency to assume that sexuality is a private *and therefore individual* matter. But the assumption that any woman can maximize a positive sexuality on her own is asking a lot of the same woman who we simultaneously see enmeshed in the deeply social conditions of patriarchy. This assumption of individualist choice in the realm of sexuality (and other areas of personal transformation) is at odds with the radical feminist critique of sadomasochism in general.[93]

---

[89]Jeffreys, p. 73.

[90] D. A. Clarke asks, "To what extent is 'sexual urge', a traditional male concept, applicable to women? Is a simple itch the basis of most women's sexual forays?" (personal communication). My point is partly that it's hard to get away from the notion of "urge" or "itch" once you're locked into the deceptive polarity of will power vs. desire. Nevertheless, if there is something that rings true to experience for me and other women about this polarity it is because, I think, lesbian-feminist practices do not yet provide the means of *fully* escaping the ways that our sexuality has been shaped in male culture.

[91]Jeffreys, p.3. I am not suggesting that Jeffreys herself is implying that responsibility is individual. On the contrary she calls on women to direct our energies into collective struggle against pornography, and in other writings to look at our sexuality in something like a new process of consciousness-raising .

[92]Andrea Dworkin, "Politics of Intelligence."

[93]For this point, as will become obvious from what follows, I am drawing on philosopher Sandra Lee Bartky's analysis of the sadomasochist debates in an essay "Feminine Masochism and the Politics of Personal Transformation," in her collection *Femininity and Domination: Studies in the Phenomenology of Oppression* (New York and London: Routledge, 1990). (Future references in text)

Radical Feminism and Bootstrap Ideology

Thus, the radical feminist critique of lesbian sadomasochism is limited by an internal discrepancy between its radical critique of *social conditions* of sexuality and its individualist conception of *change*. Despite a radical analysis of sadomasochism as how patriarchy ticks, there is the not so radical assumption that knowing this, any woman can thereby pull herself up by her bootstraps and out of sadomasochistic desires. There is a conflict here between a radical analysis of the social shaping of our desires (how we come to "want" our oppression) and the liberal notion that we can change those desires at will. "Any woman can—such is the motto of voluntarism," as philosopher Sandra Bartky describes this ideology. "Armed with an adequate feminist critique of sexuality and sufficient will power, any women [sic] should be able to alter the pattern of her desires." (57) Bartky claims that a subtle blame-the-victim ideology creeps in through the back door of this voluntarist version of feminism, in

> the idea that the victims, the colonized, are responsible for their own colonization and that they can change the circumstances of their lives by altering their consciousness. Of course, no larger social transformation can occur unless individuals change as well, but the tendency I am criticizing places the burden for effecting change squarely upon the individual, an idea quite at variance with radical feminist thinking generally.(57)

On this point, radical feminism strangely dovetails with the position that it critiques: the sexual libertarian defense of sadomasochism. Radical feminism tacitly assumes what the latter makes explicit, that the dynamics of subordination and domination can be changed at "will."[94]

Gaining Control:
The Libertarian Defense of Sadomasochism as a Flight from Memory

Pro-sadomasochists often defend sadomasochist practices as a way for women to gain power over their victimization. This "empowerment" is often cast in therapeutic terms

---

[94] Although we *explicitly* argue that this is what *cannot* be done, I'm suggesting that a lack of theorizing and strategizing about actually transforming our desires, i.e. about the decolonization process, does assume that any woman can get out of her colonization at will. Or, that feminists do not *really* have attractions to sadomasochism (as the sadomasochists say that we believe). Or, that it's a misdirection of our energies: we should be focused on changing the system. And, indeed we should. As I'll discuss below, the same individualism rationalizes a lesbian-feminist retreat from political, direct action. What I'm arguing, indeed advocating for here, is the need for a dual level of political process that reclaims the matter of personal transformation from therapized, individualistic containment into a collective process of re-politicized feminist culture and makes culture a *site* of politics rather than a replacement for it. Years ago D. A. Clarke suggested discussion groups called "unlearning S/M." (personal communication).

of "catharsis," that sadomasochism is healing with respect to memories of abuse, or so argues Carol LeMasters for whom

> [S/M has meant] living through past violation but from a different perspective . . . [I]t is not unusual for women experimenting with S/M to remember abusive childhood experiences. [S]adomasochism can be a way to dislodge such memories . . . [O]ne can relive the pain, the excitement, the guilt, the arousal but in another context, with the victim in control of the events.[95]

But it's difficult to see how replaying memories of abuse as a means of sexual arousal can be an effective way of getting *real* control of those events, not when it's those events which twisted together arousal and abuse in the first place. Lesbian sadomasochism is a *fantasy* of control, and a fantasy that indicates enormous effort taken to resist the actual pain of victimization. While LeMasters suggests that sadomasochism *draws upon memory* for *healing* this pain, another argument is that lesbian sadomasochism is an *aversion* from the power of memory on a collective as well as individual scale. It is an aversion from the history of violence that became conscious for women as a movement struggling to *free* ourselves from the violators and a system of violation—a history which hurts.[96] Given this history, the figure of the sex outlaw who "playfully" experiments with the symbols of her own violation—and the violation of women as a people—seems to epitomize an attempt to escape from memory into the sanctuary of a kind of cultural forgetfulness. Sadomasochism and its myth of the sex rebel is what British feminist Margot Farnham has called a "flight from memory":

> [The sexual outlaw represents a flight] both from the memories of each lesbian body and the political memory of the lesbian community which has witnessed different historical phases.[97]

Just as the discourse of lesbian sadomasochism distorts the history of feminism in its good girl/bad girl story, it also distorts, as Farnham suggests, the memories that individual lesbians have—it is a flight from the history of the female body.

I suggest that sadomasochism took hold in the lesbian community in a moment that was roughly parallel with the eruption of memories, within that same community, of childhood sexual violence. This most recent explosion of memory—a memory of rape—was precipitated by feminist activist opposition to male sexual violence, making the latter public and intolerable; it exemplified in a particularly profound way the politics of memory

---

[95]LeMasters, p. 27.

[96] Frederick Jameson, *The Political Unconscious* (Ithaca, New York: Cornell University Press, 1981), p. 102.

[97] Farnham, "The Body Remembers." p. 22.

for an oppressed group, a group that has been atrociously and pervasively victimized for centuries.[98] The poet Nicole Brossard evokes this memory, writing:

> We call memory a precise form of recollection which reminds us of death fire torture traversing female bodies death fire and torture like three horsemen let loose charged with diffusing over us the odour of the patriarchal plague.[99]

The sheer number of women "having memories," as the expression goes, recalls an epidemic. "She's begun having memories," is the shorthand often used among members of the lesbian community. Like a password it instantly conjures up the "patriarchal plague," as Brossard puts it, the phenomenon of women remembering perhaps for the first time in their adult lives what men (mostly) did to them as girl-children.[100] Lesbian sadomasochists often suggest that "What is most evident about anti-S/M feminists is their fear of the unconscious," as Lemasters puts it, "as though the unconscious were a dangerously overpowering force which, if unleashed, could 'take over' one's rational life." But is it fear of the unconscious spilling over that motivates radical feminist critique of lesbian sadomasochists, or is it fear of this memory on historical and individual levels, the virtual boundlessness of this memory, that motivates lesbian sadomasochism?

Using LeMasters' description, in sadomasochism there is clearly an effort to free oneself of the memory of torture, to "dislodge" memories, but in a way that binds one to this past, binds one to *reliving* it again and again, while paradoxically and futilely seeking sanctuary from it. Freedom from history, from the capacity and responsibility to transform the past, is secured in the myth of the sexual outlaw, in scenes shoring up fragments of the past against the specter of ruin by memory—memory, a terrifying force with its specter of unleashed terror and rage.

If lesbian sadomasochism *is* a way to gain control of *memory* through fantasy, it certainly is no way to gain control of the *actual* events stored up in memory, the reality of sexual violence and sexual violators.

Lesbian sadomasochism is a flight from the reality of how the female and lesbian body has been colonized by the institution of heterosexuality, through rape and battering of individual women and girls and through pornography and the pornographic culture and industry; it is also a flight from the meaning of lesbian-feminism (the "lesbian community") on a collective scale, as "a wholly different history; one which recognizes women's struggles to love their bodies in a culture which hates them or objectifies them."[101]

---

[98] The period I am thinking of is the late seventies through the early eighties, when the anti-violence movement (anti-rape, the shelter movement for battered women and the anti-porn movement) took shape and grew.

[99] Nicole Brossard, *The Aerial Letter*, trns. Marlene Wildeman, (Toronto: The Women's Press, 1988), p. 89.

[100] I am not denying the incidence of mothers' sexual abuse of children, or the sexual abuse of boys; I am arguing that, as research still indicates, it is men's violence against girl relatives that is pervasive.

[101] Farnham, p. 25.

Gaining Control and the Need for a
Radical Feminist and *Collective*
Practice of Personal Transformation

It seems to me that gaining actual control over victimization means *stopping it.* This means gaining power through political action that will stop the perpetrators. But, in my opinion, it also means creating a culture of dissent capable of confronting the "plague," the depth of conditioning that women suffer, one by one, in a society where one out of three women is a survivor of incest. Radical feminists, wary of individualist solutions (such as therapy) to a political problem, have paradoxically made the individualist assumption that any woman can change her psyche at will *and* suggested that personal transformation is not a high priority for radical feminists.[102] But the depths of memory tell us otherwise; memory tells us that decolonizing our psyches is indeed a necessary focus for feminist strategy and that it cannot be an individual task. If we agree that oppression is internalized (and this is the best way we account for the appeal of sadomasochism) then we need a way to transform this *internal* level of oppression that is not dissociated from *external* collective, political struggle (in the way that therapy has so dissociated an "internal" reality from the "external").[103]

We need, in my view, something parallel in function to the consciousness raising of the early years of the second wave movement, namely: a method of collective, critical self-reflection capable of moving between the raw areas of memory on the one hand, and invigorating our understanding of what is to be done, on the other. In other words, why not open a new conversation among radical lesbian-feminists about sex, including sadomasochism? It is not only the reserves of memory as the *plague* that we can draw upon. As Jeffreys puts it, "Though many of us have experienced fantasies and practice which incorporate SM values of dominance and submission, we also have experience of positive sexuality with egalitarian values . . . . We can have a sexuality which is integrated not into our oppression but into our politics of resistance" (81).

I see this as a process of reflecting on sexuality with an eye to the ideal, the ideal of decolonizing the body and freeing the lesbian imagination to resist with all its strength the anesthetizing effects of a pornographic culture. I see a new wave of consciousness raising as critical to a new position of reflexivity, the ability to reflect on and change ourselves, collectively, as part of the process in which we fight the world men have made

---

[102] Radical feminists have developed an astute critique of therapy as an individualist (among other things) treatment of a social problem. While this critique is still trenchant, it leaves a gap in terms of strategies of decolonization. In the absence of a collective practice of personal transformation, therapy seems an appealing option, and in some cases, an urgent one given the level of psychic devastation most of us suffer. See Mann, 1987, "Validation or Liberation? A Critical Look at Therapy and the Women's Movement," *Trivia* 10 (Spring 1987), pp. 41-56.

[103] And I would add that the "triumph" of the therapeutic is precisely this dissociation of internal psychology from external political reality and struggles, of which the defense of sadomasochism as cathartic is one consequence.

and create the world as feminists imagine it could be.[104] Perhaps the ability to take on a self-reflexive radical lesbian-feminism is a matter of political will, after all.

Self-Reflection Outside the Mirror of Sadomasochism: Rethinking Lesbian Feminist Ideology

What do I mean by alive? What I mean by alive—not to shrink from what is most difficult: to change one's image of oneself.

—Christa Wolf, *Cassandra*[105]

The Value of Reflexivity

We need a position of reflexivity in order to move from "is" to "ought." In other words, I don't think that radical lesbian-feminism can revitalize itself if we shrink from the risk of confronting the limitations of our own ideology, taking the risk of seeing our ideals as historical, thus partial and changeable. Otherwise there is a tendency to cling to them as timeless essences, a tendency which fixes feminist lesbians as a group and ideology in place and time, in perpetual defense of a static position rather than moving with political and cultural creativity between past and future. At stake in a *self-reflexive* critique of lesbian sadomasochist ideology is memory, in the deepest sense. The lesbian sadomasochist story of the good girls vs. the bad is a damnably revisionist one. However, while a nostalgic idealization of a former lesbian-feminist community is tempting, it is no closer to re-claiming memory in all its complexity than the sadomasochist version. Most radical dykes resist this temptation on an explicit level; but the story of how it all went wrong (and it did, really) that omits a good dose of self-reflection is a story that ultimately stops short of insight at the resting place of fantasy.

Letting Go of an Idealized Harmony

The harmonies of an idealized lesbian community seem out of tune with the noisy dissonance of lived experience. The mournful dirges of betrayal, of course, speak to an impossibly yet ardently clutched image of harmony. Ideals that skate over a work-a-day conception of living our values have engendered much and bitter disappointment at much and bitter failure to live up to the splendor of our expectations for our community and our relationships within it. A consequence of idealism is a tendency to hold each other accountable for ideals that become unrealistic for lack of political practices of personal transformation, of a transformation from *what is* to *what we wish to be* that acknowledges

---

[104] This is inspired by Janice Raymond's concept of feminist "dual vision," "how do women live in the world as men have defined it while creating the world as women imagine it could be?" *A Passion for Friends: Toward a Philosophy of Female Affection* (Boston: Beacon Press, 1986), p. 205.

[105] Christa Wolf, *Cassandra: A Novel and Four Essays.* Trans. Jan van Heurck. (New York: Farrar, Straus, Giroux, 1984).

the tensions and clashes between experience and ideal.[106] Thus there is a grain of truth to the charge of "political correctness"—as there is when applied to the majority of politically idealist communities. When the unity of the ideal, especially the unity of the ideal community, becomes the political goal rather than, for example, stopping oppression, conformity replaces solidarity and ideals are brandished as instruments of internal social control rather than as pivots and sparks of political imagination and creativity.[107]

Prodding the Beach Rubble

What seems most immediately relevant to the lesbian sadomasochism debate is the possibility of re-evaluating ideals of community with respect to *sexual values* by opening up "free spaces" for discussion (Pamela Allen's term for consciousness raising in the early seventies; so much more inspiring than *safe* spaces)[108] to disrupt the safe harmonies fixed by ideals of lesbian sexuality that have become dogmatic, and to reflect anew on the messiness of experience. "If you are squeamish/don't prod the beach rubble," wrote Sappho. This is precisely where we must prod, into the squeaky and the raw, zones of both delectation and disgust, if all the stories, the untold details outside the frame of *both* sadomasochist excitement *and* lesbian-feminist dogmatism are to be freed. These are stories that will undoubtedly include the sexual arousal of sadomasochist dynamics, as well as of other dramas and inscapes, both humble and grandiose, exhausting and exalted, canned fantasies and vibrant discoveries of "uncontaminated moments."[109] Can we invent a way to talk freely, *without fear of censure*, and yet *keep our focus on the common values* we are in the process of shaping?

In the face of the attack on the concept of lesbian community as "police state" wielded by lesbian sadomasochism, it is difficult to not dig in one's heels and engage in a simplistic defense of lesbian community, one that refuses to acknowledge the real way lesbians do wield power over each other[110] But the other side of a self-critique that shows

---

[106] Again, what I'm advocating here is not abandoning ethics, but replenishing ethics with viable practices, e.g. CR, through which to make lesbian community a reality. As Melanie Kaye/Kantrowitz suggests in her recent book, *The Issue is Power* (San Francisco: Aunt Lute Books, 1992) along with new CR groups which discuss sex, are needed CR groups in which lesbian violence is discussed. Both of these kind of groups, which touch upon the two major conditions of our lives, sex and violence, are certainly urgently needed for the revitalization of community and values.

[107] I do not believe that this idealism, nor this tendency to social control is *ever* wholly avoidable; it is an internal risk and obstacle to most forms of political community and movement and can only be overcome by confronting power as a phenomenon that must be *structurally channeled*, not wished away. This was a lesson, a chief lesson, of the anti-hierarchy philosophy of the second wave feminist movement and if this lesson was taken to extremes by excessive anti-leadership practices and beliefs, the lesson still remains valid.

[108] Pamela Allen, "Free Space," *Radical Feminism*, pp. 271-279.

[109] Phrase from Christine Thürmer-Rohr, "From Deception to Undeception: On the Complicity of Women," trns. Lise Weil, *Trivia 12* (Spring 1988), p. 77.

[110] A "utopian" defense of lesbian community can take the shape of a cynical retreat from this community as well as an idealist promotion of it. By this I mean that the bitter condemnation that
(Footnote Continued on Next Page)

how power works between lesbians in nasty ways is a critique that shows how we haven't made power work *for* us. How, in taking the power of sisterhood as a given, have we taken power *over each other* in unacknowledged ways and yet not worked to *take power politically, collectively*? What are the assumptions about sisterhood, community, woman loving that we shrink from changing?

Sisterhood is Power-full All Right

Confrontation with the *realities of power* has permanently fractured a version of a dream of lesbian unity that did not account for relations of power *between lesbians*, including relations of domination and subordination. The task of connecting a critique of lesbian sadomasochism and a broader critique of power inequalities among women/lesbians is crucial.

The broader critique emerged in the eighties as a corrective to certain forms of feminist/lesbian idealism that concealed political, racial, and economic power inequalities between women under a rubric of sisterly love. Space and scope of this essay allow me to raise only a few points of connection between a general analysis of power and a critique of sadomasochism, questions that urgently need to be taken up by others and/or in my own future writings. In my view, the general, relevant question is this: How do power-dynamics within feminist/lesbian institutions, formal and informal groups and relationships structurally relate to institutions of male power, white power and class power? What are the lines of influence, negative and positive, the relations of profit and privilege on the one hand, the relations or potential relations of active subversion on the other hand?

As I see it, there are two levels of power inequalities/abuses among women that have been addressed by feminists over the past decade or so. One level has to do with power differences that reflect race and class hierarchies. Although acted out personally (as racist and classist "behaviors," for example) race and class differences reflect concrete social structures resulting in different access to resources necessary for physical survival. The reality of material power differences among lesbians and women, mostly articulated by women of color and poor women, has affected the lesbian-feminist community in ways that white and middle class lesbians/feminists ignore at both our peril and our profit. For of course the peril of failing to confront race and class stratification in a meaningful way results in the profit of continued class and race privilege; thus white middle class women continue to profit directly and indirectly from the exploitation of poor women and women of color. At another level this profit is to the peril of any radical lesbian/feminist ideology and strategy that might hope to be a historically relevant force for change.

---

most of us level, at one time or another, at the lesbian community for letting us down, whether this is focused on the incursion of sadomasochism or not—and usually it is some combination of sadomasochism and endless other varieties of betrayals and rifts—is too often based on an idealized concept of community. As I will argue here, I don't advocate throwing out the ideal, only *rethinking* the ideal for the purpose of realistically moving towards it and really *creating* community among lesbians.

The other level of power inequality that has been the focus of feminist discussion in recent years is defined by relationships of authority and obedience within lesbian and/or feminist institutions and/or relationships; hierarchy or abuses of hierarchy (abuses of leadership); back-biting (trashing); lesbian battering and emotional abuse. I don't know whether to call these abuses of power an *internalization* of misogyny, *complicity* with misogynist practices, or whether some new term is needed altogether to talk about those power abuses among women that do not line up neatly with the stratification of race and class (although they may overlap).

What is the relationship between lesbian sadomasochism and these two kinds of power relations? Although the relations and distinctions between these power relations require further clarification and elaboration in lesbian/feminist discussion and writings, what *is* clear to me is that lesbian sadomasochism *obfuscates* rather than demystifies or exposes these relations.

Lesbian-sadomasochism calls itself a sexual minority, linking itself with "other" oppressed groups. It especially cashes in on the eighties language of anti-racism for its claim as an oppressed *minority* yet in this very gesture empties out the meaning of racism as a systematic structuring of social power. The term "sexual minority," furthermore, by suggesting a parallel with ethnic minority, suggests that opposition to sadomasochism is equivalent to racism. The repeated strategy of lesbian sadomasochism is to re-write the terms of the *political* conflict between lesbians in its frame of fantasy, on this point, its fantasy of itself as a persecuted minority. While lesbian sadomasochists *are* persecuted *as lesbians* by the right wing, so are lesbian-feminists. Lesbian sadomasochists, unlike lesbian-feminists, however, are not persecuted by the right wing for their ideology but for their lesbianism—whereas it is certainly the case that lesbian-feminists are attacked for feminist and/or separatist ideologies as well as for our lesbianism. Lesbian feminists do not *persecute*, we *critique* lesbian sadomasochists for their *ideology*.

While sadomasochists style themselves as "sexual minorities," implying a parallel with ethnic minorities, a more accurate parallel might be with social groups that come together around sets of beliefs, styles, political agendas, around a particular ethos or aesthetic. I am not saying that race/class conditions are not a factor in other subcultural groups: I'm saying that a subcultural group is not the same thing as a racial minority.

Furthermore, in its reliance on cultural symbols of oppression (the master-slave relationship for example) for its erotic buzz, lesbian sadomasochism flattens out the meaning of historical relations of domination and subordination in general by making them the material of "play." It suggests thereby that the reversibility of power-roles is a matter of individual consent—consent to submission, as well as to mastery.

Dyke as Dissent

The "police state" myth of lesbian community notwithstanding, lesbian sadomasochism *has* brought with it the disappointing realization that no automatic state of grace is entered into upon self-definition as "lesbian" or "lesbian-feminist." Perhaps this disappointment can be transformed into hope with the more positive insight that lesbian identity is a site of struggle.

A lesbian-feminist critique of lesbian sadomasochism cannot afford to root itself in an idealized identity or sexuality. It is not about pitting the non-violent dykes against the man-like violent ones, which would be precisely playing our part in the sadomasochist game. It's not about counter-posing a good lesbian-feminist against a bad sadomasochist lesbian: but about a sabotage of the sadomasochist text. "Good girls" and "bad girls" are both dykes that please men.[111] Lesbian feminists took a historical jump out of this paradigm of man-pleasing, inventing a new social identity *based upon loving women*. But if this jump is not to be a flight of fantasy, perhaps we ought to heed the poet Judy Grahn's words:

> not until we have ground we call our own
> to stand on
> & weapons of our own in hand
> & some kind of friends around us
> will anyone ever call our name Love,
> & then when we do we will all call ourselves
> grand muscley names:
> the Protection of Love,
> the Provision of Love & the
> Power of Love.
> until then, my sweethearts,
> let us speak simply of
> romance, which is so much
> easier and so much less
> than any of us deserve.[112]

If we are not to settle for what Grahn calls *romance*, we must realize that sisterhood and lesbian-feminism is not a given but a new social relation, a historical project of *inventing* woman loving. As Grahn suggests, the language of "love" may not have the force of reality in the absence of a culture of *dissent* to a society in which woman hatred is the norm. Love is not Love, she suggests, if it is not the *power* of love, and her meaning here is not mystical. The power to provide and to fight and to protect has sometimes been forgotten by those of us who have imagined that a love without "weapons" could magically provide all the necessary protection and sustenance women need. Or that such a love could magically fill a gap in feminist/lesbian theory and community where lesbians turn on one another with verbal and physical violence.

The idealization of lesbian love has functioned to obscure the fact that women have power over one another, not only personally, but systematically, as members of privileged groups. Lesbian sadomasochism plays on this gap with its "discovery" of power in the face of the lesbian-feminist tendency to deny or evade the reality of power imbalance

---

[111] I am grateful to Shoney Sien for this insight. Sien used the phrase good girl/bad girl to describe the parallel trends in lesbian community: sadomasochism on the one hand and assimilation, especially baby-making, on the other. I will develop this point below in the concluding section. Conversation, 1989.

[112] Judy Grahn, "Confrontations with the Devil in the Form of Love," *Work of a Common Woman* (New York: St. Martin's Press), p. 158.

between women. The sexual power emblazoned in the sex rebel myth might appeal to a real, and positive need that many lesbians have to claim agency as sexual beings. But it does so at a price. The sexual *power* sold by sadomasochism confirms women's social power*less*ness with respect to male supremacy. Lesbian sadomasochism is a myth of a lesbian power that is no threat to male domination. Power that *would* be a threat, on the other hand, would be women's power to provide for and protect one another as well as to invent a sexual intelligence outside the paradigms of pornography or romance.

The contemporary terrain of U.S. cultural politics is a climate in which what Nicole Brossard has called "the landscape of the lesbian"[113] is being eroded: lesbian identity is obscured by the show-cased visibility of queer identity, and "women loving women" are increasingly kept behind quote marks, a romanticized relic of a naive era before the discovery of "power" *à la sadomasochism* and the systematic forgetting of power as in *fighting patriarchy.*

From Lesbian Nation to Queer Nation

I have been loved by something strange and it has forgotten me
—Djuna Barnes, *Nightwood*

On the One Hand: Unleashing *What?*

Lesbian nation has been displaced by *queer nation*, on a variety of levels, including the level of public visibility/action for lesbians. An anti-AIDS agenda has catalyzed a new rapprochement between gay men and lesbians for some sound political reasons. These include a shared need to fight the intensification of homophobic violence and yes, the intensification of right wing incursions into the public sector in a backlash effort to quash urgently needed sex education strategies and reproductive rights for women. Also, lesbian activists are increasingly speaking out on behalf of lesbians and women who die of AIDS: currently a (predictably) under-studied population and perhaps another hidden body-count. What irks me, however, is not the radical health care and civil rights agenda for gays and lesbians that has admittedly been pushed to the foreground of national attention by AIDS activism, notably The AIDS Coalition to Unleash Power (ACT UP) but the *male* power that has been unleashed by the same agenda.

A crucial sign of this unleashing is the attack on *lesbian* identity by an agenda which is inextricably linked, symbolically and politically, to the promotion of a new sexual pluralist orthodoxy under which lesbian identity disappears. Queer protest is defined primarily by a political platform that has erased the specificity of *lesbianism as a challenge to the heterosexual institution.*

Lesbian sadomasochism, with its dissociation of lesbianism from feminism and from any radical challenge to the heterosexual institution, was a crucial moment in the development of the new sexual pluralism; sadomasochism remains a shaping factor as well as a norm of the new queer culture. In turn, queer politics has both normalized sadomasochism (as safe sex, see below) and popularized sadomasochism as fashion, as

---

[113] Talk given at Crone's Harvest Bookstore. Jamaica Plain, MA. April 17, 1990.

"hip." It is the "artful articulation of hip" which has launched the pop icon of dyke-as-sex-rebel into mainstream culture in flight from the memory of second wave lesbian-feminism.[114]

Boys 'R' Us?

One concrete outcome of queer ideology has been the regularity with which attacks on autonomous lesbian and/or woman-only spaces have been revived in a queer context.[115] The taboo, as it were, on woman-only and lesbian-only spaces has re-surfaced with a vengeance in the post-seventies era of queer. If anyone has any lingering doubts as to the potential force of lesbian-only space try in your own town to establish one measly lesbian-only, or even woman-only event—and take cover as the rhetoric flies: *intolerant, bigoted, reverse sexism—how unfortunate that oppressed groups become like the oppressor, feel they need to keep insulated, insular* . . . all coming mostly from the lesbian-gay-bisexual contingent. The old-fashioned demand that men be allowed into lesbian spaces has evolved into the present-day demand that lesbian identity itself include anything that anybody wants it to include. Hence the latest: transsexuals are back, in this round as "transgender," and they even have their own *transgender nation*. This development *was foreseen* in the discourse surrounding transsexuals and lesbian identity in the seventies, back in the time when lesbian-feminists were closer to winning the argument that no, Doctors—and all the King's horses and all the King's men—could *not* turn men into women.[116] Responding to a recent wave of letters in the *San Francisco*

---

114 I allude here to the verbiage of a male writer who praises Andy Warhol for "the artful articulation of hip" which "made being gay hip" by spreading "the gay appreciation of cock into the hetero culture through his art . . ." The context is a comparison with Madonna: "No one will be able to avoid the existence of hungry cunt again. That's art!" Now, if there's one thing that hetero culture "appreciates" it is cock—and the distinction between gay and hetero appreciation is arguable—and the notion that "hungry cunt" is likewise a transgressive "articulation" is a typical gesture of the new wave of apologists for porn. The "emperor's new clothes" again, that's "hip." (See Joan Wypijewski, *Review Sex. By Madonna," The Nation.* December 14, 1992, pp. 744-748.)

115 See Julia Penelope, "Wimmin- and Lesbian-Only Spaces: Thought into Action," *Call Me Lesbian: Lesbian Lives, Lesbian Theory.* (Freedom, Ca.: Crossing Press, 1992), pp. 52-59, for several examples of these attacks as well as an analysis of this phenomenon. Other events include lesbians' (mostly unsuccessful) struggles in both Santa Cruz, California and Northampton, Mass. in the late eighties and early nineties (and undoubtedly other towns and cities across the united states) to preserve the gay/lesbian yearly march as gay/lesbian and not gay/lesbian/*bisexual*. In Santa Cruz this same struggle took place over the local gay/lesbian community center. In this city the attempt to even have one all-lesbian day at the center, per week, was roundly rejected.

116 See Janice G. Raymond, *Transsexual Empire: The Making of the She-Male* (Boston: Beacon Press, 1979), for an analysis of discourses (medical, psychiatric) surrounding transsexualism in the seventies and the events within lesbian contexts which precipitated debate about "lesbian transsexuals". Like Raymond, the emphasis of my critique of "transgenderism" is not on the "transgendered" *individuals* who have suffered the violence of compulsory heterosexuality, but on the professionals and pundits who perpetuate and profit from the notion that men can be changed, surgically, into women. While "transgenderism" foregrounds the reality that femininity is a male construct, it does so by *preserving* sex difference, i.e. the heterosexual institution, by further
(Footnote Continued on Next Page)

Bay Times elevating "transgender" identity (and vilifying lesbian protest as, for example, "hate mail") Caryatis Cardea writes:

> No further proof should be needed that this whole transsexual/bisexual assault on lesbian identity has only one end: to render lesbians completely invisible and obsolete . . . This *is* the patriarchy, after all. Lesbians exist publicly only insofar as we can make our presence known. We have been doing so for some years now, and the world gets a good deal of assistance in counteracting our presence by a 'gay' world and a 'queer' world in which there is really no such thing as a lesbian.[117]

There is no such thing as a lesbian in a queer world because lesbian, a word representing the ultimate threat of *separation* between men and women, has been turned around in this world to mean the ultimate *fusion*: any *body* can be a *lesbian* body, even a *male* body. Nicole Brossard has written:

> A lesbian who does not reinvent the word, is a lesbian on the verge of disappearing.[118]

In my opinion, the visible record of this disappearance is the full scale *incorporation* of "lesbians" into the official (well publicized, and saleable) story of lesbian/gay/bisexual (and now *transgender*) *nation*, in short the invention of "queer" as the latest, or rather final phase in the phasing out of lesbian-feminism. Reinventing lesbian identity takes on a particular urgency in this climate.

On the Other Hand:
The Queer *Positive* Revitalization
of Direct Action

Queer politics, it must be said, has also been a way for lesbians to "act up" and get rowdy in public. The dyke rebel of today's queer nation has *some* substance; she's not only gloss and style. The militancy of queer nation politics, for example, gives those of us who still yearn for the spirit behind the words "lesbian nation" something to think about.

---

empowering the male "priests" of medicine (and thus the patriarchal social order) to *create* this category, in contrast to being a strategy of *disempowering* (politically destroying) the social system which generates the category. Like Raymond, I have been sympathetic to the individuals who are maimed by the governing categories of male and female and who believe that they are truly woman (or man) inside their physical "shell". But this sympathy reaches its limit with recent events in which "transgenders" are militantly demanding inclusion in political space defined as queer, and receiving that space. As obvious from the debates then (15 years ago) and now, the meaning of *lesbian* identity is the contentious issue at stake. Thus the recent "transgender" militancy is a clear indication that feminist lesbian fears in the 1970s were not paranoia, but a realistic apprehension of the significance of "lesbian" transsexuals as a *penetration* of woman-only space by men.

[117] Caryatis Cardea, "Letter to the Editor," *San Francisco Bay Times*. December 3, 1992, p. 3.
[118] Brossard, p. 122

52

The positive features of queer politics cannot be denied. They include a new tradition of creative, sometimes militant direct action capable of feeding hope in an era of despair.

Still, when Queer Nation organized its queer patrols in New York City, patrols of armed dykes and gay men responding to queer-bashing, I couldn't help but ask, "Where are the feminist and dyke patrols armed against woman-bashing?" "Why aren't we screaming that sexism kills?" the late Jackie Winnow (AIDS and cancer activist) exclaimed in a critique from the inside of the anti-AIDS movement.[119] Indeed, the figures recording woman-slaughter are still staggering and they include death by illness in a society unwilling to provide adequate health care for women, especially poor women and women of color. As Winnow pointed out in a keynote speech to a lesbian "care-givers" conference, while community mobilization for the caretaking of dying gay men has been breathtaking in scale and quality, no comparable mobilization of resources exists for dying women, dying lesbians.

The increased difficulty of mobilizing lesbian community is certainly due in part to the current queer terrain in which lesbian identity is devalued if not altogether erased, in which attacks on autonomous lesbian space are consistent and in which the paucity of our material resources is in striking disparity to the economic resourcefulness of gay male dominated community projects. Partly, but not wholly as an effect of queer ideology, the *material* poverty of lesbian-feminist community coexists with a poverty of *vision*. This poverty is expressed in the near absence of any lesbian mobilization of resources for lesbians and women, and near absence of vision with respect to any truly radical agenda of community politics, one that would include a mobilization of resources for survival and self-defense.[120] This is changing in significant if small ways with the founding of the Women's Cancer Resource Center and Charlotte Maxwell Clinic in the Bay Area of Northern California—Winnow was a primary organizer of the former—and in Santa Cruz, a women's cancer resource center called WomenCare. There are also several lesbian economic redistribution projects in progress at the moment. including The Lavender

---

[119]Jackie Winnow, "Lesbians Evolving Health Care: Our Lives Depend On It," *Sinister Wisdom 39: On Disability*. (Winter 1989-90), p. 23.

[120] Undoubtedly, economic scarcity is one important condition for lack of vision, but unless conditions for protest and resistance are reducible to economics (and I don't think they are), it is not the only condition. Nevertheless, the relationship between economics, privilege and vision should not be underestimated. Many lesbians who I've talked to about Queer Nation actions have been similarly struck by the ferocious sense of entitlement that seems to power the militancy of (predominately white) gay male activists. The latter appear to experience a severe conflict between their white male privilege and severe homophobic attacks on basic rights such as health care. This conflict spurs a capacity to mobilize at a time of great crisis. The parallel emergency facing women on the other hand, the daily war against women by men and the state, is exactly that—daily, everyday, normal. There is no sense of entitlement attacked, as there is no parallel reality of entitlement. As a result, political vision for women continues to require the two-fold task of, on the one hand, exposing that there is an emergency situation confronting us, and on the other, conceiving of a different reality. This is another version of what Janice Raymond called the "dual-vision" of feminism.

L.E.A.F. (Lesbian Emergency Action Fund) in Oakland, California.[121] Without the kind of radical agenda for community and resistance that these kind of projects represent, does woman loving become just a romance?

If Love means protect then whenever I do not
defend you
I cannot call my name Love.
if Love means rebirth then when I see us
dead on our feet
I cannot call my name Love.
if Love means provide & I cannot
provide for you
why would you call my name Love?[122]

In my opinion, the historical meaning of *lesbian separatism* is central to the task of reinventing women loving at this moment of cultural amnesia called "queer."

Dyke as Dissent: Lesbian Separatism

The meaning of separatism, in my view, is to live out the meaning of lesbianism as dissent, by which I do not mean taking a purely reactive stance. While creating a radical alternative to heterorelations, that is, creating a culture based upon a *positive* vision of loving women (not just "reacting" to men) we still must live in a hostile social context that works to oppose this vision at every turn. Lesbian feminism—especially in its most radical U.S. embodiment in separatism—is *inherently* antagonistic to heterosexual culture.[123] But it is not inherently a *politics* of dissent, by which I mean an *activist* confrontation with dominant institutions of the social order as heterosexual. A myth of *peaceful co-existence* with the dominant society is implied by some lesbian separatists who believe that separating from the malestream and creating our own cultural enclaves is a *sufficient* and *sufficiently political* form of resistance to patriarchy.[124]

---

[121] There are undoubtedly other notable exceptions to the picture I am presenting. Grassroots projects move with stealth outside the limelight of media attention and sometimes outside the boundaries of what has been scoped out as "feminist" or "lesbian" (I'm thinking of the women's cannery strike in Watsonville some years back which would not identify itself as feminist but is an example of women's collective resistance to conditions created by patriarchal as well as capitalist structures).

[122]Grahn, p. 157.

[123] As radical lesbians in Quebec, Ariane Brunet and Louise Turcotte write, ". . . these two political forces are antagonistic by nature, since the one, heterosexuality, can ensure its political power only through the destruction of the other, lesbianism. The first is the political institution of the dominating class and the second, the power of revolt." "Separatism and Radicalism: An Analysis of the Differences and Similarities," Hoagland and Penelope eds., *For Lesbians Only* (pp. 448-449).

[124] The notion that creating a separate culture can *replace* political action against the dominant society assumes that this culture can more or less peacefully co-exist with the dominant society, or
(Footnote Continued on Next Page)

54

Recent attacks on the autonomy of lesbian space indicate that the significance of this autonomy extends beyond the sheer existence of such spaces. All the recent attacks on the autonomy of lesbian and woman-only spaces and/or projects are attacks on *separatism*, thus, in my opinion, on lesbianism as a political identity.

In my view, lesbian separatism is an urgent and necessary (but not sufficient) condition for women's liberation.[125] However, there is a historical tendency among U.S. lesbian separatists to de-historicize lesbian separatism and render it a fixed identity rather than a *strategy and political philosophy*.[126] By this I mean that, in the U.S at least, the project of creating women's space has taken on the meaning of getting space for lesbian separatists as one more marginalized, oppressed, silenced group, rather than being defined as a project of making love the *power* that Grahn calls for.

As *open dykes* we *are* marginalized, and we are marginalized by the same homophobes who "queer bash" any lesbians. As *separatists*, however, we are marginalized because we *dissent* from the social order. We are marginalized, trivialized and in fact erased for our *political beliefs*, and for living our lesbian identity in terms of those beliefs, beliefs that threaten the core of patriarchy. The significance of lesbian space has to do not so much with protecting and defending a marginalized group as with the possibility of creating contexts of rebellion, of opening channels for qualitative leaps outside the hetero-scene.

As Hess and Langford and Ross address the issue in an internal critique of separatism published in the 1989 anthology *For Lesbians Only* (but first written in 1980):

> . . . Our little enclaves can exist only with the tolerance of the larger society [liberal-pluralist]. Separatism, racial or lesbian, is somewhat acceptable to liberals as long as it is not armed and militant. That is, as long as it remains a life-style alternative . . . [127]

---

else embraces the idealist view that change will happen through the transformation of ideas rather than social structures. I will elaborate upon this point in the sections that follow.

[125] Here I differ from radical lesbians who dissociate from the term and practice of "feminism" as heterosexual. While I agree with the critique, radical lesbianism as a political identity (in contrast to a lifestyle choice) means nothing if it does not mean that it is one crucial site of women's liberation. Which is precisely why it is a threat to heterosexuality. Nevertheless I take this position knowing full well that in feminist contexts that erase or minimize lesbian-feminist politics and/or that erase or minimize a critique of heterosexuality, I will insist upon a strong lesbian-feminist position. The emphasis on feminism—as in lesbian radical feminism—in the present essay is motivated by what I see as the most urgent threat to radical lesbian identity, namely the sex liberal (queer/sadomasochist) attack on the connection between lesbianism and women's liberation.

[126] Contributors to the British magazine, *The Revolutionary and Radical Feminist Magazine*, Harriet Wistrich and Julie Bindel make this same point in an article entitled "An Ism of one's Own" in which they embrace the strategy of separatism but critique the making of lesbian separatism into a new "ism" that gets to be oppressed and so forth. (Issue 19, 163 Abbeyfield Road London SE16 2DQ). Also, radical lesbians in Quebec, unlike most U.S. separatists (or most publicized) focus on a political critique of heterosexuality and are wary of a strategy which emphasizes building an alternative culture. (See *Amazones D'Hier/Lesbiennes D'aujourd'hui*)

[127] *For Lesbians Only*, p. 131.

As we can see, ten years later, the statement doesn't completely hold given an increasingly sex liberal climate where "anything goes" *except* lesbian separatism. Nevertheless the point stands that a separatism without "weapons of our own," as Grahn might say, is not one that will last as a culture of *resistance*. I would argue that rethinking the very concept and reality of *resistance* as it has functioned or not functioned in lesbian ideology is very much at stake in the reinventing of lesbian identity today.

Lesbian *Resistance*: Culture *and* Politics

Lesbian culture, for it to belong to and represent most lesbians, will be pro-woman, pro-working people, and multi-racial . . . a genuine culture of lesbians will always be in danger of repression, co-optation, and absorption, until such time as lesbians have control of our lives.

—Melanie Kaye/Kantrowitz[128]

Really, I don't want to live my life resisting—I want to live my life by creating, loving, building. But I live in a world where my creativity is, by definition, resistance—which means, in order to act I must always know I'm acting against something as well as for something. This isn't fun.

—Elana Dykewomon[129]

Are we, as Dykes, willing to sustain each other?

—Elliott [130]

LeMasters and Johnson?

"I'm talking about organized, political resistance," Andrea Dworkin once stressed in a speech given in the late eighties.[131] The simple phrase resonates powerfully for me in a climate where it is increasingly difficult to conceive of this simple political necessity—no less a necessity for women than any other oppressed group in history. But there is a tendency among feminist lesbians in the U.S. to affirm separatism as a new option *in distinction from* resistance. While not representative of separatists by any means, Sonia Johnson epitomizes this tendency. "Resistance doesn't work," she claims:

---

[128]"Culture-Making: Lesbian Classics in the Year 2000?" *The Issue is Power*, p. 182.

[129]"Notes for a Magazine," *Sinister Wisdom 48: Lesbian Resistance*, p. 4.

[130]"Funeral Food," *Sinister Wisdom 45: Lesbians and Class*, p. 39.

[131]Speech given at a full-day conference, "The Sex Liberals and the Attack on Feminism," Saturday, April 4, 1987, New York City.

When we look at the world what we see is patriarchy at its Nadir . . . I think this is not *despite* women's resistance but because of it . . . . Resistance is an acknowledgment and an acceptance of powerlessness.[132]

This philosophy is one extreme version of a fairly wide-spread notion among some (mostly white and middle class) lesbian-feminists, namely that focusing on the enemy gives the enemy more power, that fighting the enemy is another form of identifying or relating to him and makes us more powerless. *Take the eyes off of the guys* is Johnson's call. But the idea that liberation from patriarchy or any social system of oppression can be achieved without resistance is another fantasy. With Johnson's outright repudiation of resistance, we re-enter a strange mirror dance between lesbian sadomasochist ideology and feminist lesbian ideology. Indeed it could almost be Sonia Johnson but in fact is pro-sadomasochist Carol LeMasters who writes:

To revolt outright against the patriarchy is to affirm its authority. To righteously confront it is to see patriarchy as a monolithic whole free of contradiction and more powerful than it is.[133]

The point of convergence between the two positions is striking. While for Johnson, patriarchy is not in our heads but *actually* monolithic, both writers agree that resistance against patriarchy helps *create* patriarchy. What is fantasy for LeMasters may as well be for Johnson, if patriarchy is a matter of belief. "And if we perceive ourselves as powerless, presto, we *are* powerless," Johnson asserts.[134] For both Johnson and LeMasters, patriarchy becomes an *internal* reality to be accepted or rejected. The two positions, ethically opposed on the issue of sadomasochism, converge on an *idealist* view of change; patriarchy is a mind-set and change is *choosing an attitude.*

It is certainly strange to be comparing these two authors, these two positions. In doing so I risk glossing over their significant differences. Johnson is rooted in radical feminism and has done much in her feminist career to inspire women to radical feminism. Whereas Johnson has done much to name the actual horrors of patriarchy, and is committed to a positive vision of lesbian reality outside the frame of these horrors, LeMasters virtually trivializes these horrors in the same stroke that she accepts them as inevitable. This is a difference in values and vision; my motivation in comparing the two thinkers is precisely to sharpen these differences by revealing an undesirable—and changeable—point of commonality.

Patriarchy Is in the Eye of the Beholder

As Johnson makes explicit, there is a scary connection between the position that says revolt against the patriarchy gives the patriarchy power and the position that power,

---

[132]Carol Anne Douglas, "Wildfire: Igniting the She/Volution [Book Review]" *Off Our Backs*, Aug/Sept 1989, p. 20.
[133]LeMasters, p. 28. (Further references in text)
[134]Douglas, p. 20.

in general, is in the eye of the beholder. This denial of social reality works to mystify and reinforce inequalities between lesbians. "No woman really needs to work in the patriarchal system if she doesn't want to," Johnson asserts, ". . . I choose to believe that neither I nor any woman has to work in patriarchy in order to live, and that our conviction that we do is part of the brainwashing that keeps us imprisoned there."[135] I see no difference between this proposition and the right wing and neo-liberal position on "the welfare mother": that she is responsible for her condition of poverty. She chooses to believe, therefore it is so; any woman can choose to believe that she is powerless or powerful, rich or poor, capitalist patriarchy is an "attitude" problem and what she needs, presumably, is to pull herself up by her bootstraps.[136] Carol LeMasters, for different reasons, sees patriarchy as a state of *mind:*

> Better to acknowledge patriarchy and undermine from within, gently erode, recognize discrepancies, play with the roles, the language and the symbols, and let the play itself rob them of their terrifying power. (28)

The proposition here is that women, unlike any other oppressed group in history, have the option of *playing with* the power of their oppressor rather than *fighting* it. Interesting that one would never apply the same logic to other political contexts. Could anyone ever conceive of suggesting to Black South Africans, for example, that they refrain from outright revolt, and "play" instead with the symbols of apartheid? Why is it that the same people who clearly see the need for militant resistance (whether armed or non-violent) in other political contexts, consistently fail to see that *women* live in a state of emergency? LeMasters' flippancy contrasts somewhat with Johnson's earnest repudiation of patriarchal violence, but the two converge on the radically idealist assumption that patriarchy is a mind-set. Lesbian sadomasochist transgression meets Johnsonesque lesbian transcendence: one would play with power, the other would leap over it.

Resistance and U.S. Separatist Ideology

Johnson's notion that "resistance doesn't work" takes an idealist tendency that pervades U.S. lesbian separatism and pushes it to its extreme conclusion. This is a tendency that *contrasts* separatism with "outright revolt" and suggests, implicitly or explicitly, that direct resistance to patriarchy equals *participating* in patriarchy, "giving it more energy." Sarah Hoagland, for example, in her discussion of separatism, distinguishes "separation and withdrawal" as "a significant type of choice" from "choosing to challenge the system from within"[137] but fails to account for resistance to the system which doesn't fall neatly into either category. "Withdrawal/separation" vs. "working within"

---

[135]Douglas, p. 20.

[136] And her unwillingness to do so is what makes her the "sponge"—and scourge—of society. Such a "right wing" view is, of course, tacitly endorsed by the pernicious Clintonite "new liberal" promotion of "work fare."

[137]Hoagland, p. 3.

are false alternatives; they exclude the option of fighting and *destroying* the system. Do *confrontational politics* come under Hoagland's heading of "challenging the system from within"?

Sidney Spinster seems to imply as much when she writes, "There is a glaring contradiction between my desire to confront patriarchal behavior and my commitment to female Separatism."[138] She goes on to explain, "There is a glaring contradiction between the strategy behind the tactics employed by most activist Feminist groups and my strategy."[139] Whether there is a contradiction between forms of feminist activist tactics and separatist strategy or not, and I'm sure there often is, why is this contradiction taken so often to mean a contradiction between *confrontational tactics* per se and separatist strategy?

Hoagland makes an analogy between separatism and strategies of philosophical argument, a move which points up the idealist tendency at work. "Philosophically," she writes, "there are at least two ways to challenge a basic statement or idea: we can argue that it is false or we can render it nonsense," the latter being analogous to the separatist strategy. She continues:

> Rendering it nonsense is to treat it as unintelligible, as in having no sense. Arguing that it is false may bring a certain kind of satisfaction, but it is nevertheless to agree that the statement is possibly true—that it makes enough sense to debate. Thus while challenging it this way we are, at a deeper level, validating it.[140]

With respect to moral argument, Hoagland's point is profound—as she illustrates convincingly with an example of debates around race. While many liberals, for example "come up with a raft of arguments to prove that [a claim about Black genetic inferiority] is false . . . in so doing, they are tacitly agreeing that the claim is intelligible and debatable . . . Another choice is to refuse to engage in the debate, to separate from it, to treat the claim as nonsense, to say it makes no sense."(4) This speaks to the moral undertone of separatist strategy, namely the refusal to "dialogue with men" about, for example, something along the lines of the proposition that women—or Blacks, or Jews, etc. etc. —are human.

> Some things cannot be proven. And one of them, it strikes me, is the right of Jews to exist. Simply speaking, the only thing one can do is fight for one's own right to exist.[141]

---

[138]Sidney Spinster, "Warriors of the Luniform Shield: Lesbians and Direct Action." eds. F. Delacoste and F. Newman, *Fight Back: Feminist Resistance to Male Violence* (Minneapolis, Minnesota: Cleis Press, 1981) p. 306.

[139]Spinster, p. 306.

[140]Hoagland, p. 3. *For Lesbians Only. (Further references in text)*

[141]Jacobo Timmerman, *Prisoner Without a Name, Cell Without a Number* (New York: Alfred A. Knopt, 1981) p. 79.

But while Hoagland's discussion illuminates something about a radically lesbian strategy of challenging "a basic statement or idea" it falls short of illuminating separatism as a *political* strategy: patriarchy is *not a basic statement or idea*, it is a *social reality*. While "truth" can be challenged by repudiating it or rendering it nonsense, *power* is not a matter of *argument* and cannot be rendered nonsense in the same way that propositions or arguments can. *The only thing one can do is **fight** for one's own right to exist.*

There is a convergence between Hoagland's discussion and the lesbian sadomasochist position which calls on lesbians to let "the play" "rob" patriarchal "symbols" of patriarchal power, as if the reality of patriarchal power was merely symbolic. Both positions attempt to flatly translate strategies of theory, argument, and art on the one hand into political strategies on the other.[142]

It seems to me that separatist strategy is about withdrawing *care-taking* attention from men, including the care for male approval which maintains our dependency on male validation within their system of logic. What I reject is the translation of this strategy into the strange assumption that political confrontation, keeping warrior eyes on the guys, is tantamount to asking for male approval or validation. What is true *escape artistry* in the realm of thought and emotion *can* become *escapism* in the realm of political action, if the two are taken as one, rather than seen as interconnected. There is a confusion here, I suggest, in the notion that withdrawing our *payment of attention to men* in terms of securing their approval and "protection" means that we stop *paying attention to* the attempts they make to track us down when we "disappear."

Escape Artists

"Take the eyes off the guys" in one sense flashes a notion of lesbian genius, in the sense of the woman who has "her wits about her"[143] and can spit in the face of "the man in her head"[144] and *escape the scene* of thought entirely. It is a principle I'm studying in feminist self-defense classes: do whatever you can do to *change the scene*; defense of

---

[142] Argument and debate depend on appeals to value and logic, whereas political strategies are focused on transformations of power, including destruction of, seizing, and/or re-channeling power. The two types of strategies almost always work together inextricably. I think for example of any feminist campaign, such as campaigns against rape. *Defining rape* (which has included seeing that men define rape as sex) and *stopping rapists* through organized resistance are overlapping strategies but not identical. This overlap between argument and political tactics is pointed up when feminists emphasize changing the law and thus narrow their focus to tactics of persuasion or argument. Contrast a strategy focused on law however, with that of organized groups of women who retaliate against rapists and/or who patrol the streets. The two cases are contrasting ways of combining "argument" or discourse with confrontations of power. Neither of them however, is *necessarily* invested in "proving" to the enemy women's right to exist, though they might be.

[143] The title of the anthology of women's self-defense success stories, eds. Denise Caignon and Gail Groves, *Her Wits About Her: Self-Defense Success Stories by Women.* (New York: Harper and Row, 1987).

[144] The title of a 1970s lesbian-feminist song by Kathy Fire, *Songs of Fire: Songs of a Lesbian Anarchist* (New York: Folkways Records, 1978).

self[145] means disrupting the scenario that's in the man's—the attacker's—head. This amounts to getting him out of *your* head as you go about disrupting his assumption: that you share his belief that you are his victim/plaything. Of course this principle animates lesbian creativity of all kinds, and at its best is a spirit of wild *irreverence* for patriarchal rules of discourse, often expressed in furious humor.[146]

The call to take the eyes off of the guys is inspirational when it speaks to the urgency of sustaining an intense focus on the positive affirmation of a *lesbian culture*, as well as on the oppositional strategy of *stopping the men*.[147] Indeed, as my self-defense teachers have discussed it, a most effective way to change the scene of an attack is to put oneself first, to sustain a focus on what one wants that is fierce enough to match one's will to stop the attacker. *This is not the same as taking your attention away from the attacker.*

On the streets and elsewhere, taking your eyes off the guys is a good way to get shot in the back. *Fighting* power is not the same as *affirming* it, no matter what the new age pundits say about giving energy to negativity. Furthermore, a strategy of confrontation which requires a certain burning attention paid to "the guys" may undermine male *logic* with far more effective force than a strategy that limits separatism to a focus on the building of feminist/lesbian culture. A woman who fights back, and even better, women and dykes organized into groups fighting back, patrolling the streets perhaps, render *non*sense what is fundamental to patriarchal "sense"-making, the belief that women cannot and will not fight back.

When a woman fights back she is withdrawing from the argument, from the game in which she must ceaselessly prove her humanity to the man with the foot on her neck.[148] In that sense fighting back is also a disappearing act in the attacker's scope of vision, as the traceable object of male fantasies, the female victim, dissolves before his eyes and a *thing* or *movement* his logic cannot quite track takes its place: a "crazy" woman, i.e. a woman enraged, a man hater, a god damn dyke, are some of the names of this moving target.

Does Politics = Altruism?

What I'm rejecting in my critique of idealist separatism is the unnecessary and detrimental dichotomy in separatist ideology between withdrawal and confrontation.

---

[145]Phrase from Melanie Kaye/Kantrowitz, *The Issue is Power.*

[146] I think most of Mary Daly who consistently infuriates what she calls the "professor yessirs" (*Pure Lust* Boston: Beacon Press, 1984) by eluding their cognitive snares. Despite efforts to track her down and fix her in place with such caricatures as "essentialist" or "cultural feminist," the movement that is untraceable in Daly and other revolutionary thinkers is a rupture in the very categories with which attempts are made to contain her —a leap free from the metaphysical gridlock of the straight mind.

[147] Inspiration, Heather Horak's (unrecorded) 1988 song, *Stop the Men.*

[148] Thanks to Bonnie Mann for this formulation of the issue. Speech given at Feminist Rally: "Naming The Real Criminals." Northampton, Ma., August 26, 1989.

There is a confusion here between withdrawing energy from caretaking and withdrawing from politics, a confusion based on the notion that politics *is* caretaking.

> All we can get by struggle is more struggle, more pain and more misery. [T]he truth is that our simply being alive, simply being *us* gives us the right to rainbows, and it is neither necessary nor useful to continue to try to *earn* happiness by rescuing first everyone else who is suffering.[149]

Escape artist as she is, Johnson seems unable to escape a christian panorama which reads political struggle as a drama of salvation in which "happiness" is "earned" through saving "others." But who is the "we" "saving" the "others"; who are the "others" and how did the dichotomy "we" and "others" come about? Magically? By strength of will? Imagination? And when did liberation struggle come to be seen as altruism? Is feminism the Mother fantasized by sadomasochists after all? If so, there is a more than a hint of a racist and classist undertone to an ideology which upholds a bourgeois individualist stance of looking out for oneself, but does so under the name of rejecting the role of mother and affirming the autonomous lesbian self. Indeed "altruism" presumes a position of power from which one is saving others.

To reject politics *as altruism* is to implicitly affirm that altruism (self-sacrifice) and egotism (self-aggrandizement) are the only alternatives. These are false alternatives which exclude the option of a collective struggle for liberation (not "happiness," although happiness is part of it) that is as much love of self as it is a commitment to others.

Withdrawing from Men, not Politics

What is the chance of *maintaining* a culture and community that is not *also* politically organized to combat the external forces of heteropatriarchy? The man is not *only* in our head, but all around us. When separatism is defined as separating from *politics* (not men), separation becomes a retreat, a dropping out, as if there was no other alternative to working within (and thus, the argument goes, energizing) the system. But the alternative to working within the system is not *only* dropping out. As Valerie Solanas once said, *"Dropping out is not the answer; fucking up is."*[150] Sabotage and subversion, not retreat, in other words. What this implies is *extending* the meaning of separation and withdrawal.

Separatist strategy as lesbians such as Mary Daly, Marilyn Frye and Sarah Hoagland first discussed it, is a strategy of withdrawing *access*. Thus, separating ourselves physically and psychically from men can mean depriving men of energy resources as well as regenerating ourselves, *on a variety of levels*. It can mean creating new contexts of meaning *and of material survival* outside the heterosexual system that sucks women dry. Lucia Valeska points out that:

---

[149]Johnson, p. 21

[150]Solanas, Valerie. "The Scum (Society for Cutting Up Men) Manifesto." [Excerpts] Ed. Morgan, *Sisterhood is Powerful.*, (New York: Random House, 1970) p. 517.

As a grand conductor of the quality of human life, and the largest world-wide distributor of private, public, psychic and economic resources, the institution of heterosexuality and the ideology which implements it are never to be taken lightly.[151]

What follows is that lesbian separatism, defined as *a strategic attack upon this system*, cannot be taken lightly:

It is also true that the only institutional and ideological alternative available is lesbian-feminism. *Not because the act of women loving women is in and of itself revolutionary (potentially yes, actually no) but because it provides the soil for revolutionary growth*.[152]

If this soil has not seemed so fertile, this is perhaps partly due to a certain idealizing and thus *underestimation* of separatism as a *political* strategy of withdrawing access. Creating a separate culture has been taken as an end in itself, as if freedom could be achieved without changing the dominant structures of power.

When the maintenance of a separate culture becomes its sole aim separatism becomes non-revolutionary. It tries to evolve towards freedom with cultural and psychological changes (changes internal to, confined to, the community or the individual).[153]

Separatists have *idealized* the strategy of separatism as if withdrawal and regeneration could take place as cultural events alone, without a political fight to withdraw access (what else, for example, is the destruction of porn but a withdrawal of access?) and a political strategy to regenerate community resources for purposes of physical as well as spiritual survival—for example, for economic redistribution, as well as for concerts and bookstores. I would argue that abstention from political struggle under the name of creating lesbian culture serves to mystify predicaments of class, race and sex oppression that can hardly be challenged by culture (ways of thinking; new values; beliefs; consciousness) alone. This rejection of *politics* in the name of *culture* mystifies and reinforces social inequalities among lesbians and thus idealizes, in the worst sense, lesbian community. On this last point, Elliott's words on class oppression are pertinent,

Stopping class oppression isn't about needing a better philosophical understanding of privilege. It's not about being anti-oppressive or being a more effective ally ... *Class is about survival, about which of us will and won't make it*. [154]

---

[151]Valeska, Lucia. "The Future of Female Separatism," *Quest : A Feminist Quarterly*, vol. II, no. 2 (Fall 1975) p. 12.

[152]Valeska, p. 12. (emphasis mine)

[153]Hess, Langford, and Ross, *For Lesbians Only*, p. 130.

[154]Elliott, *Sinister Wisdom* p. 39, (emphasis mine).

Without strategies of fighting the dominant, capitalist system as well as strategies for the redistribution of resources, the question of survival (who will make it, who will not) becomes individualized. A conception of freedom as psychological, spiritual, intellectual freedom alone, tacitly resigns itself to a world in which every individual woman is condemned to her collective fate in a class system. This of course holds equally true for the collective fate of women and lesbians under race war, and the war of sexual violence against women. This individualism (which results in extreme isolation) is the shadow side, the undertow of futility beneath the optimistic face of an ideology promoting a "right to rainbows." Elliott pointedly asks:

> Are we, as Dykes, willing to sustain each other? And I mean *really* sustain, not just entertain, challenge, instruct, appease, or even please and delight each other.[155]

We have depended too long on the notion that lesbian community and culture is a matter, primarily, of inspiration and emotional support, and not one of sustaining one another at the level of material survival. This is about self-defense at the level both of economics and of confrontational direct action against male violence. An ideology which promotes the belief that poverty, racism and misogyny can be transcended in feats of the lesbian imagination is an ideology which buffers the privilege of those lesbians who can (literally) afford the illusion—temporary though it might be—that they have so transcended these conditions, and further isolates those who cannot afford it but embrace this illusion anyway. (The majority of separatists probably fill the latter category. The fact that many lesbians are not privileged does not mean that some of them do not also subscribe to the kind of mystifying ideology that upholds other women's privilege). I say "temporary" because this illusion depends upon a contingent safety for lesbians and lesbian social space in the U.S. and elsewhere. But a lesbian whose existence is contingent on a climate of fluctuating tolerance (speaking now of the U.S.), namely tolerance for the remnants of lesbian-feminist culture in a queer world, in a right wing world, is not lesbian as dissent but a false transcendence of social categories. As if we could secure an isle of freedom by leaps of the imagination, or the category of "lesbian" itself offer magical sanctuary from the material conditions of the world.

Can We Sustain Our Culture Without Politics?

Culture *is* essential for revolutionary politics. The philosopher Raya Dunayevskaya discussed "The dual rhythm of revolution which is not just the reorganization of objective material foundations, but the release of personal freedom, creativity and talents." And a vital lesbian culture would seem to have the following dual meaning: on the one hand, culture defined as collectively sustaining the survival of *lesbians*, and thus recycling the material resources otherwise channeled into the heterosexual system; and on the other sustaining the survival of *lesbianism*: inventing, remembering, celebrating lesbian identity

---

[155]Elliott, p. 39.

in the release of creativity and talents long suppressed, negated, crushed by heteropatriarchy. In the interface between these two meanings of culture is glimpsed the urgency of politics; politics sustains culture as much as the reverse. In another, but relevant context A. Sivanandan writes of the limits of a separatism (in this case Black separatism or "cultural nationalism") that makes cultural identity its political goal:

> Creating ourselves in terms of our culture and reshaping our society in terms of that creation are part and parcel of the same process. To abstract our culture from its social milieu in order to give it coherence is to lose out on its vitality. [156]

The social milieu of lesbian-feminist culture, of separatism, I have been arguing, is shaped by women's liberation politics; a historical context of opposition to the existing dominant order as heterosexual. When we abstract feminist lesbianism from this milieu, from its historical dynamic as women's liberationist, values such as "women loving" become abstract indeed, losing vitality, because we *cannot really sustain* them without political militancy.

A culture such as lesbian culture which has its roots—the roots of its symbolism, its languages, its values—in the historical context of a political movement loses its dynamism when it separates from politics; it loses the force of its language and its intensity of vision wanes to fantasy; it loses a certain ferocity of longing to bring about dreams in the real world and settles for carving out small, shrinking spaces where lesbians can buff our values and hone our already-carved-out ideological positions.[157] To quote Hess, et. al. again,

> . . . too often the construction of a new lifestyle and institutions becomes an end in itself. So the strong community base which is a valuable part of separatism (and feminism in general) comes to be a substitute for a movement, instead of a support for it. . . Instead of pushing forward more we stop at defensive positions of survival, self-improvement and shelter from the outside world.[158]

---

[156] Sivanandan is a Black writer in Britain critiquing cultural nationalism in Black liberation contexts. There are indeed striking parallels between separatism in feminist/lesbian contexts and in other liberation contexts such as Black movements, where oppressed groups prioritize the building of a "counter-culture" and re-claim a positive cultural/ethnic/sexual identity as a political strategy of decolonization in the face of the degradation of identity, history, cultural memory that the oppressor has waged upon this group. See A. Sivanandan, "Culture and Identity," *Liberator* (New York, Vol. 10, No. 6 June, 1970.

[157] And often "we take from the oppressor the instruments of hatred and sharpen them on our bodies and souls," as Aleticia Tijerina points out in a different context. We sometimes use these very instruments to turn *lesbian* values and ideological positions into weapons against ourselves, each other. "Notes on Oppression and Violence" *Haciendo Caras: Making Face, Making Soul,* ed. Gloria Anzaldúa, p 152, quoted by L.M. Kenney, "Some Notes on Resistance," *Sinister Wisdom* #48: *Resistance,* p. 53.

[158] *For Lesbians Only,* p. 131.

The attempt to choose culture as an option *over* politics is an illusory choice which deprives lesbian-feminism of its vitality, its dynamic *movement* as political culture. Separatism is not a meaningful choice *over* resistance, it *is* resistance—but only if extended beyond its current contentment to build culture as an end in itself instead of building culture that, *actively confronting* heteropatriarchy, would become a site of women's activism. Separation and withdrawal are urgent if they do not imply retreat. Separatism is revolutionary if it is taken to mean a withdrawal of access from heteropatriarchy that throws a wrench, indeed a bomb in the machinery of what Valeska calls "the largest world-wide distributor of private, public, psychic and economic resources, the institution of heterosexuality."[159]

Realism and Idealism

While lesbian sadomasochism presents a picture of itself as filling a void hollowed out by sexual repression and denial of power, I would like to suggest that it moved into a space voided by political inertia (not sexual repression) a space where lesbian values have become abstracted from their historical *movement* in women's liberation struggles. When lesbian separatism becomes idealist rather than visionary it creates a vacuum that, for many lesbians, appears to be filled by, among other things, the apparent "realism" of sadomasochism.

But what "real lesbians" do in the sadomasochist script is little more than opt for a good fantasy. And the biggest fantasy of all is that in doing so they are *transgressive*. Transgression needs a law in order to exist; it needs a barrier to cross. If Feminism isn't Mother, sadomasochists will have invented her to provide this barrier. Since it isn't, they did. It is feminist lesbianism that is "gently" eroded from within by lesbian sadomasochism. Lesbian sadomasochism is a shaping factor of a social terrain which works at eroding the *landscape of the lesbian* by assimilating it into itself as a factor of patriarchal realism—by *including* it, rather than *outright resisting* it. It is not the *eruptive resurgence* of a *downtrodden* element in the lesbian community but a sign of the assimilation and *absorption* of lesbianism into heteropatriarchy. Lesbian sadomasochism consents to the idea that lesbianism is (inevitably) the same as anything else under the heteropatriarchal sun.

It is precisely the reality of assimilation that is obscured by the bad girl/good girl fantasy, a fantasy of conservative lesbian-feminism that masks the real, good girl face of lesbian sadomasochism.

Conclusion

Question Authority.
Question Reality.
> —Bumper Sticker Slogans in the Eighties

Well, they got women on T.V.

---

[159]Valeska, p. 12.

but I still ain't satisfied.
'Cause co-optation's all I see,
and I still ain't satisfied.
They call me "Ms.,"
they sell me blue jeans,
Call it "Women's Lib,"
they make it sound obscene.
Whoah, they lied.[160]
—Bonnie Lockhart

Questioning Reality and Killing your Television

Escaping the narrative snare of patriarchal realism, a plot where even the "bad" girls please men, compels me to turn from a preoccupation with challenging the notion of what is "bad" and to ask, finally, what *is* "good" about lesbians, or will the real "good" girls please stand up? Idealists, for all our flaws, are usually good at *questioning reality* —a strategy undoubtedly appropriate in a country where *reality* is primarily a television production. The "progress" which has put *lesbians* on national television is an object lesson, if ever there was one, about lesbian identity and patriarchal reality.

I refer here to Barbara Walters' show, "20/20" which featured a story on lesbian life in a New England town.[161] The show highlighted stories of white, upper class lesbians, almost exclusively couples (one couple owns both a Porsche and a Rolls Royce); it exposes the flip side of lesbian sadomasochist transgression, namely its bourgeois all-american face. This, reader, is the real good girl/bad girl story. The bourgeois, consumerist aspect of lesbian culture is of course also explicit in the media flirtation with "new" lesbians discussed previously, the "adventuresome" lesbians who are tired of "screaming women's liberation" and would rather be taking Olivia cruises or opening "girl spot" sex clubs. But the recent "20/20," which coddles a conventional U.S myth of suburban "respectability," spotlights (in my opinion) the decisively "good girl" fantasy underlying all "transgressions" popularized by lesbian sadomasochism. Indeed, like heterosexual pornographers and sadomasochists, lesbian sadomasochists participate as fully in the bourgeois world as their supposedly moralizing counterparts; they *are* that world. Lesbian sadomasochism is the transgression of a lesbian culture defined *not* by feminist principles but by rapidly congealing norms of white, middle class American life-styles. Transgression needs a norm and norms need a transgression; the patriarchal moralist needs the pornographers, he needs to drive pornography underground to savor its excitement and linger over its "forbidden" details à la Meese Commission and Jessie Helms. The story is not altered by its placement in a lesbian frame; an increasingly bourgeois lesbian culture will need its transgressions, it will need its sadomasochism.

Broadcast at a time when hard-won, basic gains for gay/lesbian civil rights were under ferocious attack, the recent "20/20" show may have tempted liberal viewers to

---

[160]Verse 1 of "Still Ain't Satisfied" by Bonnie Lockhart. Paredon Records, 1974.
[161]October 3, 1992.

resign themselves to its "sympathetic" perspective on lesbians as "regular" people.[162] We're not being shown as monsters, after all, but as "wholesome" beautiful people living in beautiful homes. In this "20/20" it is particularly fitting that one of the couples has one pregnant member and before the time of the show is up gives birth to a *baby boy*. It's the American Dream dyke style: two lesbians, two cars, house, VCR, and boy baby too. What better proof that lesbians are the same as everyone else? But then how "regular" *are* the lives of lesbians who own Rolls Royces and Porsches? How "real life" are the lives of those who live the American Dream?[163]

The "realism" of each side of the true story of good girl and bad girl lesbians *is* as realistic as the American Dream; both provide a *fantasy* of assimilation which in turn betrays the source of lesbian power as truly—politically and ethically—deviant. Again, a line from Rich's (seventies) writing springs to mind: "denying/ her wounds came from the same source as her power."[164] Dykes who do access the American dream are denying that the source of their power is the source of their wounds—their privilege is based on the system of exploitation they've only temporarily escaped, and provides no lasting buffer against the anti-lesbian violence of that same system. At the same time, the wounds we endure as the survivors of heteropatriarchal attacks and censure also have a source in our potential—a *potential political power*—to fight these attacks. We are attacked because of the threat lesbianism poses to the dominant culture, because of our potential to undermine the heterosexual social order. A source of our wounding is also its cure—our potential power to really sustain this threat, making it a promise of active rebellion. *This* is what is, or *could be*, really good about lesbian-feminism.

It is not incidental, then, that the central question mused upon by the "20/20" show was the great mystery, Is lesbianism biological or not? Both the apparent ingenuity of the question and its response, that lesbianism was as natural as anything else, was most

---

[162] At the time of its showing gay/lesbian anti-discrimination legislation was under attack by referendums in Amendment 2 in Colorado and Proposition 9 in Oregon.

[163] Radical lesbianism does not fit the good girl/bad girl paradigm but that does not mean that radical dykes do not partake of the pie. As I argue below, some, perhaps many, of us do, which is why we need to get out of the idealism which rationalizes inequality and work to make ideals of an autonomous, empowered self-sufficient lesbian *community*—not just *individuals*—a reality. The consequence of lesbian idealism has been a kind of political correctness, a tendency to irritate, if not manipulate each other with holier-than-thou standards. This dynamic is endemic to most political communities and in the case of lesbian-feminist community, a result of the difficulty of grasping that the process fro "is" to "ought" as a dynamic one. This is not only a process of decolonizing ourselves with respect to the internalization of misogynist violence (and thus confronting and transforming batterers and patterns of abusiveness among ourselves, confronting and transforming patterns of eroticized domination and submission within ourselves). It is also a process of identifying the concrete stakes that privileged lesbians do have in a capitalist, white supremacist society *and demystifying the ways that lesbian ideology has sometimes functioned to conceal these stakes under a rubric of lesbian identity and/or feminist principles.* Radical lesbianism (if it is truly radical and deviant) cannot be accommodated by mainstream heterosexual society and an investment in a fantasy of assimilation is to avert our "eyes" from the reality that it will always be dykes and women *without* access to the American Dream who will be most brutalized by its empty promises.

[164] Adrienne Rich, "Power," *The Dream of a Common Language* (New York: Norton, 1978), p. 3.

dumbfounding in its leap over a little historical phase known by a little word that no one mentioned, namely "feminism." Particularly in this cultural context—Northampton—the erasure of political lesbianism is stunning given the history of lesbian and women's liberation politics in this town.[165] No, it is not incidental that a twenty year history was glossed over and that a "realist" view of lesbianism was presented as if a lesbian/feminist movement never happened.

The historical possibility of lesbian-feminism as a culture of dissent has been erased by lesbian sadomasochism, itself both a catalyst and rigidified symbol of the "new" mood of "realism" sweeping the lesbian nation. This is a "realism" that would rather lie back and enjoy than continue to question the *sense* of an ideology hastening women's and lesbians' return to men and to heterosexual conventions of culture, sexuality, and politics. This "realism" is its fantasy and it depends upon a propagation of the idea that feminism never happened, that radical lesbianism never happened, that a historical conjunction of lesbianism and feminism never happened. This eventlessness is pressed upon us in the two-faced dyke of men's dreams, the baby-booming, house-mortgaging, cruising (on Olivia and elsewise), and (mostly) white, middle class lesbian and her counter-part who is often herself, the bad and sexy rebel who poses no threat to male power.

Lesbian sadomasochism as an ideology delivers a resounding message, and that message is: "nothing happened."[166] There is a hole in history where a revolt against heteropatriarchy is supposed to be; and heteropatriarchy isn't really happening to revolt against anyway. In this gap is a "screen memory"[167] called "the politically correct good girls vs. the sex rebels."

But even in this fantasy frame, the politically correct have a virtue worth noting—the virtue of obnoxiousness. In a time of utter complacency, "politically correct" obnoxiousness may be the weak signal of someone still shouting somewhere about what is still happening to women, about who is doing what to whom, and how brutally, even when everyone else is submerged in the consoling thought that it isn't really happening, not to them anyway. Even caricatured, these figures, the *fantasy* "good girls" (vs. the real ones showcased on T.V.) are the lingering gadflies of the era who "still ain't satisfied." As gadflies we stick around, and even when our voice is heard as no more than an irritating buzz, it persists in its single shrill note of insistence that something happened. And this something may just be the terrible daughter of the women's revolution that we have not yet become.

---

[165] Indeed Northampton is rumored to be a separatist center of the lesbian world.

[166] *Nothing Happened* is the title of a Norwegian novel by Ebba Haslund (Seattle: Seal Press, 1987) out of print for 40 years because of its lesbian content. The book itself, like the love story between women in the novel and like woman-loving in this society, "never happened."

[167] Mary Daly writes, "[Screen memory] is 'an imagined or real recollection of early childhood that is recalled with magnification of importance or other distortion that aids in the repression of another memory of deep emotional significance.' The stages and screens of the Fathers' Foreground, the state of fabrications/fictions, flash forth terrifying and murderous shapes that constitute a mass of man-made magnified, mummifying 'memories,' repressing women's ancient Other Memories that are of deep Emotional significance." (*Pure Lust* Boston: Beacon Press, 1984) p. 21.

Acknowledgments:

The work in this paper has been nourished and incited by struggle and friendship with many lesbians. Study groups in Northampton, Ma. on feminist/lesbian militancy and in Santa Cruz, California on pornography were hot beds of thinking from which the ideas in this paper originally crystallized three to five years ago. Ellen Scott, Sandy Goodman, Jamie Lee Evans, Katy Geraldine and Ger Moane gave valuable feedback on early drafts of the present incarnation. Julia Chapin was a sharp editor of the final draft. D. A. Clarke fortified me with rigorous comments and conversation through more drafts than either of us care to remember. Elise Ficarra's brilliant comments and conversation have helped me clarify key arguments in this paper. I feel especially grateful for the editorial genius of Bonnie Mann as well as for years of intellectual co-conspiracy. Irene Reti's compassion, patience, and vision as an editor has been an inspiration. And I especially thank Katy Geraldine, Ellen Scott, and Elise Ficarra for friendship which has given place and flesh to lesbian utopia in the past two years.

Anna Livia

I arrived in California in August 1990 and everyone I knew had just left for the Michigan Women's Music Festival. When they came back they regaled me with stories of the goings on. Apparently while sadomasochists had their own camping area, they had not been allowed to perform sadomasochist acts on stage. They had protested vehemently, hiring a low-flying plane to spray the area with fliers to explain their position. My friend E said she was concerned that some of the fliers might have been picked up by the wind and blown beyond the Festival grounds into the gardens of the local population. Thus outsiders would find out what was going on and the Festival would be endangered. I was not up to this sophisticated level of analysis and stood there going, "Yuk, do they have to do that to each other? I mean, doesn't it hurt?" Whereupon another woman, a therapist, said, "Hell, Anna, can't you think of anything good to say about sado-masochists?" I racked my brains accordingly and wrote this story for E's birthday a month later.

Look on the Bright Side

I.

Once upon a time in the State of Michigan, in a part of the country so hot in summer that the shedding of clothes and flesh and skin would still not cool the bones, so cold in winter that skin sticks to ice, splits and peels like skin on fire, there lived a happily married woman, mother of two fine sons. The house was well supplied with dishwashers and microwaves and electric ovens and walk-in refrigerators, so there was nothing for the happily married woman to do but cook and clean and wash and freeze and mother her two fine sons, as well as providing hand relief for her inestimable husband who was scared of contracting AIDS and had interesting ideas about causes.

One day the happily married woman was washing dishes, in the sink the old way because it made her feel virtuous, when a piece of paper landed in the soap suds. It was mauve. It was covered with words. She threw it in the trash, but clumsily and it landed on the floor where her inestimable husband slipped on it, soapy as it was.

"Goddamn stupid bitch," he observed, and she set about pouring him a beer, and one for herself while she was at it. She put his on a little tray, with a second bottle so he could get a refill as and when, and brought it out to him in the garage. Her own she sipped at the kitchen table, for the first three sips, after which she chucked it back and reached for another. The mauve paper with the words was sitting on the top of the trash can as she passed.

" . . . Lesbian . . .," it said, and " . . . Michigan . . .," and " . . . Sadomasochist . . ." The happily married woman began to read, but one of her two fine sons came in to find out when dinner would be ready, so she had to put the paper down.

But the seed had been sown and that night the happily married woman sneaked down to the trash can to consider the evidence by dint of a flashlight. There was in the State of Michigan a land where only women lived, and listened to music; a lesbian civilization so well-established that special facilities were provided for each of the many different kinds of woman. Except one, apparently: couples in which one woman hit another for sexual pleasure. These women were excluded, hence the mauve paper with the words which they had dropped from a low-flying plane to express their dissatisfaction.

Tick tick tick.

And a year later and in another country, though only an hour's drive from her inestimable ex-husband's house, the much happier, no longer married woman said,
"Thank heavens for sadomasochists, without them I never would have heard of the land where women live, a land where there are no fine sons and no inestimable husbands."

II.

Once upon a time in a far off country where they strip to the blade to keep cool in summer, where they pack snow round nails to hurl in the frozen winter, and hurling them keep warm, there lived a small lesbian stretched taut as skin. If you held her to the light you would see only unsunned flesh and blue veins sharp as a right angle. And yet she breathed and her body was visited by the woman she loved.
The small lesbian put on her clothes, brushed her teeth and took public transport to her place of work, the place where she worked for the woman she loved. For who else would employ a small lesbian with no skill and much silence? It was not a question the small lesbian dared ask. Fortunately the woman she loved asked for her,
"Where would you be without me, silent as you are?"
"Who would employ you who cannot add or subtract or divide by nine, who make so many mistakes and cost more than you earn?"
"Why do you find it so hard to make friends, don't people like you? All our friends are my friends, who would you have if I left you?"
The woman she loved was an activist in many important campaigns to create a lesbian civilization while, simultaneously, purifying it of undesirable elements.
"What undesirable elements?" asked the small lesbian, eager for political insight.
"There are women," said the woman she loved, "who do terrible things to each other. Couples where one woman hits another for sexual pleasure, humiliates her partner and calls it consensual."
"Well at least we don't do that," said the small lesbian with a stab of half-forgotten humor.
"What?"

"You don't ask my permission before you humiliate me."

"What do you mean?"

"Nothing."

The small lesbian went to the toilet. There was nowhere else to go. She sat and cried bitterly. She was not naturally small, she had been flattened inside a small perspex box whose only communication link was with the woman she loved.

"What are you doing in there? Communing with the devil?"

The small lesbian flushed the toilet, washed her face and went back to the woman she loved. There was nowhere else to go.

But the seeds had been sown and the small lesbian in her small solitude had many hours to think. There were women who deliberately humiliated their lovers because it gave them pleasure. These women were undesirable and nice lesbians steered clear of them. Even the woman she loved said humiliation was a terrible thing.

Tick tick tick.

And a year later and in another country the small lesbian, who was now quite large, said,

"Thank heavens for sadomasochists, without them I never would have known you could consent to humiliation and therefore," she said, "withhold consent."

Jamie Lee Evans

Rodney King, Racism and the SM Culture of America

I believe the not-guilty verdict against the batterers of Rodney King was a decision based on racism as well as a product of analysis brought forth via a culture indoctrinated with violence and sadomasochistic beliefs.

Working class cities reeled with righteous anger and disorganized violence all over the country after the not-guilty verdict of the batterers of Rodney King. "No Justice, No Peace," became the warning of protesters and rioters, most of which were young men and women of color. Indeed it seemed that the streets of South Central Los Angeles had been taken over by young men and some women who lived there. However, our capitalist and authoritarian government wasn't about to stand for young men and women controlling the cities in which they live with violence. No, *this* kind of violence is something specifically set aside for the government and in specific our then President, George Bush. What eventually suspended (or replaced) the riots in Los Angeles was government violence against neighborhood residents, mass arrests and police-inflicted community terror.

There were many power struggles and scenarios that were played out throughout the trial to convict the batterers of Mr. King, one being the multiple viewings of the video taken of the beating. Mr. Bush, in a televised Presidential address to the nation, commented briefly on how "sickened" he was by the videotaped beating of Rodney King. He then admitted that he had watched the video more than a dozen times. I wonder about the motives of a man sickened by a video but who watched it more than 12 times! I also question whether it was an act of media responsibility that kept the news almost sadistically playing the video nightly. In the same vein, I wonder: was it for investigative examination or *enjoyment* that the American public continued to view the video over and over? Stern and ever thoughtful of the lives of South Central residents, Mr. Bush also said, "The [street] violence will stop, and I will use as much force as necessary to do so." He said that as our president he had his promise/oath of maintaining "domestic tranquility" in the forefront of his mind. *What tranquility is he talking about? Is ending domestic violence and rape a part of the tranquility plan and if so how come the feds are cutting battered women's shelters and rape crisis centers to the bone?*

After listening to Mr. Bush's threats guised in the form of promises of protection, my lesbian housemates and I all loudly told Mr. Bush to eat his words and other such indelicate suggestions. They set off to attend an anti-racism rally in San Francisco and feeling ill and afraid to be an Asian lesbian in the middle of rally during a time of severe cross racial hostility, I waved good-bye. I didn't see my housemates until two days later, as they were arrested for walking towards the protest and for acting as if they were free.

The martial law that was passed in San Francisco and Berkeley, California during the uprisings was all a part of our government's show of force. Mass arrests and violence against advocates of free speech were not called violence, but protection. This is how our culture distorts reality. It's the same theory that lets deadly first strike nuclear missiles be called "peacekeepers." It is also a distortion that extends into the language and beliefs of sadomasochism and allows for someone being tied up to call it a liberating experience. Under martial law you are supposed to have a choice about whether or not you are arrested or protected, but in fact, there are certain classes and races of people that are the main groups of people arrested and certain property owners who are protected. There are also the arresters and the arrested, and very little crossover between the two groups.

He asked for it. He deserved it

In sadomasochism it works the same, the backgrounds of masochists are usually of those who have been victimized and those who are sadists are usually people who hold power positions in their family, workplace, etc. Of course some sadomasochism advocates would disagree with this, while others would admit to it. The question this brings up for me is about consensuality and when you take someone's choice away or they don't have a choice to begin with, (for example, when a woman grows up being abused by numerous perpetrators in her life, and has not been able to stop the abuse)— can it be called consensual? There are parallels in the ways our government treats its constituents and how a sadist treats her victim. But back to case in point.

In the case of the Rodney King beating, the jurors' justification for their decision was ladened with heavy sadomasochistic ideology. Some of the jurists from the Simi Valley (which is commonly known to anti-racist activists as Klan Country) jury released a statement about their decision which brought it all together for me. They said their verdict was based on the belief that *Mr. King* was the party in control the entire time he was being beaten. They said that *Mr. King* determined how long and how severe his beating would be and that *he* was in control of the situation. They also used horrific racist descriptions of Mr. King, stating he was "snorting like a bull," and that he was "acting like an animal that needed to be tamed." The jury also revealed that because Mr. King himself did not testify, he was not human to them, he was not real. In other words, his silence made him the guilty party not the brutalizing cops that were documented on video.

Although a friend of mine thinks that perhaps Mr. King was kept from testifying in an effort to protect him from further brutalization, I believe it was a legal strategy that kept Mr. King from the stand. His legal counsel feared that he would discredit his case by speaking, and would have to admit to having a past in crime and drug abuse. Silenced and without his own self-defense, Mr. King is a lot easier to see as an object. And we all know that when someone is no longer a human but an object, it is much easier to do violence against them or forgive those who have done that violence to begin with. After all, he was an "animal" and was giving off non-verbal signs that he was in the powerful position, right?

How interesting that Mr. King's past would do anything to change the way the viewers of that video would see him. Kind of like the lie that the prostitute or the wife can't be raped? *She asked for it. She deserved it. She liked it.* "Mr. King laughed afterwards in the squad car." It didn't hurt. It didn't affect his sense of humor. The beating wasn't as bad as it looked. This is not the first time that a person of color has had to remain silent in order to protect themselves in front of a panel of racist judges and it isn't the first time a person of color has not been seen as human.

As far as the verdict justification goes, maybe I'm not the one to give the commentary. I am an urban woman of color, raised in the low-income housing of Los Angeles County, just south of Watts, and I may be a bit biased. I grew up first-hand knowing that Officer Friendly was *not* my friend; but, really how could *anyone* think that an unarmed grounded man surrounded by more than four armed and violent, battering cops could be *in control?* Well, two thoughts: Racism and indoctrination into sm thinking.

The jury was predominantly white, the plaintiff, black. Racism. The jury described Mr. King as an untamed animal, inhuman to them. Racism. The jury said that the cops suspected Mr. King was on PCP (this is before they had identified him as someone with a drug history) and thus felt he had to be *dominated* before cuffed. Mr. King was a black man, the cops who beat him were white. Racism. I could go on here, but do I really need to?

The only way anyone could think that someone on the bottom of a beating was in control, is by way of sm thinking. The common belief and propaganda in sm is that the bottom is "in control." We are told that they are in power of "determining" *how long, how much and how severe* their violent violation will be. Sound familiar? The person being beaten, dominated, etc. is also supposed to have the power to stop the violence any time they wish, simply by whispering out their pre-determined "safe word," that is usually not, "No," "Stop," or "Get off me!" It's usually not a word that is traditionally used to decline or refuse something, I am told that is part of the thrill. (Maybe the cops didn't hear Mr. King murmuring out "*artichoke, artichoke?*")

There was no "safe word" in the Rodney King beating because the truth of the matter is *there is no safe word when you are being beaten!* It is inconceivable how a person under the blows of a baton, a gun, a whip, or a chain could be seen as in control. It holds the same logic as a statement which implies a woman who is raped has "asked for it," or could've stopped it at anytime. The justification of the King verdict was one built in a sadomasochistic culture where George Bush decries senseless street violence and then sends out 11,000 troops to settle the violence (or the score?). Surely the next comment will be something like, "those looting street mobs had control the entire time whether or not they would be shot in the back by a cop/national guard/business owner/marine, etc.," and the conservatives and most others of the American public will agree. Ah, the wonderful world of patriarchy.

My Story

As a feminist lesbian, I take it as my personal responsibility to denounce patriarchal doublespeak anytime I can. And as a lesbian living in the San Francisco Bay Area, the prevalence of lesbian sadomasochism has effected my life more than I can say. While American heterosexual males get away with murdering their girlfriends and wives under the upper-class legal understanding/forgiveness of "rough sex play," (she asked for it, she got it), they lick their plates clean of sm and all the new privileges this thinking affords them in hurting, beating and murdering women. Although the danger seems clear: sm is simply another way for heterosexual males to abuse women and get away with it, another "rule of thumb" ruling, lesbians are not only endorsing the meal plan, but asking for second helpings.

I write on this issue because so many newly out lesbians are now under the impression that sm and lesbianism go hand in hand. In fact when I organized a panel of feminists against sadomasochism, I was asked by more than one conference organizer what my stand on sm was, even though my position was made clear in my proposal, and my proposal had been accepted and supposedly agreed upon by the organizing collective. It seems lately that people have a hard time separating sm and lesbianism, and I am of course, offended by this. During this time of backlash against feminists and anti-racist activists (also known as multi-culturalists), not Audre Lorde, Angela Davis or Naomi Wolf, but pop singer Madonna has become the inconceivable yet popular "feminist" icon to many apolitical lesbians and women. After all she is the woman who "cuts to the edge" with near nude infantilizing photos in *Vanity Fair Magazine*, drinks milk out of a cat bowl on music videos, and makes brave challenges? to patriarchal censors by using sm and "queer" interactions in an expensive, and tired pornography collection of fantasies and photos. Currently, beside Madonna, many influential and powerful women are gaining a lot of popularity by encouraging women to "experiment with their power," in the bedroom and give up their analysis of patriarchy. *(As one postcard from England said, "Post Feminism: Keep your bra, burn your brain.")* SM dykes are promising heightened sexual pleasure, taboo-breaking fantasies galore, and the one that gets me the most and seems the most dangerous, *liberation* beyond your wildest belief.

Right now there is an sm dyke somewhere offering a moneyback guarantee: if you choose to be her bottom you'll feel like submission "never felt soooo good" during the sex scene of *her* choice. But listen, my advice is simple, if a woman is telling you that by whipping and chaining you, simulating a rape scene, holding you down, scarring your body, piercing your clitoris, carving into your skin; that by playing a nazi, or a slave keeper, or a cop, while you are a sexy incarcerated Jew, a slave, a protester, she will liberate you, then you should run as fast as you can in the opposite direction! There is nothing liberating about buying into sm doctrines. Tied up is exactly how George Bush and his brothers would like to see lesbians and Rodney Kings and anyone else who isn't white, straight and middle-upper class. And if we do it to ourselves, well then we save the master planners a lot of work.

Ritual Abuse and Sadomasochism?

I am a lesbian who has survived direct attacks against my life, including being whipped, beaten, burned, chained, tied down, tied up, gagged, gang raped, choked, and forced to witness all of the above being done to other children, in a Satanic foster home subsidized and supervised by the State of California. Believe me when I say there is nothing liberating about being the bottom of these types of assaults. In fact, a common practice of these Satanists (who were all white in the mostly black city of Compton, California) was to tell you what they wanted to do to you and then make you request that treatment. Just as in many jails today they make the inmates lock their own cell doors, as a psychological mind-fuck, I was forced to *ask* to be raped, beaten, burned. Just as teachers make you "repeat after them," I was forced to say, "Yes, I want to lie in a coffin of snakes, yes I want the lid to be closed, yes, I want to be buried in the earth."

77

Sometimes I think the reason I am alive today is that I did every damn thing they told me to and I performed the perfect victim. My ability to forget/deny most of it until a few years ago was also a large part of my survival. My refusal to accept sm ideology now, as a lesbian whose culture seems to be surrounded by it, is a large part of my daily survival and struggle to feel good, vibrant, alive. There ain't no way that anyone is ever going to get me to play the slave, the geisha, the courtesan, the Chinese laundress, the Hawaiian hula girl, or any other eroticized racist stereotype they have of the mixed-blood Asian American Lesbian Woman. It would be an insult to my survival of abuse to willingly play the role of victim. Additionally, playing the dominator or perpetrator would not be subversive to anything or anyone, it would just be giving in to old programming. Participating in or endorsing sadomasochism would be a danger to my mental, physical and emotional health.

And so this is my position and my background and from this I encourage all lesbians to reflect on their present and past realities when investigating sadomasochism. You must consider the violent context in which we all live and reject the false conclusion that taking on the role of violator or learning to *like* being violated will set you free.

Irene Reti

Remember the Fire:
Lesbian Sadomasochism
in a Post Nazi Holocaust World

Introduction

Before

You see it was just statistics to me too
before it was my family.
Just another chapter in the horror of human history
before it was *my* history.
Just another oppressed group
before I knew I was Jewish,
before *they* were *my* people,
before it was *me*.

Before I counted my lost cousins—
Yuki, my grandmother's favorite brother,
who looked like my brother, Steve—
dark-haired and sensitive,
taken to a Czechoslovakian mining camp by the Nazis,
miraculously survived that experience,
came back to Budapest,
only to be deported to the camps,
disappeared.
Another cousin shot outside the synagogue
in the town square,
two red-headed women named Irene,
with delicate dispositions and
a penchant for clean houses,
soft feather beds—
disappeared.

My grandmother's beloved uncle
killed himself and his wife
with morphine
when the Nazis came.
When the Nazis came
the rich cousin who was a lawyer
working for a Baron
scoffed when my grandmother warned,
get out of the country!
said nothing would happen to him
under the Baron's protection,
disappeared.
A litany of disappearances
disappeared people
For Holocaust survivors
disappeared
is a noun.

I am a lesbian and a Jew and a child of two refugee survivors of the Holocaust. My parents were not in the camps but were among the small percentage of Jews to escape Nazi-occupied Europe. Both came to the United States, and chose the path of assimilation. They decided not to tell their children they were Jewish. Hence, I had no idea I was Jewish until I was seventeen when my family had a Jewish funeral for my grandfather.

It has taken me years to piece together this history of my family from the fragments of memory I collect like a hungry bird from my mother, my father, my grandmother. I write these words against the weight of a silence generations deep. I have no resentment against my family for their silence; it is the silence of healing, of the snow of years falling softly, mercifully, on a withered family tree, on piles of disappeared relatives; the silence of fear, of survival. What do I do with these holes in history, these voids in the family tree? Will these words fill the silence? How can I cope with something as immense as the Holocaust? What do other Jews do with their feelings about it? I was brought up without any defense mechanisms, Jewish identity, or Jewish pride which I could use to cope with this horror. It is only because I am a generation removed from the ovens, shielded by the relative safety of the United States, that I can begin to gain some of the distance necessary to dig through these snowdrifts.

But I have nightmares. I am told this is a common experience for children of survivors—we dream of barbed wire and trains clattering through countries we've never seen. I dream I am a lesbian in a concentration camp, making intricate, hopeless plans to escape. I dream I have somehow survived the war but now I have to register with the CIA because they are after me. I awake in the night, sobbing, nauseous—awake, saying over and over, "How shall I grieve? How can I mourn?" The bedcovers and the walls are mute; my flannel nightgown wraps around my neck; the next morning I am white-faced, exhausted, wondering if the people on the bus can tell what I'm dreaming.

I'm dreaming. I dream I am standing by the side of a cattle car. Five old women lean out of the train and hand me their memoirs wrapped in dirty plastic, saying, "Take these.

Do something with them." I know they are on their way to Auschwitz. I awake incredibly sick and sit by the heater trying to get warm, arguing with these spirit women in the dark, women who I have no doubt existed. I tell them I'm doing the best I can. I write. Finally, I go to sleep.

I write, but I keep wondering—What's the point? Who will want to read this? Is this just airing of family laundry or personal exorcism? I'd rather write love poems.

But I am also a lesbian. I have been to the Gay Pride Parade in San Francisco and seen lesbians and gay men wearing swastikas and stormtrooper outfits. I have listened to the debate in my own community over whether *On Our Backs* (a lesbian sadomasochism magazine published in San Francisco) should be carried in the women's section of the local bookstore. I have read *Coming to Power* (the anthology edited by SAMOIS, a support organization for SM lesbians) and other writings by SM lesbians. And I feel extremely disturbed. I feel disturbed by the pictures of women wearing stormtrooper costumes in *Coming to Power*. I feel disturbed by the playful endorsement of torture, humiliation and slavery. And I feel disturbed by Pat Califia's claim that:

Sadomasochism is more a parody of the hidden sexual nature of fascism than it is a worship of or acquiescence to it. How many real Nazis would be involved in a kinky sexual scene?[1]

Contrary to Pat Califia's claim, sadomasochism was an integral part of the Holocaust; there were many "real Nazis" involved in "kinky sexual scenes." One of the purposes of this essay is to demonstrate that fact. Whips, chains, racks, shackles, and other instruments and methods of torture are our inheritance—passed down through history. They existed in the Roman Empire, during the medieval Inquisition (in which millions of women, Jews and gay people were murdered), during Black slavery, during the Holocaust, and persist in modern-day South Africa and Central America. The legacy continues. In a world where torture, slavery and violence are our legacy, I believe we must question why we find handcuffs and chains alluring, slavery erotic, torture pleasurable.

Sadomasochism has been around for a long time, but the Holocaust was a particularly recent and virulent occurrence of SM. The central point of this essay is that lesbian sexuality (and sexuality in general) has been imprinted with the images and scenarios of the Holocaust. I believe we cannot think of lesbian SM as something accidental or as some activity conceived in the privacy of bedrooms with thick walls. We must face our desires with a fierce inward staring, and ask—which of these are really *ours*?

This essay will trace the boot prints the Holocaust left on SM lesbian sexuality, the images of the concentration camps reflected in sadomasochistic lesbian mirrors, the scenes of Nazism re-enacted for SM lesbians' "pleasure." I will particularly focus on *punishment* and *discipline, humiliation, handsome sadism* and *beautiful masochism* as they operated during the Third Reich and are reflected in lesbian SM.

I write this essay to document the blatant and more subtle ways in which sadomasochism fueled the Holocaust. I also write this essay to break familial silence, to

---

[1] Pat Califia, "Feminism and Sadomasochism," *Heresies #12.* pp. 30-34.

81

claim my identity as a child of survivors, and to avenge five old spirit women with moldy diaries. In this writing I choose to combine my own poetry with a more analytical voice because I believe the Holocaust must be both ruthlessly analyzed with the tools of the intellectual and mourned in the raging voice of the poet. I also ask the reader to bring both her intellectual and emotional sensibilities to the reading of this work, and all of her courage to grasping this terrible and complex history.

There are a number of things this essay is not. This is not an essay proposing that lesbian SM be banned or censored, for such techniques are likely to backfire on all feminist/lesbian/leftist people. Nor am I claiming that the only ground upon which to oppose SM is its anti-Semitism. One might also argue that SM is racist, or that it duplicates the dominance/submission patterns of heterosexuality as it is constructed under patriarchy. I refer interested readers to the anthology *Against Sadomasochism* for elaboration of these arguments. Nor am I claiming that the lesbian SM scenes described here are identical with the scenes in the Nazi death camps, or that the women described here *are* Nazis. The SAMOIS statement calls SM, "a form of eroticism based on a consensual exchange of power," and emphasizes that SM, "must be consensual, mutual and safe."[2] Over and over again SM lesbians say that they *enjoy* SM sex, whether they play sadists or masochists. Obviously the people in the camps were not enjoying themselves, nor were they there out of any kind of choice. But I think we must ask ourselves—*why is this enjoyable?* What are these rituals doing in our sexuality?

Punishment/Discipline

The SS sergeant cracked his whip through the air. At the very first strokes the Czech's skin already burst open and started bleeding, but the SS commander continued unperturbed . . . . The camp commander stood right by, and looked visibly more than a little interested in the proceedings. At each stroke his eyes lit up, and after a few strokes his whole face was red with excitement. He buried his hands in his trouser pockets and could clearly be seen to masturbate, quite unperturbed by our presence. . . . I myself witnessed on more than 30 occasions how this camp commander got sexual satisfaction from watching the lashings inflicted . . . and the perverted lust with which he followed each stroke and the screams of the victim.[3]

The heavy strands of black braided leather bit into my ass and shoulder blades once more. And again. And again. And my cries continued, breathless, reverberating in my throat, barely making it into the air. My body, bound and helpless, jerked at the blows, writhing without my will . . . . The heavy black whip hissed through the air landing over and over on my thighs, shoulders and

[2]SAMOIS, "SAMOIS: Who We Are," *Coming to Power: Writings and Graphics on Lesbian SM* (Boston: Alyson Publications, 1982).

[3]Heinz Heger, *The Men with the Pink Triangle*, trns. by David Fernbach (Boston: Alyson Publications, 1980) p. 55.

ass. What marks there would be when we were done! At each stroke I twisted, moaned, strained, wanted to come. [4]

The Men with the Pink Triangle by Heinz Heger is a first-hand account by a gay man who survived Sachsenhausen brick-works, known as the death pit, the "Auschwitz" for homosexuals. It is one of the few books available on gay men and the Holocaust. An essential part of Heger's account is his detailing of the sexual sadism practiced by the SS guards against gay prisoners. The above scene took place after a Czech gay prisoner tried to escape the camp. Scenes like this in which gay men were tied onto a bench called the horse, and beaten with a dog whip, a stick, or a horse whip, while the other gays were forced to stand in rows at attention to witness the whipping took place quite frequently.

In the Holocaust Museum in Israel there is no exhibit revealing the execution and torture of thousands of gay men by the Nazi Regime. We aren't told that during the years just before the Holocaust a large gay liberation movement flourished in Germany, led by Magnus Hirschfield and his Scientific-Humanitarian Committee. One of the goals of this movement was to abolish paragraph 175 of the penal code by which male homosexuality had been a criminal offense throughout Germany since 1871. But in 1935, two years after the Nazis took over Germany, paragraph 175 was re-written to be even more repressive: "any form of 'lewdness' between two men was included in the offense of homosexuality. This could mean, and indeed did mean, as little as a mere kiss or embrace, or even fiction with a homoerotic content."[5] By 1939, 24,450 men had been convicted under this law. At first the punishment for these gay men was six months imprisonment. But after 1936, Himmler, who was commander of all Nazi security services, established a policy of eliminating homosexuals by sending them to concentration camps. Thousands of gay men were sent from the prisons to extermination camps. Thousands more were sent directly to the camps from their homes, simply because their names were mentioned in the extensive police files the German government had been collecting on the gay movement for years.

Sexual punishment and discipline were essential tools used by the Nazis against all of their prisoners. Klaus Barbie was one Nazi who made extensive use of this tool. Known as the Butcher of Lyon, Barbie managed the Ecole de Santé, a prison in Lyon, France, where members of the French Resistance were imprisoned and tortured, where hundreds of Jewish people were locked up in a dark, stinking cattle shed for months, where thousands died. After the war, the U.S. government hired Barbie as an agent to help them keep communism out of Germany. This business of the U.S. intelligence using German Gestapo agents was quite common in post-war Europe. "Who knew Germany better than anyone else? Who were the most organized? Who were the most anti-communist? Former Nazis."[6] Eventually Barbie ended up in Bolivia, where he aligned himself with leaders of that right-wing regime.

In Bolivia, Barbie sat in cafes and drank. When he was drunk:

---

[4]Janet Schrim, "Act II, Scene I," in *Coming to Power*, p. 47.

[5]Heger, p. 9.

[6]Brendan Murphy, *The Butcher of Lyon*, (New York: Empire Books, 1983), p. 43.

... he was different. In his drunkenness he spoke of his life before, the things he did in France, in Lyon, and how he enjoyed torturing people. He was very proud of this; he never denied he was an SS official . . . . More than one survivor of the Ecole de Santé has described Barbie as having a sadistic nature, of taking pleasure in personally breaking his prisoners . . . . I think it gave him pleasure . . . . I had the impression this man was happy to be giving out punishment, to be hitting someone. He seemed quite pleased to be in power.[7]

Barbie particularly enjoyed torturing women. Blardone, a member of the French Resistance imprisoned in the Ecole de Santé remembers that Barbie:

... burned them on the breast with cigarettes. I never saw women tortured with their clothes on. When the session began Barbie immediately ordered them to strip, part of his technique of humiliation. This apparently added to the enjoyment of the tortures. With Barbie it was a pleasure as it was for the others. It was a pleasure for them to say, "Take your clothes off!" Barbie had a French secretary with whom he would toy between and even during interrogations, embracing and kissing her in front of the prisoners.[8]

Sexual punishment and discipline are also key elements of lesbian SM. As Susan Farr writes in her article, "The Art of Discipline: Creating Erotic Dramas of Play and Power":

For the past three years I've been exploring my feelings through physically hurting my lover and through submitting to her physically hurting me. We spank each other with our hands, tie each other up and deliver a beating with a belt or paddle, discipline each other with a switch or whip. The punishment is always by mutual consent, and the severity, though most often mild, is sometimes sufficient to leave an occasional bruise or a faint welt the next day. It does hurt and it feels very good to me, whether I'm on the giving or receiving end.[9]

The fact that discipline rituals like this one occur with the consent of both women involved does not keep me from feeling disturbed by them. Once again I ask—why is punishment erotic? *Where* do these desires come from?

Humiliation

There was one latrine for thirty to thirty-two thousand women, and we were permitted to use it only at certain hours of the day. We stood in line to get into

---

[7]Murphy, p. 43.

[8]Murphy, p. 43.

[9]Susan Farr, "The Art of Discipline: Creating Erotic Dramas of Play and Power," *Coming to Power*, p. 181.

this tiny building, knee deep in human excrement. As we all suffered from dysentery, we could hardly wait until our turn came, and soiled our ragged clothes, which never came off our bodies, thus adding to the horror of our existence by the terrible smell which surrounded us like a cloud. The latrine consisted of a deep ditch with planks thrown across it at certain intervals. We squatted on these planks like birds perched on a telegraph wire, so close together that we could not help soiling each other.[10]

'Shit! Oh no! Shit—I'd never touch that!' my lady protested. I'm telling her that not only would I like it if she ate my asshole, but I might require her to savor the contents . . . . After a delightful meal, I order her to fetch me a large china bowl in which I deposit a tidy pile of after-dinner turds. 'No, no' is in her eyes as she also begs for my love. 'Eat them or eat me,' I tell her. Her choice is obvious. Kiss my sweet smelling turds or you will spend half an hour tonguing my asshole.[11]

Humiliation was another major technique used by the Nazis during the Holocaust. "Almost every woman referred to the humiliating feelings and experiences surrounding her entrance to the camp: being nude, being shaved all over—for some being shaved in a sexual stance, straddling two stools, being observed by men, both fellow prisoners and SS guards."[12]

"Excremental assault," as Terrence Des Pres calls it in his book *The Survivor*, was an essential tactic used by the Nazis to debase and humiliate people in the camps.[13] Conditions like this were not accidental; they were part of a deliberate policy designed to humiliate prisoners. The purpose of this policy was twofold: 1) It prevented cooperation among prisoners who couldn't face each other with respect as human beings when they were caked with mud and feces. 2) It reduced the prisoners completely to the sub-human so the Nazis would be able to kill them without feeling that they were killing something human. If society scorns street people who haven't washed in a few weeks and are dressed in shabby clothes, how much easier it must have been to degrade filthy, emaciated concentration camp prisoners.

The filthy, emaciated concentration camp prisoners were my people, members of my family. I am a child of two people who barely escaped this fate. I am also a woman, a Jewish woman, whose body is forever marked by this experience:

---

[10]Terrence Des Pres, *The Survivor: An Anatomy of Life in the Death Camps* (New York: Simon and Schuster, 1977) p. 58.

[11]"Handkerchief Codes: Interlude II," *Coming to Power*, p. 151.

[12]Joan Ringelheim, "Women and the Holocaust: A Re-consideration of Research," in *Signs: Journal of Women in Culture and Society*, 1985, Vol. 10, no. 41.

[13]Des Pres, p. 57.

Humiliation

to reduce to a lower position in one's own eyes
or other eyes
Extremely destructive to one's self-respect
or dignity—
humbling
humble
from humilis meaning low
humus meaning earth.

Humiliation—
to reduce to earth
to ashes.
The bodies of my relatives in Germany and Hungary
make the grass grow lush and tall.

I curl under a blue quilt.
My hands search
for my breasts
warm and firm
the nipples soft as down.
I press and smile
think of your eager kiss,
press
and think
they made soap out of breasts like these.

I comb my mother's hair
in a winter cabin
waves of brown and gray and silver
spread across her strong back.
My own red fire
wild, unfettered—
you love to play with it.
Hair like this they shaved
made into blankets, stuffed mattresses.

My skin brushes against your hands.
I shake with pleasure,
my skin
hot against your jeans
my skin
the skin
they made lampshades from.
Ashes.

Or, as Andrea Dworkin has written:

> The Nazis in reality created a kind of sexual degradation that was—and remains—unspeakable. Even de Sade did not dare to imagine what the Nazis created and neither did the Cossacks. And so the sexualization of the Jewish woman took on a new dimension. She became the carrier of a new sexual memory, one so brutal and sadistic that its very existence changed the character of the mainstream sexual imagination. The concentration camp woman, a Jew—emaciated with bulging eyes and sagging breasts and bones sticking out all over and shaved head and covered in her own filth and cut up and whipped and stomped on and punched out and starved—became the sexual secret of our time. The barely faded, easily accessible memory of her sexual degradation is at the heart of the sadism against all women that is now promoted in mainstream sexual propaganda: she in the millions, naked in the millions, she utterly at the mercy of—in the millions, she to whom anything could be and was done—in the millions, she for whom there will never be any justice or revenge—in the millions. It is her existence that has defined contemporary mass sexuality, given it its distinctly and abashedly mass-sadistic character.[14]

The connection between humiliation and love is deeply embedded in our sexuality. While I have never participated in scenes like the one described at the beginning of this section, I have often found myself courting humiliation in relationships—deliberately placing myself in situations where I feel emotionally powerless and sexually vulnerable, unsafe. And the more powerless and tormented I feel, the more romantically "in love" I feel. I believe sadomasochism can be emotional as well as sexual. I am certain I would not be acting in ways that jeopardize my self-respect were it not for the legacy of sadomasochism embedded in the culture that shapes my sexuality.

Handsome Sadism

Thunderous cries of Heil! Heil! greeted him right and left as row after row of people raised their arms in the Nazi salute. Suddenly he was right in front of me. There was his brown shirt and shoulder straps, his hand raised in salute, his dark hair falling across his forehead. He stared straight ahead, past the crowd. It seemed if he saw no one. His eyes were very blue. I wanted to scream but I could not. I saw him slowly striding in high boots . . . my feelings had been stirred. I swore in my head that I would die for the Führer if that was what he wanted. And I dreamed of that man with the slow stride, his eyes directed at something far away which no one else could see.[15]

---

[14]Andrea Dworkin, *Pornography: Men Possessing Women* (New York: Perigee Books, 1981), p. 26.
[15]Wendelgard von Staden, *Darkness Over the Valley* (New Haven, Conn.: Ticknor and Fields, 1981), p. 145.

There was a little stir at the head of the stairs. I looked over crossly, unwilling to break my introspection. Then I saw who was causing the commotion. She had come back. It was Jessie.

I had an immediate physical reaction to her presence: my clit jumped. Then it started throbbing in time with my heartbeat. As I watched her speak to acquaintances here and there, moving on before a greeting could turn into a conversation, I began to shake a little—an erotic attack of fear.[16]

Imagine it is 1933, Germany. The Great Depression chokes six million people out of work, including large numbers of skilled metal and construction workers, secretaries and government employees. Shopkeepers are having a hard time staying in business. People feel hungry, depressed, restless, powerless.

Into this grim environment marches a Party of soldiers in handsome uniforms, a militaristic, masculine Party of men and women full of purpose, a Party which offers some virile hope of power. "Uniforms and fifes impressed not only the girls but also many a young fellow tired of his humdrum apprenticeship to a trade."[17]

Nazism seduced the people of Germany, seduced them with handsome sadism, with the attractiveness of its masculine character. Hans Frank, Hitler's lawyer and later Governor-General of Occupied Poland, said at the Nuremberg Trials:

You know the people are really feminine . . . so dependent on mood and environment, so fickle—[they] idolize virility . . . not merely obedience but surrender—like a woman. That was the secret of Hitler's power. He stood up and pounded his fist, and shouted! I am *the man!* and he shouted about his strength and determination—and so the public just surrendered to him with hysterical enthusiasm. One must not say that Hitler *violated* the German people—he seduced them![18]

While many people describe the incredible charisma of Hitler's character, few delve deeper to discover the source of the charisma the above quotation reveals. But the sadomasochistic underpinnings of Nazism extended far beyond Hitler's personality—and drew on the sexuality of ordinary people like the woman quoted above recalling when she first saw Hitler, ordinary people who found stormtrooper uniforms handsome. I want to ask *why*? Why is sadism handsome? Why are we attracted to people who have power over us, who could hurt us? Why do we have "erotic attacks of fear"? Why are soldiers considered handsome? Outside the museum in Tel Aviv an American businessman gestures towards the group of Israeli soldiers in uniform, leans close to me, leers, "Don't you wish you were in the Israeli army so you could be with those handsome soldiers?"

at what age do we learn to worship the uniform, the soldier, the gun, the scornful aristocrat, the prize fighter, the gangster, the tough cop, the bad boy,

---

[16]Pat Califia, "From Jessie," *Coming to Power,* p. 156.

[17]Peter Merkl, *The Making of a Stormtrooper* (Princeton, N.J.: Princeton University Press, 1980) p. 101.

[18]G. M. Gilbert, *Nuremberg Diary* (New York: Signet Books, 1947) p. 137.

the tall dark stranger, the villain, the hero, the chain, the whip, the firm chin, the cold eyes, the big muscles, the mean look, the tight mouth, the clenched fist, the wide belt, the steel buckle, the high boots, the armour, the invulnerable, the Hell's Angel, the storm trooper, the rich man, the Marine, the executioner, the inquisitor, the leader, the officer, the winner, the owner, the murderer, the Marquis, the Boss, God?"[19]

This worship of the uniform of militarism, the rituals of militarism, extends to lesbian SM as well:

I'm wearing army fatigues and a form fitting black military shirt. I apply a gash of cruel red lipstick to remind her that I am all woman within my command outfit . . . . I put her through her paces, watching her tits jiggle, her ass sweat, her cunt drip. Yet she's not quite sexy enough for me. Nor, really, for her own pleasure. So I put her in the cage and allow her to lick my big black boots through the bars. When we are both thoroughly aroused I return to my bed and we listen to each other masturbate. Later I punish her for experiencing pleasure unsuitable for a prisoner and for spying on an officer. When I take her across my lap for punishment she follows instructions to keep her fist in my cunt as I paddle her. She comes just seconds before I do and she is punished for preceding an officer . . . . [20]

Beautiful Masochism

"The Jews just sort of accepted it and went off to the concentration camps like sheep."[21]

In a world of handsome sadists there must also be beautiful masochists. In the world of the Holocaust, Jewish people played the role of the submissive masochists. I will discuss the implications of this role in two parts: 1) the Jewish script of survival in submission, and 2) the idea that Jewish submission and suffering are beautiful and romantic.

1) Survival in Submission

The Holocaust did not begin with a crematorium. It happened in stages. First came laws forbidding Jews and Aryans to marry, laws prohibiting Jews from entering public parks, riding buses, the requirement that Jews wear the yellow star—a whole host of laws. At the same time came propaganda against Jews, and riots such as Kristallnacht (November 9, 1938), in which Jewish businesses were destroyed, synagogues burnt,

---

[19]D. A. Clarke, "to live with the weeds," (stanza 5), in *To Live with the Weeds* (Santa Cruz, Ca.: HerBooks, 1985), p. 47.

[20]"Handkerchief Codes," *Coming to Power*, p. 153.

[21]Lucy Steinmetz and David Tzony, eds. *Living After the Holocaust: Reflections by the Post-War Generation in America* (New York: Bloch Publishing Company, 1976), p. 101.

people beaten, some killed. Then came forced concentration of Jews in over-crowded ghettos like the Warsaw Ghetto. Many starved to death in these ghettos or died of disease. Next came massive deportation to labor camps. It was not until the spring of 1942 that Jews began to be deported to camps specifically set up for killing—death camps. When Hitler rose to power in 1933 virtually no one, Jewish or non-Jewish, perhaps not even Hitler himself, knew what the ultimate result would be.

The fact that the Holocaust happened in stages is part of what made it possible. For oppression is almost palatable in stages, almost bearable. We get used to it. The Holocaust comes quietly. A new leader comes to power. Reality changes. We cannot ride the bus; our children can no longer go to public school. At first this seems outrageous but we get used to it. Think of how much daily oppression most of us live with today—rape, ever present homophobia, poison in our fruit. We have even become accustomed to living in a world that could be blown up any minute. We get used to it. We eat the fruit. We get up and go to work in the morning as if things were normal. We are happy things aren't any worse, grateful nuclear Holocaust hasn't happened yet. The Holocaust comes quietly. We get used to it.

And we don't want to rock the boat. When they seized Jewish property many Jews were afraid to protest in fear that their lives would be seized as well. The survival strategy for both Jews and women has often been submission. Don't make Daddy mad or he'll get violent; don't say no to your husband in bed or he'll hurt you. We believe our submission is inevitable. I did. The night I was almost raped—he told me to come with him in the dark on his motorcycle. He was a stranger. I was lonely. I wanted someone to watch stars with, maybe cuddle. I didn't want sex. He did. I didn't believe I could resist, that I had the right to resist. I felt like I was watching myself submit, as if I was helplessly re-enacting an ancient, pre-ordained script, one I was compelled to carry out. I did fight him off but it took me years to realize this, years to stop blaming myself for what happened, years to stop believing I had asked for abuse, gotten *what I deserved*. We are told this is how it's always been, this is who we are. We are women and women have always been raped. We are Jews and Jews have always been persecuted. We cannot imagine a world in which this is not so. Small wonder that when the knock comes at the door, when Daddy says take off your pants, small wonder that we go obediently.

My grandmother and I walk through the Holocaust Museum in Jerusalem. I am afraid to be with her here—she who actually survived this history. This is not a museum for us, this is a family album. On one of the walls is a picture of a family, an ordinary family, about to be shot by the Gestapo. The grandmother is holding a baby, trying to quiet its cries. The older daughters remind me of my mother and my best friends Leslie and Diane—dark curly hair, deep blue eyes. They look ordinary, as if this was an ordinary event, being shot by the Gestapo in a mass grave outside your home town. Perhaps they believed this was inevitable; this was their ultimate, pre-destined role in a script engraved upon history.

This *was* a script engraved upon history. The story of anti-Semitism is very old, dating back thousands of years before Nazi Germany. As Ben Hecht writes in his fierce book on anti-Semitism *A Guide for the Bedeviled*, written in America during World War II:

The line from Phoenician anti-Semitism to its present Nordic child in Germany is unbroken. It makes a spiral through time but never breaks. It threads the councils of dead and living nations, wraps itself about the steeples and minarets of new religions, crawls in and out of the windows of philosophers, and grows like a moss on the paving stones of villages and cities. Its outer tracks are easy to locate. The historian with a strong stomach can follow it neatly. (Name the cities of Europe and you have the tombs of the Jews.) . . . Here Jews burn themselves alive in their synagogues in Coblenz, Munich, Magdeburg. Here they flee down Spanish roads to the sea and the peasants seize them and cut open their bellies, looking for hidden gold. Here they hang in the villages of France, guilty of having slyly attacked Christendom with the Black Plague. In Basle, Freiburg, and Cologne they make an almost continual bonfire. Cossacks to the east bash them to death against stone walls. Englishmen to the west halloo at their heels and go home at night with tales of their day's bag, a hundred Jews, a thousand Jews.[22]

But despite this history, there has always been Jewish resistance. The Holocaust years were no exception. Indeed resistance was only possible if you accepted the fact that you might die for it. Yet resistance did take place.

Armed and unarmed rebellion occurred even in the death camps of Sachsenhausen, Auschwitz, Sobibor, Treblinka, Kruszyna and Kryschow. The fact that people in such dehumanized, weakened and degraded condition could still rebel is a tribute to the strength of the Jewish spirit. In October 1944, the 300 people who were forced to dig up the bodies of Jews who had been gassed earlier during the war and buried in mass graves, and burn them, revolted by throwing stones at the SS and setting fire to Crematorium No. 4 with explosives that young Jewish women had smuggled into the camps. A number of SS guards were killed or wounded and some prisoners were able to escape the camp. But of the 650 involved in the uprising, 450 died, and almost all the rest were recaptured. In addition to these revolts in the death camps, there were massive uprisings in at least twenty ghettoes including the famous Warsaw Ghetto uprising. And there was a large and organized Resistance movement composed of both Jews and non-Jews who risked their lives daily to fight Nazism. The Resistance movement deserved far more space than I can give it here; I recommend Vera Laska's book *Women in Resistance in the Holocaust* to interested readers as one of many books available on this subject.[23]

The picture of the Jews *all* lining up for the ovens is a myth, a lie which has been passed down in history until even we believe it. It is lies like this which present Jews as submissive masochists that made the Holocaust possible. I had no idea the Resistance existed until I started researching the Holocaust. What does it mean to be a Jew carrying around this picture of submissive Jews in your head, or a Jewish woman carrying a double burden of lies—passive woman and passive Jew?

---

[22]Ben Hecht, *A Guide for the Bedeviled* (New York: Charles Scribner's Sons, 1944), p. 101.
[23]Vera Laska, *Women in the Resistance and in the Holocaust: the Voices of Eyewitnesses* (Westport, Conn.: Greenwood Press, 1983).

2) The Romance of Suffering

I think there is a belief that the Jews should not have allowed themselves to be led to the slaughter and that they should have taken up arms and used Nazi tactics, an attitude which I find abhorrent. I think there was something beautiful in the way they went.[24]

I had my own theories about the Holocaust. I saw a face that was Sophia Loren's face: skin stretched tight and blazing eyes, a very dignified lady. She was suffering silently, trying to preserve her dignity . . . Somewhere I got the idea that suffering was a noble thing. All our relatives who were so brave and noble had suffered. I thought if I wanted to be a special, noble person I had to suffer too. And I tried. . . I *wanted* to suffer.[25]

Submission and suffering bring purity and beauty. This is the ideology that says the only way to be a good Jew is to be a submissive Jew. Indeed many of the survivors of the camps encountered this attitude after the war:

I know a survivor, a woman had told me. That man at the meat market with the blue number on his arm. Sweet man. Never raises his voice. Not like the others I've come across. You'd think they'd have learned something from their experience, wouldn't you? No those people seemed to have learned nothing.[26]

This insidious form of sadomasochism tells us that punishment purifies, suffering is good for the soul. This is the ideology that "elevates" oppression to martyrdom, that claims the oppressed are better than the powerful because they have suffered. We have heard this story before, played out in countless chapters of history. It is the story of the noble Indian romanticized even as her land is taken, her people are sterilized into oblivion. It is the myth of the woman on the pedestal who really has no power. It is the tale of the handsome dyke drinking herself to death, the romance of alcoholism and co-alcoholism.

The problem with this romantic story is that it confines the oppressed to our suffering role. If you love me as a ravaged alcoholic I am afraid to stop drinking because then you might not love me any more. If you think I am heroic because I have nightmares about the Holocaust, you confine me to a world in which there must *be* a Holocaust. Helen Epstein talks about how people reacted to her mother's tattooed number in *Children of Holocaust*,[27] "Her tattoo was a mysterious flag. It made some people blush, turn their eyes aside, mumble odd, garbled things. Others acted as if my mother was some species of saint."

---

[24]Steinmetz and Tzony, p. 102.

[25]Helen Epstein, *Children of the Holocaust* (New York: Bantam Books, 1981), p. 32.

[26]Epstein, p. 10.

[27]Epstein, p. 43.

We buy this insidious form of sadomasochism. We believe there is some kind of redemption in our suffering, that our suffering makes us beautiful. Judaism seems to have internalized this idea:

> According to the Bible, God has always punished his chosen people more harshly, and just as often as their enemies. But they have gone on believing in him and loving him. They have always believed—and so do religious Jews to this day—that their own errors and sins were to blame for all their tribulations, that their God punished them most because he loved them best and wanted them to be perfect.[28]

If we believe punishment is a demonstration of love we are buying the ideology of sadomasochism. If we believe we are "chosen to suffer" we are endorsing sadomasochism. If we accept the picture of the Jews lining up submissively for the ovens as a beautiful picture, or even a true picture, we are accepting sadomasochism, accepting the lies of sadomasochism.

We must be on guard against this form of sadomasochism which Joan Ringelheim calls the "valorization of oppression," in her article on women and the Holocaust.[29] "Oppression does not make people better; oppression makes people oppressed. There's no sense in fighting or even understanding oppression if we maintain that the values and practices of the oppressed are not only better than those of the oppressor, but in some objective sense, are 'a model for humanity in the new society.' If sexism makes women better able to survive, why get rid of it? Does suffering make us better people?"

For lesbians to play masochist in bed is to endorse a world picture, *a reality* in which masochism is used to rationalize suffering. To play masochist in bed is to endorse the Nazi picture of reality in which there are sadistic torturers who believe their victims enjoy being punished and humiliated.

Implications for Lesbian Feminism

> In every detail, the concentration camp resembled an enacted pornographic fantasy. Even the hardware of SM was present. Men and women were chained and shackled; and the SS officer, who wore high leather boots, carried a whip.[30]

In a sense, the Holocaust was an exercise in pornography. As we have seen, camp inmates were transformed into living pornography for the entertainment of the Nazis, and then disposed of, like women in snuff films. There were brothels in many of the camps. Jewish and Gypsy women (large numbers of Gypsies were also murdered by the Nazis) were told that if they gave "six months of service to clients" they would be released from the camps. In six months they submitted to over "2,000 acts of love." But after this period of time was up they were not set free. Their used up bodies were disposed of in the

---

[28]Lynne Reid Banks, *Letter to my Israeli Sons* (New York: Franklin Watts, 1980) p. 11.

[29]Ringelheim, p. 758.

[30]Susan Griffin, *Pornography and Silence* (New York: Harper, 1981) p. 189.

crematoria at Auschwitz. The SS officers drilled holes in the brothel room through which they spied on the prisoners having sexual activities. Another woman remembers when the camp guards decided to open the gates of the men's camp and allow them to go over to the women's. "The men came. I was pretty young then. Strangest thing—so many of these men tried right away to screw. They were like a horde of animals. I had this vision for a long, long time—this horde of sick men, jumping."[31]

These scenes acted out the Nazis' pornographic fantasy of Jewish sexuality as animalistic, of Jewish men as rapists, Jewish women as dark and mysterious whores. This myth dated back before the camps to the Nazi propaganda effort in the early days of the Holocaust. Central to this effort was Julius Streicher's magazine *Der Stürmer*, which published many cartoons depicting the Jew as "sex offender, seducer and rapist, exploiter of teenaged employees and accoster of respectable women."[32] The most disturbing cartoon I came across in *Der Stürmer* showed an "Aryan" woman lying on her back, helplessly bound and gagged, being tortured by a Jewish male. Pornography like this was a key instrument in enforcing laws that prohibited Jewish businesses from employing non-Jewish women. It also strengthened the idea that Jews were not human; Jews were beasts with beastly sexuality; Jews were the Other. Finally, pornography like this draws on sadomasochism, pleases the sadism in the reader who enjoys seeing women tied up and tortured. Once again sadomasochism fuels the Holocaust. As Andrea Dworkin points out, "Hitler's first and most basic anti-Semitic appeal was not economic, that is, the Jews control the money; it was sexual—and it was the sexuality of the Jews, as portrayed by Hitler, that provoked the German response."[33]

The parallels between these pornographic lies about Jews and the depiction of Black men as rapists and Black women as whores in America are rather striking. It could certainly be argued that sadomasochism fueled slavery as well, and that it is no accident that sadomasochists incorporate the technology and scenarios of both slavery and the Holocaust into their sexuality:

> I have other toys; leather wrist and ankle restraints, handcuffs, a g-string, some chain. Never underestimate the feel of cold metal on a hot body.[34]

Nor do I find it an accident that many Black women find lesbian sadomasochism disturbing:

> If it comes to the point where a large part of the women's community is supporting sadomasochistic activities, then I will not choose to be in the women's community because it would be totally against what I see the direction of Black people having to be in this country, and it would totally alienate Black people, it would totally alienate other cultures. I don't want to live out the fantasies or to remind myself of the people that are living out the fantasies of

---

[31] Ringelheim, p. 744.

[32] Dennis Showalter, *Little Man, What Now?: Der Stürmer in the Weimar Republic* (Hamden, Conn.: Archon Books, 1982) p. 65.

[33] Dworkin, p. 147.

[34] Juicy Lucy, "If I Ask You to Tie Me Up, Will You Still Want to Love Me?" *Coming to Power*, p. 35.

power when those same powers are used against me in the struggle for survival.[35]

SAMOIS considers itself "a lesbian/feminist SM organization" and claims that "S/M can and should be consistent with the principles of feminism." They say, "as feminists, we oppose all forms of social hierarchy based on gender."[36] I have serious problems with this conception of feminism. The kind of feminism I believe in also opposes social hierarchies based on race, anti-Semitism, class, age and other differences. I believe sadomasochism is both racist and anti-semitic and to advocate SM is to seriously contradict feminist ideals.

Furthermore, to advocate SM, a primary factor in the Holocaust, is to ignore the history of what happened to lesbians during the Holocaust. A large and active lesbian movement existed in Germany before the Third Reich. There were *Vermittlungsburos*— agencies run by lesbians that specialized in fixing up single lesbians. A number of lesbian social clubs met frequently in cafes, such as the Jewish lesbian club of Berlin, which met from 4-6 in the afternoon to talk and play chess. Balls were held regularly, run by and for lesbian women. A plethora of lesbian journals flourished, including—*Frauenliebe* (Womanlove), *Ledige Frauen* (Unmarried Women), and *Die Freundin: Weekly Journal for Ideal Friendship Between Women.* "From 1918 on, lesbian journals were part of the culture, usually presenting a perspective that was part political, part educational. What emerges then, is a picture of lesbian life as a widespread phenomenon, surprisingly aboveground, organized around its own publications, clubs and rituals."[37]

This thriving lesbian culture was virtually destroyed by the Third Reich. Lesbians were among those women imprisoned as asocials considered a threat to German society before 1939. Also on this list were prostitutes, vagrants, murderers, thieves and violators of laws prohibiting sexual intercourse between Aryans and Jews. Those lesbians who were not arrested went into the closet, for fear of their lives. Information on what exactly happened to lesbians during the Holocaust years is almost nonexistent. In his introduction to *The Men With the Pink Triangle*, David Ternbach mentions that paragraph 175 did not designate lesbianism as illegal and that legal measures against lesbianism were considered but dropped.[38] So we can surmise that lesbians were not thrown into the camps specifically because of their lesbianism. However many lesbians must have died in the Holocaust because they were left wing politicos considered a threat to the Reich, or because they were Jews. We know that the Holocaust years were hardly years favorable to lesbian culture. Therefore, I find SAMOIS' claim that they are opposed "to all social hierarchies based on sexual preference."[39] inconsistent with their support of sadomasochism, since sadomasochism fueled the Holocaust. The silence on what happened to lesbians during the Holocaust terrifies me. I believe it is political suicide for

---

[35]"Racism and Sadomasochism: A Conversation with Two Black Lesbians," Karen Sims and Rose Mason with Darlene Pagano, *Against Sadomasochism: A Radical Feminist Analysis* (East Palo Alto, Ca.: Frog in the Well Press: 1982).

[36]"SAMOIS: Who We Are," *Coming to Power.*

[37]"Maedchen in Uniform: From Repressive Tolerance to Erotic Liberation," *Jump Cut* No. 24/25.

[38]Heger, p. 9.

[39]SAMOIS: Who We Are," *Coming to Power.*

lesbians and gay men to wear swastikas and stormtrooper costumes at Gay Pride Parades.

Conclusion

Although the Holocaust was a complex historical event with a multiplicity of causes, it was stimulated at least partially by the Nazis' appeal to sexual sadomasochism. This began with handsome uniforms and a Party that made depressed and helpless citizens feel attractive and powerful. It continued with the usage of propaganda which depicted Jewish women as whores and Jewish men as rapists, and drew on the age-old stereotype of Jews as passive masochists. The result was the provocation of a violent sexual response from the German people—a sadistic response which involved the actual enactment of an elaborate pornographic scenario in which millions of people suffered punishment, humiliation and death, their bodies turned into soap, blankets and lampshades in the ultimate example of objectification.

The sadomasochistic virulence of the Holocaust is deeply embedded in our most "private" sexual selves. We live in a post Nazi-Holocaust world. We wear stormtrooper costumes, swastikas and play Nazi/Jew in bed. We call this making love. Even lesbians have not escaped. We too are caught in a great chain of history, a sadomasochistic chain which has persisted so long we have learned how to live with it, how to adapt to its weight, to walk differently, love differently, desire differently. We get used to it, so used to it we no longer notice it is there.

For lesbians to re-enact the power dynamics which existed in the horrendous historical scenarios of the Holocaust, not for educational or dramatic impact, but for *sexual entertainment*, seems to me an incredible trivialization of the suffering and deaths of millions of human beings. We live in a world which trivializes the Holocaust enough already. Auschwitz today is a tourist trap. The supporting poles of the station where Jews and other prisoners were once selected for death are now painted red and white like pieces of peppermint candy. The litter baskets are shaped in the form of penguins with their mouths open. A hotel and two restaurants have been built on the premises of the camp. A souvenir stand sells pendants depicting the prison uniform on one side and a drawing of a guard on the other. You can also buy lapel pins and picture postcards. Little children play in halls where ghastly medical experiments were once performed. Teenagers listen to rock music and laugh. A sixty-year-old woman climbs into the crematorium and smiles as a twelve-year-old boy takes her picture.[40]

It may be a thrill to sit in a crematorium and have your picture taken, but it is a horrendous insult to the people who died there. It may be a thrill, a *real turn-on* to re-enact discipline rituals, scenes of sexual punishment and humiliation in the bedroom. You may feel very attractive as a handsome sadist or a beautiful masochist. But what you are doing is an incredible insult to my dead, a horrifying trivialization of burnt flesh. Remember the fire. I ask you—is what you are doing really free of the bootprints of history? Which of these desires are really *yours*? Do you have the courage to take my words seriously and ask yourself these questions?

---

[40]Heger, p. 12.

I am a Jewish lesbian, a child of two survivors, digging through snowdrifts of silence trying to uncover some remnant of dignity, some kind of hope. I'm dreaming. I dream of five old women who stretch out their hands and say, "Take these. Do something with them." I dream I have somehow survived the war but now my own lesbian people are betraying me. I awake in the night, sobbing, nauseous—awake, saying over and over, "How shall I grieve? How can I mourn?" My people are silent, mute; do they see my exhaustion; do they wonder what I'm dreaming?

Bibliography

Banks, Lynne Reid. *Letters to My Israeli Sons.* New York: Franklin Watts, 1980.

Bauer, Yehuda. *A History of the Holocaust.* New York: Franklin Watts, 1982.

Beck, Evelyn Torton, ed. *Nice Jewish Girls: A Lesbian Anthology.* Trumansburg, New York: Crossing Press, 1982.

Bridenthal, Renate, Anita Grossman, and Marion Kaplan eds. *When Biology Became Destiny: Women in Weimar and Nazi Germany.* New York: Monthly Review Press, 1984.

Califia, Pat. "Feminism and Sadomasochism," pp. 30-34, *Heresies* Issue #12.

Clarke, D.A. *To Live With the Weeds.* Santa Cruz, Ca.: HerBooks, 1985.

Des Pres, Terrence. *The Survivor: An Anatomy of Life in the Death Camps.* New York: Simon and Schuster, 1977.

Dworkin, Andrea. *Pornography: Men Possessing Women.* New York: Perigee Books, 1981.

Epstein, Helen. *Children of the Holocaust.* New York: Bantam Books, 1981.

Gilbert, G.M. *Nuremberg Diary.* New York: Signet Books, 1947.

Hecht, Ben. *A Guide for the Bedeviled.* New York: Charles Scribner's Sons, 1944.

Heger, Heinz. *The Men With the Pink Triangle.* Boston: Alyson Publications, Inc., 1980.

Klepfisz, Irena. *Keeper of Accounts.* Watertown, Ma.: Persephone Press, 1982.

Laska, Vera, ed. *Women in the Resistance and in the Holocaust: The Voices of Eyewitnesses.* Westport, Conn: Greenwood Press, 1983.

Linden, Robin Ruth et. al. *Against Sadomasochism: A Radical Feminist Analysis.* East Palo Alto, Ca.: Frog in the Well Press, 1982.

Merkl, Peter. *The Making of a Stormtrooper.* Princeton University Press, 1980.

Murphy, Brendan. *The Butcher of Lyon: The Story of the Infamous Nazi, Klaus Barbie.* New York: Empire Books, 1983.

Reed, Lannon D. *Behold a Pale Horse.* San Francisco: Gay Sunshine Books, 1985.

Ringelheim, Joan. "Women and the Holocaust: A Reconsideration of Research," *Signs: Journal of Women in Culture and Society.* Vol. 10, No. 4 (1985), pp. 741-761.

Roth, Cecil. *A Short History of the Jews.* New York: Schocken Books, 1961.

SAMOIS: *Coming to Power: Writings and Graphics on Lesbian SM.* Boston: Alyson Publications, 1982.

Showalter, Dennis. *Little Man, What Now? Der Stürmer in the Weimar Republic.* Hamden, Conn.: Archon Books, 1982.

Steinmetz, Lucy and David Tzony eds. *Living After the Holocaust: Reflections by the Post-War Generation in America.* New York: Bloch Publishing Company, 1976.

Von Staden, Wendelgard. *Darkness Over the Valley.* New Haven: Tichnor and Fields, 1981.

Sharon Lim-Hing

The Rules of Love

She took me down the thin corridor. On the right side was an unpainted concrete wall with slits for windows. On the left was a row of about fifteen metal doors painted years ago, now a chalky blue with rust spots, no graffiti. She pushed one of the doors open.

"I live here," she said.

Inside was a narrow bed, a chair, a TV, and a window. Walls of plaster. A standard workers domestic cell. I tried to turn the TV down. She laughed.

"How do you sleep?" I asked, not being used to constant stream boxes.

"You just dream deeper in the night."

I crossed the cell in two steps. Outside, a field covered with luxuriant, prickly, poisonous weeds. Across that, another unpainted concrete tower with slit windows rose among the evening stars. In the distance, a rusting railroad.

"You didn't come here to look at the landscape," she said, and took my hand. We kissed. Her peachfuzz bushed against my face. My hands found their way under her clothing, and gently, I stroked her back, traced her ribs, as we kissed.

"Wait." She stopped me from undressing her. "This is too soon."

"Too soon?" I was puzzled. Her saliva was sticky on my lips, and I wanted more.

"I don't even know you. I have read books, you know. And this is too soon. We have to get to know each other first."

She was right. I was not following procedure.

Suddenly, a chain hit the other side of the wall. Then a gruff bark, a soft sigh.

"I don't want it to be like this," I said. "I'm going now."

She nodded.

In the tight hallway, a dominatrix in well-worn leather made a pass at me. Like the barker and the sigher in the adjoining cell, she was intent on getting her quota in. I kicked her shin to get by.

"Hey, I'm supposed to kick you, dumb class-I bitch!" she yelled after me. I turned around and made a gesture of hostility. "I'll slit your face up too, you yellow bitch!" For that I almost stopped to beat her up, but I kept walking.

How did we get this way? As a historian I knew that the structure put into place in the twentieth century now solidly encased the entire globe. When television began saturating people's waking hours, they read less and less. In any case, all types of media were bought by a handful of transnational corporations. A single version of reality reigned, that which was propagated in the interests of a shrinking minority of ultra-

100

wealthy. In my spare time, I tried to gauge how much my predecessors had bent and reshaped their data. As state historian, my job was to manipulate the same material for the benefit of the present government, which is the permanent government. I told the official version, that we currently benefited from the most equitable distribution of wealth, the most efficient use of each member of society, and the most united set of beliefs in the history of the Republic. And perhaps this was true, too.

As for sex, same story. Things simply continued according to the drift taken a few centuries ago.

I entered the main public space, the shopping area. I approached the soldier. If he wanted to apprehend me, he could.

"Where's the restroom?"

"Right over there, Doctor," he said politely, pointing his laser slicer. I accepted his respectful misidentification of my profession.

I went in and washed my hands. I knew it was irrational, but I had to do it. I felt dirty. I had looked into her eyes. I had felt her soul. She had felt mine.

A week later I went to meet her as she came out of the filing factory.

"My eyes are tired," she said, but she looked pleased to see me.

"Come over to my place," I invited. She looked at me warily. "I made us dinner," I added quickly.

We made an incongruous couple as we walked through the shopping area: two disparate class members, neither of whom was wearing a leash.

"I'm so sick of filing," she said. "Every two years the system changes and we have to start all over again, from zero or A or whatever it is."

"Really? How wasteful."

"That's political change for you."

"If it really exists. I'd have thought they'd be using artificial intelligence for state filing by now."

"Humans are cheaper to maintain than robots. Besides, it helps cut down on unemployment revolts. Anyway," she looked at me challengingly, "if they really wanted to, they could do away with your job too. It's not as if writing books or whatever it is you do has such an impact on the world."

"Well . . ."

"It's kept you off the streets. Till now," she smiled at me, perhaps my discomfiture.

When we got home, she marveled at the all-wool carpet. Wool was scarce, as Phoretoxine, the cure for HIV37, was derived from sheep's brains when they died in agony. It's true, I'd forgotten such material goods were impressive to someone whose bare floor echoed the sounds of the next cell's sexual paraphernalia. The same color carpeting came with every dwelling of my class, although I didn't know what they were using as wool now and wouldn't want to ask.

"Where's the box?" she asked, looking around for the TV.

"Here, here, and here," I pointed to the books in my library, my heart and hers. "And now for something new, or rather, old." From an envelope pasted under my desk I took out a sepia, dog-eared document, *Passion's Fire* by Edwina Kingston. It was the story of Juliana, a governess, who goes to Leedsworth Estate to care for the Carrington brood. She must contend with strange fires she sees burning at the nearby monastery in ruins late on moonlit nights, and also her growing fascination for the widow Mrs. Carrington.

Despite the differences in age and station, they try to have an egalitarian relationship. Of course this is impossible, and they end up jumping off a cliff together onto wave-assaulted crags.

"A friend of mine once had a facsimile of one of these things. They found it under his bed and took him away."

"When did you know that you were . . . different?" I asked.

"I've always known I was different. When I had my first ritual, I hated it. And as I was growing up, it didn't matter if I was master or slave or was with a man, a woman or a group. I never liked it. It doesn't work for me. How about you?"

"Thanks to my profession, I've had access to certain archives that are kept as examples of perversion. I've read them in secret, always afraid I would be caught. I knew that there was nothing wrong with my reading them, but I wasn't interpreting them in the correct way.

"Continuing my research, using related topics as a cover, I read articles by scholars in the last century who believe that . . . there's nothing inherently wrong with, with, this way of being or thinking."

"I've always felt that there's nothing wrong with who I am, or what I do," she said. "I didn't need books to tell me so. I just have to be careful who I tell."

"Don't worry, it's okay," I said. I too was afraid I would tell the wrong person.

She reached over and held my hand. For a long time we just sat there, looking at each other now and then. I felt happy.

One day we went to the park. It had three big trees, two smaller trees, and a flowering bush. These were hardy species.

"Aren't you sad you don't speak Korean?" I asked, remembering what she'd told me of her long-ago ancestors.

"You don't speak Chinese. Are you sad?"

"Not today."

We left the park and walked among the towering buildings. Today, even their opaque glass windows and geometric uniformity looked pleasing to me, against an optimistically blue sky.

The next time I went over to her place. We sat on the slim, sagging mattress.

"I'm having incest flashbacks," she said. "And nightmares." It was about time. Usually they hit by adolescence. Most people got over it.

"Who did it?"

"My father, my brother. I don't know."

"Did you tell your section's therapist?"

"That's just a way to let off steam. So you don't go crazy and can go back to work. It doesn't solve anything . . . What do you think? Does it really happen?"

"Probably a lot of it does happen in a physical sense. Some of it telepathic. Some of it symbolic. What matters is that it keeps us atrophied, subdued."

"And you?" she looked at me.

"My father and my mother, at different times." She started to cry. For me, for herself, for every molested child, every citizen. I had gotten over my pain. I had grown up to be a successful member of a privileged class. Not that that meant a great deal, as I was discovering. She trembled, trying to hold it in. I held her like a baby I once dreamt about.

Tears and saliva dripped across my arms. All I could do is be with her. All my tears had been cried out a long time ago.

One day we were walking to her place. In order not to be noticed by security, I had taken to wearing a fake emerald-studded collar with a little bell. Sometimes she led me on a leash. It made me laugh to think that this was considered "normal," that unknown to the shoppers around us pranced a subversive couple. I felt elated and silly. I looked over at her. We had gotten accustomed to the strong exchange of emotion that happened when we looked into each other's eyes.

At that moment I felt compelled to tell her that I loved her, a way I had been feeling every now and then for the past few weeks. I didn't know why. I wondered if I knew enough about this thing, love, to know if I loved someone. Still, it was like an itch on the inside of my skin, an obsession, something tugging at my brain making me want to say the sacred words.

"There's someone following us—don't turn around," she hissed. "Let's walk over to that toy store, not that one, the other one with the mannequins in the iron maiden."

We joined a group of people admiring the new window display.

"Look at the reflection, the man in the overcoat," she whispered. Then in a loud voice, "Oh honey, it's lovely. I wish we could afford one." I saw him, an ordinary, ugly-looking white man in a blue coat and carrying a rumpled plastic bag. It's true, I had noticed him earlier outside my house.

We continued on our way, careful not to touch or look at each other. When we got to her place, we talked about what we could do.

"Before, or if they get us, I just want you to know. I love you," I said, holding her hand and drinking up the feeling of skin on skin.

"I love you, too." Instead of satisfying me, our mutual declaration made me want to tear away the barriers that made us two people, not one.

"I don't want to stop seeing you."

"Me neither."

"We don't know that he's from security."

"Maybe we should stop seeing each other exclusively, have a few other sexual contacts to put them off our trail."

"The thought of being chained up or beating someone up disgusts me."

"Can't you handle a little verbal humiliation?" she reasoned. "Or would you prefer a lobotomy? What did you do before we met?"

"I did the minimum quota. You saw the scars. But that was before we met."

"Sometimes I think you're taking this too seriously." She looked at me with a mixture of pity and pleading. "Some parts of what we have are just a game, you know."

"It's not a game for me."

"We have to be alive first. Then we can talk about whether it's a game or not."

"Maybe it's something worth dying for."

That night she sent me away and told me to have some normal sex with someone. I tried, but in my despair I would forget what part I was playing while negotiating. I left the bars alone.

When I got home, he was waiting for me. Not the man in the blue overcoat, but another white man, just as ordinary, just as ugly.

"Follow me. You are now in state custody," he said, "as you always have been." He led me back towards the shops and into an information store. On one side videos, on the other computer programs, and in a corner books and magazines. A few late night shoppers browsed under the harsh lights. We went through a door marked *Employees Only* and up a stairway to the second floor. In the large office with several desks lay unpacked boxes, and computers blinked stoically at one another.

"You own the info stores?" I asked, puzzled.

He pushed me through the office to an unmarked door. The door opened. Inside was a real-wood desk. An older white man with dull grey hair sat there. Elbows propped up on the desk, he caressed his own chin. Then he sat back, returning my stare with no particular emotion.

"The state *controls* all important concerns, Professor. What more appropriate offices for state intelligence?

"I want her alive, too," he said, dismissing his subaltern with a small head movement. The man left quickly.

He motioned me towards a chair. I refused to sit down.

"How did you find out?" I asked, fighting to keep my voice from warbling.

"Your therapist."

"But therapy is confidential. That's the law!"

"Your therapist tried to dissuade you, but you were too stubborn. After a while you stopped talking about your little love affair, but by that time she had already reported you."

"You're getting sloppy. We spotted your man today," I shot back.

"Oh, he wasn't one of ours," he said casually. "He is, or I should say *was*, one of yours. Belonged to a group of romance agitators, trying to get in contact with you. But we'll soon destroy all their little nests." What might have been a smile caused the corners of his mouth to crease upwards, but he began pulling his chin, so it looked like a grimace.

"But why?" I wanted to know.

"What do *you* think, Professor?" His grey eyes narrowed.

"Because 'loving' another person is inimical to the functioning of the economy. Having an emotional exchange with another person instead of using her as an object would help people feel connected," I said, as if I had always known it, "instead of being divided. If people knew that sex is not a thing to be bought or sold, that love is shared, then—"

"Ah, you're so smart, but again you've reached the wrong conclusions. That's why you're going back to school. To learn to interpret properly. We'd like to salvage your mind, since we've already invested considerable training and resources in you." He tapped a pile of computer read-outs on the desk, as if he was out of patience.

"Your friend will be taken to a different kind of school. She will be taught to enjoy sex the correct way. If the lesson doesn't take, and she isn't dead, the state can use her. She might make a modest contribution to science."

Dizziness, incomprehension, then anger like a shot of adrenaline, a rush of heat and power.

I observed myself as I lost control. I grabbed a pen from the desk and stuck it through his left eye. He screamed and tried to pull it out. He was spreading blood all over his chin. I shoved his clawing fists in deeper. The pen must have hit his brain. He still made noises and scratched at his face. I picked up the chair beside me and heaved it wildly at his head. I was lucky. He fell and lay still.

I kneeled to wipe my hands on the plush carpet. I had enjoyed it. None of us is pure.

In complete clarity and calmness I walked out of the info store and to her place. She had just killed a man. We took off towards the old railroad track. I didn't know where we were going, but we kept running. I heard dogs behind us, but we kept running together.

D. A. Clarke

Consuming Passions:
Some Thoughts on History, Sex, and Free Enterprise

Choosing Sides

I did not go to a Gay Pride march this year or last year, neither the small one in my town nor the large one in San Francisco. It was a conscious decision. I am not, at this time, proud of the gay community, and I don't feel like pretending that I am. At one time I was an organiser[1] and active participant in Gay Pride; something has changed, but what?

Increasingly the gay community, that uneasy coalition of lesbians and gay men whose culture is dominated by gay male traditions and aesthetics, is identifying itself with the sex industry and with "kinkiness" and "decadence" of various kinds. This has led to the bitter debate in the lesbian and feminist communities between advocates and critics of sadomasochism/pornography/prostitution, but the issue is deeper than that (and wider than just the gay world). Unfortunately the majority of the gay community and its media leaders seem to be on what I believe to be the wrong side.

The result: what I might charitably call confusion, and less charitably call arrant hypocrisy, in the gay media. Take my home-town gay newsmagazine,[2] for example. On page 5 of the Fall 1991 issue Frances Lawrence of Rutgers College is proudly quoted: "It must take a generous spirit to believe that cross-burning, swastika-painting, and racial and religious hate slogans are brave gestures of free speech." The paper implicitly supports her efforts to uphold Rutgers' anti-harassment codes and protect gays on campus from insult and attack.

On the other hand, on page 6 we find a full page ad thanking a club called Bulkhead Gallery for its support and its commitment to "free speech." It was at this club that a live sadomasochistic sex show called "The Torture Circus" was recently presented; the show drew a certain amount of feminist response because of a number involving a woman (in collar and leash) whose clothes were cut from her body with a knife by another woman. When some businesses were requested to withdraw sponsorship and advertising for the club, there was a firestorm of accusations of "censorship" which ended with a public apology to "the gay community" from one restaurant. Apparently we are to extend a very

---

[1] The author is originally a British citizen, and has requested that her Briticisms be retained for publication. Ed.

[2] *Lavender Reader* (Fall 1991).

generous spirit indeed when violence against women (as opposed to Jews or Blacks) is being symbolically evoked and enacted.

On page 20 the news clips include triumphant mention that "The Canadian Radio-Television and Telecommunications Commission has announced a proposal that would ban negative comments about gays and lesbians from the air." But on page 33 a local artist and writer comments that "we are witnesses to a sexual revolution that is shaking all the most solid, archaic, and conservative of systems . . . art's free spirit . . . greatly disturbs the tranquility of those who demand 'respect' and 'morality'." This double standard on the part of gay and lesbian writers and publishers is not uncommon; it has become the rule. The gay community wants respect, legal protection from hate speech against queers, yet it defends and praises any and all sexual imagery and speech, even when violent and hateful towards women. Public, ideologically defended lesbian sadomasochism is a visible and (for many feminists) distressing manifestation of this trend.

Sm fashion and mystique are sometimes seen as a passing style among younger people, like various youth trends which have come and gone in the past few decades. Youth culture in the US, whether gay or straight, exaggerates the national attraction to things flashy and exciting, and to whatever seems to shock our parents. And sex still passes for a "shocking" or "rebellious" activity—particularly among queers, still accustomed to public ridicule and discrimination for their choice of lovers.

However, the appeal of sm is not new. There is a long cultural tradition in the industrial West (and other places) of eroticised violence; there is a strong tendency in male-supremacist societies for violence itself to be found sexually arousing and satisfying. The inclusion of violence and death in pornography is as old as Western culture.

Neither does sadomasochistic chic appeal only to the young, or only to queers. Department stores reorganise their window displays to include a hint of "b&d" (bondage and discipline). Mainstream women's magazines encourage women to explore their enjoyment of being spanked by their husbands. And ambitious members of the newly-respectable university departments of Women's and Gay Studies capitalise on the popular trend by contriving hip new philosophies and politics of "deviance," "sex rebellion," "gender radicalism," and so forth.[3] (The prevailing economic and physical conditions of women's lives seem to have become too unoriginal, too boring, or perhaps too depressing for the serious academic attention they rated fifteen years ago. Derrida[4] is more fun.)

---

[3] The appeal of this essentially adolescent stance to so many adults says something about the status of queers, and about the particularly American obsession with youth culture and "rebellion."

[4] Jacques Derrida, French philosopher whose concept of textual "deconstruction" is currently fashionable among many academics. Highly simplified, Derrida's philosophy is a denial of the possibility of absolute meaning in text or other cultural materials; his adherents are fond of "deconstructing" text and visual art to discover "subversive" counter-interpretations. Particularly, pro-porn advocates have "deconstructed" pornographic materials and claimed the revelation of hidden, positive messages about women's sexual and political power. The physical and economic meanings of the porn industry are sufficiently present and obvious that I see no need to apply obscure analytical methods in search of other (albeit more palatable) interpretations.

I don't believe this mini-phenomenon[5] within the gay and lesbian subculture (from its lowbrow commercial roots to the highfalutin theories of the academicians who hope to make a dissertation and a reputation out of it) can be isolated from larger trends in youth culture and popular culture in general. In browsing through a discography of heavy metal bands I was struck by the same self-conscious "decadence"—what was at one time known as "fascist chic"—expressed in band and album names. An iconography of violence and violation is shared between the "queers" and the often queer-hating, queer-bashing young metal-heads. And a common thread runs through the album art, the sm sex magazines, the pornographic prose and film, the flyers for the sex shows, the promo posters for the spandex-boy bands: it is the thread of shrewd, calculating, manipulative commercialism. The gay subculture is merely responding to the prevailing social winds. And those winds are blowing ill for women.

There seems to be a turning away from any serious material analysis of the conditions of women's lives, the problems of global capitalism, and the challenges to democracy. The emphasis of the eighties and nineties is far more on self-actualisation (or self-indulgence)—on individual adjustment and accommodation to the mechanisms of society—on entertainment and "art"—than on a search for practical ways to maintain justice and prosperity for a whole society. Even among those leftists who are seriously studying global economic and ecological crises, the issue of sexual exploitation of women is last on their list. And there is an increasing tendency to focus on "sexual liberation" as a primary goal of, or a replacement for, feminism.[6]

It seems to me that many women, lesbian and straight, are uncomfortable with the current trends in lesbian and "feminist" thought and practice; we feel something is amiss, that the movement or the community has somehow lost its way, lost its ideals, lost its mind. But we are often prevented from leveling any criticism at those things or people which disturb our sense of rightness.

One factor which can shut us up is too narrow a focus. Arguments and justifications which seem reasonable within the very small, closed room of (white US) academic feminist theory or lesbian political infighting suddenly lose their appeal when you step back and take a wider (economic, historical, or ethnographic) perspective.

Another discouragement is the clever and well-developed rhetoric which centers around "sexual liberation"—meaning the sex entertainment business. In this dialectic the standard response to questioning or critique is a counterattack in which the questioner is dismissed as narrow-minded, naïve, repressed, "sex-negative," or worse: neo-conservative, fascistic, anti-gay, anti-life, anti-fun. Most of us are understandably reluctant to be identified with any of these unlovable characteristics, let alone all of them at once. Particularly, we are reluctant to appear in any way supportive of the Rightists who have done such damage to American life and politics in the last decade.

But there are very good intellectual and political reasons for feminists (indeed, for anyone committed to simple social justice) to have *and to express* strong doubts about

---

[5] i.e. the popularity of sm and legitimisation of gay porn, and attempts to establish "politics of deviance" as a primary agenda.

[6] I am surprised every time I hear the term "post-feminist": it never occurred to me that feminism could be over until women were free.

the value and impact of sadomasochistic style and practise, prostitution, and pornography. I do not refer here to revealed religion, fear of nudity, or a fascistic desire to control what everyone does in their bedrooms. I am talking about a sensible distaste for unfairness, exploitation, manipulation, and the unlovelier aspects of capitalism; about an aversion to male supremacy and its inevitable side-effects; about a perspective that is *woman-positive.*

"Welcome to Fantasy Island"

A couple of years ago I saw on a bumper sticker one of those newly-manufactured slogans which come and go like the daisy sticker and the smiley face. It said something very like "Having abandoned my quest for reality, I am now looking for a good fantasy." I cannot think of a better slogan for the nineties, or for the particular people and subculture which I am trying to challenge: the new lesbian "feminists" of the last decade before the millennium, who have perhaps so despaired of getting or wielding any power and control over a hostile and incomprehensible world, that they prefer to devote their time and energy to elaborate fantasies of absolute personal, sexual power.

I have, actually, nothing against fantasy. No one who has read as much science-fiction and eagerly watched as many movies as I have, could earnestly uphold such a position. I do have a problem with fantasy as the basis of relationships between adult human beings.

Childhood fantasy play may be an important developmental stage, and is sometimes (though by no means always) harmless; but after a certain age I think it indecent to assume that other people should or can be props and actors in one's private fantasy productions. It makes me reassess the literal meaning of the term "objectification"—once much used in feminist rhetoric, now tarnished with age, no longer hip or trendy. I find it a really essential word, indispensable in trying to understand human error and wrong-doing.

The sm social scene, for example, places strong emphasis not only on costumes and accessories, but on categorizing individuals by what they are and aren't "into" or willing to do. The handkerchief colour code is the classic public expression or advertisement of these categories, and I use the word "advertisement" with purpose. This convention reminds me strongly of a shopping mall, where potential buyers shop for the correct accessory, the proper cast for their current movie. It reminds me also of the anterooms of certain whorehouses where the merchandise is on display, and the male customers decide whether they want the Asian girl or the white one, the blonde or the redhead, the young one or the more motherly type. It is a selection among goods on a shelf.

There is a sense in which the redefinition of our sex lives into a set of fixed requirements, according to which we shop around for compliant partners, means that we regard each other more and more as prostitutes: as service providers or as commodity. Of course, it's trendy these days to defend not only prostitutes, but prostitution in general. Hookers certainly need defence, against harassment from police as well as violence from customers. Their working conditions are appalling; but sympathy and support for women enmeshed in the commercial sex trade is now being manipulated into support for the trade itself. It's beginning to be "old-fashioned" or even reactionary to think that there is anything wrong with prostitution at all. And maybe that's a good place to begin.

Obscure Objects of Desire

The objectification of a person means the conversion of that person into an object. Extreme cases spring to mind easily: slavery is one, in which human beings are bought and sold like any other form of property. Cannibalism of certain kinds (not, for example, ritual funeral cannibalism) is another, and rightly horrifies us: we would not like to be regarded dispassionately as someone else's lunch. Objects can be consumed, and for a human being, being consumed means spiritual or physical death.

Certainly nothing more accurately expresses the chattel or object position of women in male supremacy than the twin mechanism of marriage and prostitution. It's been said that traditional marriage, as legally defined, differs from prostitution only in that one is a sale and the other a rental.[7] That which is sold or rented is an object. Certainly some have argued that a woman has a marginally better chance at autonomy as a whore than as a wife (though most of these arguments conveniently ignore the institution of pimping). Too seldom is the argument forcefully made that women's "choices" are meaningless if limited to these two alternatives. Whether sold or rented, women remain (as Levi-Strauss[8] pointed out long ago) the *currency* of transactions between men.

And yet (no matter how much we know about objectification) prostitution and the sex industry in general are nowadays hyped as inherently progressive. Because the American Right makes a traditional—and bogus—show of opposition to "immorality," millions of wannabe radicals leap to the easy conclusion (in which they are naturally encouraged by the sex-capitalists): being consumers for the sex trade is somehow revolutionary or subversive.

For gays and lesbians, long associated in the public mind (since the writings of the ancient Greeks, at least) with the sexual underworld,[9] the sex trade is now being sold as a *community.* There are academics among us (well-paid, in no danger of resorting to prostitution for grocery money) now proposing a "politics of deviance" which should embrace all queers, prostitutes, pornographers, pimps, fetishists, transsexuals, bestialists, sadists, masochists, and perhaps even paedophiles in one community of queerness, united in resistance to straight middle-class values.

Ironically, this only confirms the most traditional bourgeois stereotypes of what homosexuality is about. The bourgeois have always believed that gay men and lesbians lead sordid lives as paid companions and prostitutes (after all, queer sex is so disgusting that no one would possibly do it without pay!) Gay sex, like other kinds of kinkiness, is then merely another flavour in the sexual marketplace where straight men shop. Or, correspondingly, gayness is a sign of depravity and therefore belongs with the violence,

---

[7] I've certainly said and written this, but it's so good that I doubt it was original. If you can identify its originator, please write to HerBooks and let me know.

[8] Claude Levi-Strauss, social anthropologist, who viewed cultures as primarily systems of communication and used concepts from structural linguistics and information theory in this sociological analysis. He studied Native American cultures in Brazil and the Pacific Northwest, and strongly influenced a generation of sociologists and cultural anthropologists.

[9] In fact the Attic Greek for "lesbian" is *hetairistria*, related to *hetaera*, prostitute; we'll get back to ancient Greece later.

coercion, double-dealing and general ugliness of the sex trade. Attempts to *reclaim* epithets like "slut" and "whore" and to propose bad-girl-ism and prostitution as a revolutionary feminist path would make me laugh, if they were not so essentially tragic.

It's difficult to imagine what might be considered deviant about the sex trade, known as "the oldest profession" (though this is inaccurately applied to prostitution, when it should be applied to pimping). No one can dispute its antiquity. From the beginning of written history, what we call "civilisation," men have bought, sold, and rented women, girls, and boys for sexual entertainment. Those who propose a politics of deviance or a "community of queerness" conveniently overlook the fact that large sections of that community, as they define it, constitute a service industry patronised by those same respectable middle-class males whose values they claim to despise and reject.

Yes, the same respectable men who preach about family values have always known where to go for a night out with the boys; they would be completely at a loss if the sexual underworld vanished overnight. Even if their only contact with it is a few tattered porn magazines hidden in the garage, they rely on its existence, on the knowledge that somewhere, if they choose, they can go and find someone who needs a few bucks enough to give them a blow job.

This attempt to invent a politics of deviance also misses a beat in its happy assumption that *all* the standards and beliefs of the bourgeoisie are false, and that anything which contravenes them must therefore be good. (If the bourgeoisie think suicide is a crime against the Lord, then obviously we should all go out and kill ourselves right now. That'll show them!)

People fall into this trap constantly—not just feminists and queers—when they become unable to realise that the opposition may actually be *right* about one or two things. Too often we end up demonstrating our purity and righteousness by refusing to agree with Them about anything at all, no matter how ridiculous this makes us. Certainly this is the tactic used over and over again by the sex-capitalists in their own defence: Jesse Helms hates pornography; you hate pornography; therefore you are (or at least you like) Jesse Helms.[10]

The attitude we take to the sex trade is relevant to other points of dispute among lesbians and feminists. The struggle over lesbian sm and pornography has been described as "differences around commercial sex,"[11] which may in fact be quite accurate. It may be that what we disagree about most fundamentally is the *commercialisation* of sex, about the basic premise, about whether it is right or wrong to rent human beings for

---

[10] This game is played over and over again wherever amateur rhetoric prevails; anti-abortionists liken voluntary first-trimester abortion to Nazi eugenic murders because the Nazis advocated forced abortions. Nuclear engineers liken anti-nuke protesters to anti-evolutionists because the anti-nukers cast doubts on certain aspects of modern science. Reductionism abounds. My favourite illustration of this is the vegetarian one. Hitler was a vegetarian; should you be afraid to defend vegetarianism, for fear of being thought a Nazi? Unfortunately, when it comes to the sex industry, many of us *are* afraid to stand up for our non-violent, anti-racist, anti-capitalist, or feminist beliefs because someone might call us Jesse Helms. And this, I fear, has something to do with our concept of ideas and politics as just something else that we "shop around" for, that we have to buy in pre-packaged chunks from the chosen supplier. It ain't so.

[11] Wendy Chapkis, panel discussion at Kresge College, UCSC, Spring 1991.

111

sexual use, or to use women's bodies as a commercial resource; and by extension, whether it is right or wrong to objectify each other in our private dealings.

Some women argue that prostitution cannot and must not be considered different from any other line of low-paid, sometimes demeaning, sometimes dangerous work: sharecropping, for example, or waiting on tables. It's not the best job, they say, but surely it's no worse than the assembly line or the fast food kitchen. I have been stumped by this objection for a long time, but I believe there *is* something about prostitution which makes it different from, and more questionable or unacceptable than, other kinds of work.

First there is the fact that the overwhelming majority of customers of the sex trade are male and adult, and that its workers are women and children. This is not merely a byproduct of capitalism, but has to do with the nature of male sexuality and fantasy. Although, as one rather whiny essayist has recently pointed out,[12] there are more homeless men than women and fewer social services and supports aimed at helping homeless men, nevertheless there are not large influxes of homeless adult males into the prostitution trade.

There are other trades in which the vast majority of workers are female, mostly the textile and food-packing industries and the "service sector" of receptionists, manicurists, waitresses, and so forth. It strikes me as very significant that the "service sector" is disproportionately populated by women workers. Smiling, soothing, and kissing ass have traditionally been women's work and still are; long after the equivalent white-folks' fantasy of the subservient black male has become socially uncomfortable and embarrassing, it is still normal and reasonable for women to be required to smile and cajole while on the job.

Most of us consider this component of ass-kissing, placation, subjugation of our pride or temper when outraged, as an unwelcome "extra" part of our jobs, to be endured with gritted teeth and much bitter wit shared with co-ranking co-workers when the more powerful are out of hearing. Now consider the prostitute. All these things we have just described as annoying extra stress in the average job *are* her job. And she is expected to do a lot more than smile and say, "Thank you for shopping at Safeway."

The prostitute is not really paid for not running away, for passively submitting to being fucked.[13] She is expected to provide active sexual service to the client on demand. She is further expected to provide make-believe at various levels: to pretend that she enjoys it, that he is physically impressive and a good lover, that she finds him attractive; depending on her rank and place in the sex industry she may be required to pretend to be somebody in particular, to act out some simple or complex scenario of the client's choice. [1] (numbers in brackets refer to endnotes beginning page 148)

The fact is that her job is about lying, and lying at the most intimate level. The more intimate the lie, the more it costs the liar; and this cost, like so many others in our economy, is concealed. Men often describe pretty women as being endowed by Nature

---

[12] Peter Marin, "Why are the Homeless Mostly Single Men," *The Nation*, July 8, 1991.

[13] When women are held as captive prostitutes they are seldom paid at all, and never directly; a pimp or manager receives the money from the customer.

with an inexhaustible source of pure profit, as if there were no cost at all to be borne in selling one's body and one's lies.[14]

There is another side to this situation, which is that intelligent slaves despise their masters. Anyone who survives by manipulation and deceit cannot help but develop a certain contempt for the person who is so easily manipulated and deceived. This aspect of the man/whore relationship is often highlighted as proof that the woman really has the power in the arrangement, that men are merely helpless dupes of their own biology, which is exploited by mercenary and street-smart females. (In this mythology, note that once again the pimp has vanished from the picture.)

It doesn't really matter if the richest man in the world is stupid. The fact remains that he and other members of the Old Boys' Club have *material power* over my life and other people's lives, *which we do not have over theirs*. The fact that a pretty girl in a short skirt may be able to talk her way into a good job with a rather dim and egotistical male employer does not change the situation: he is the boss, he can fire her.

The fact that a hooker is clever enough to interpret and manipulate a client's fantasies and obsessions does not for one minute obscure the facts: he has the money and she needs it. Manipulation and deceit are the survival tools of the powerless; they would not need them so much if they had real, genuine, power.[15]

I think we are generally right in our intuitive perception that "slavish" submission and catering to the egos of those in power are not good for us, and are a distasteful blight upon the already-complicated relations of power in a workplace. So I think there is good reason to conclude that prostitution lies at the extreme worst end of a long continuum of jobs; at the other extreme we find those lucky people who are expected only to supply their skill or strength to the work in hand, and are not used as some kind of emotional puppets by those who employ them.

This is one simple reason for feminists to strive for general progressive goals like social justice, unemployment insurance, and full employment programs; without a job, food, or shelter, any woman or child (you or I, dear reader) is a potential prostitute. Frightened and hungry people have difficulty exercising little luxuries like choice and dignity in a free country. Servitude, no matter how objectionable, is generally preferred to death; few of us would nobly freeze or starve to death on the street rather than buy food and shelter with anything or everything we had.

I am willing to say that in a fully-employed, fully-enfranchised, and fully-fed world, where male violence was strictly curbed and punished, a nation of healthy and fearless women, youths, and children would provide very few prostitutes. The industry would die for lack of labour. May we not also say that—since the one runs on the other—those who defend and praise the sex trade are defending and praising the poverty and fear that keep it alive?

---

[14] We'll take a closer look later at the parallel between this belief and the corresponding belief that Nature itself is merely an inexhaustible storehouse for the sustenance of human beings, and that what we take out of it is "free," or the belief that the market economy is a boundless system capable of infinite expansion.

[15] Not only men, but women often believe or wish to believe these myths of female sexual power over men; I think they are at best a consoling fantasy.

There's No Business Like Big Business

Prostitution is business, when it comes down to essentials, and how we feel about it depends largely on how we feel about business, money, and the ethics of trade. Pornography, prostitution, gay sadomasochism all take place in a global economic context which shapes people's thinking as well as their daily, material lives.

The roots of recent trends in the gay subculture are found in the surrounding mainstream culture. Events in the larger world drive events in all the smaller worlds of ethnic, sexual, religious and political affinity. The shift among "out" lesbians from a "women's movement" orientation to an individualist, consumer-oriented definition of self and community is not due to some individual moral failing, nor is it a sign of inadequate leadership or scholarship on the part of earlier organisers. During the eighties (and continuing as I write), the US and other industrialised nations have been swinging to the right, rapidly or gradually as their unique circumstances demand. The tightening global economy is stepping up the pace and pressure for production and marketing, and eroding socialist programs the world over. The income gap between rich and poor has been growing for a decade. The US is no exception.

A major philosophical schism is arising in the industrialised nations; it has been coming for some time, but recently it grows clear and (to many people) threatening. Large numbers of people are questioning the basic values of industrial capitalism; what has awakened them is the degree of environmental damage finally being admitted and publicised the world over, damage which is a direct result of the apparent wealth and success of the "over-developed" nations. Many people are waking up to the concept of hidden costs attached to everything they wear, play with, and eat.

This awakening threatens corporate interests and (therefore) established political interests more than almost any other citizen action could, short of revolt in the streets. A backlash is inevitable, when the corporate pseudo-states feel themselves sufficiently threatened. It will probably not go so far as John Brunner predicted,[16] with the arrest of anyone suspected of buying health food or belonging to an ecological interest group. But it is here already, and during the Reagan/Bush years it manifested as a strong resurgence of the *libertarian* or *laissez-faire capitalist* position, also known as "free-marketism," "Logical Positivism," etc.[17] Very few Democrats of the new administration are willing to challenge laissez-faire capitalism as a philosophy, so we should not imagine that it will fade away with the change of regime.

Free marketism is based on the old Adam Smith model of economics, in which the "invisible hand" of competition in a free marketplace will result in maximum prosperity, freedom, and happiness for everyone.[18] The free market is the abiding icon of the

---

[16]John Brunner, *The Sheep Look Up* (New York: Ballantine Books, 1973), scathing dystopian satire.

[17] The prolific anti-socialist writer Ayn Rand popularized Logical Positivism for two generations (at least) of American readers. See her *Atlas Shrugged* for the definitive fictional expression of the philosophy.

[18] Unfortunately, it doesn't seem to work that way; see Blumberg's *The Predatory Society* for some insights into the free market's encouragement of dishonesty.

American Right, though not all libertarians can safely be classified as rightists (for example, they despise all drug laws). [3]

The mythology of the free marketplace has a strong hold on most of us; it is seldom challenged except by the old American Left. Corporate values are, as never before, American values. Many people identify more strongly with the products they buy than with the church or neighbourhood they belong to. Groups which once identified themselves with a belief or ideology now are more easily identified by their consumption patterns than by their public speech or action. "The personal is political" has been opportunistically interpreted by petty and grand capitalists to convince wannabe radicals and good-hearted liberals that the best way to express their beliefs is by purchase power. The idea of *voting with your dollars* has gained currency far outside the circles in which it was first coined.

The free marketeers share certain beliefs with the Libertarians: the public sector and government must be as small as possible, laws as few as possible, taxes as low as possible, and the rights of the individual absolutely the primary social agenda. Their definition of rights tends towards 17th and 18th century Rights of Man theory (which they do not see as a weakness). Any interference by government in the free marketplace is totally unacceptable to them.

This package has its attractions, particularly for American gays and lesbians. Breaking the stranglehold of Church dogma on the morals of public life is attractive to those whom the Churches and States have despised and sometimes put to death. A strong emphasis on the rights of the individual appeals to those who have been harassed, arrested, beaten by police for the mere possession of gay literature. "Leave me alone, and let me read and watch whatever I can afford," seems a reasonable demand for America's queers.

Unfortunately, it is also the slogan of corporate America, a corporate America whose most rapidly-growing sector is entertainment and information. The basic ethic of capitalism is that good business is good for everyone; and *good business* simply means *lots of sales.*

One of capitalism's great strengths, emphasised by its fans, is its tremendous flexibility; like pornography, it is able to digest and render profitable almost any trend, innovation, or event. Big business has made earnest attempts since the early seventies to subsume the new feminist movement into a defined market sphere.[19] The mainstream media took only a few years to move from open mockery and defamation of the women's movement to glossy advertising directed exclusively at the "new woman." One of the most glaring and (to feminists) infuriating examples was the Virginia Slims "you've come a long way, baby" campaign, but it was merely one of many. (The first incarnation of *Ms.* magazine eventually died a humiliating death, buried under heaps of ads—including that one.)

Similarly, it has not taken the pornographers long to make their bid for the new market; from the days when *Hustler* magazine ran Wanted posters of feminist

---

[19] US capitalism is particularly good at commercialising the rebellious urge. "The commodification of dissent is the great ideological innovation of our time . . . Insincere insurgency is now standard in advertising for beer, fast food, cigarettes, radio stations and cars." (T. C. Frank, from "Buy Hip: Why Non-Conformists Make Model Consumers," first published in *The Baffler* and excerpted in *Utne Reader* #52 (August 1992) pp. 102-103).

spokeswomen, to the latest mutation of "porn for women" rhetoric, has been barely ten years. The push to recruit women as consumers for the sex trade reminds me of nothing so much as the immensely expensive Reynolds Co. campaign (circa 1920) to induce American and British women to smoke, after a couple of centuries when it was (in Western lands) thought absolutely unacceptable for women to do so. [2]

But that's capitalism: it is not the seller's business to comment on the nature or worth of the goods; if the customer wants them, the customer is always right. And if the customer doesn't want them, perhaps she can be persuaded to want them. If the buyer has the cash, anything is for sale; we don't make judgments about the nature of the transaction. The ethic of laissez-faire capitalism is, in short, the ethic of pimping, and increasingly the ethic of the entertainment industry. It therefore bears a closer look.

The Invisible Hand at Work and Play

The interaction between marketplace and morals is clear in the Libertarian world: let the market decide. Free-marketism also encourages a simple three-value classification of the world: consumer, entrepreneur, and raw material. The right way to live is make sure you belong to class 1 or 2, not class 3 (Libertarians are profoundly anti-slavery). It is a Libertarian ethic, then, which informs current attitudes towards the sex trade among lesbian "feminists": women can resolve all questions about the industry by making sure that they are either entrepreneurs (hence the recent disproportionate emphasis on the independent hooker, who represents a tiny fraction of prostitutes in the US and the world) or consumers (hence the proliferation of lesbian sex shows and clubs, Chippendales calendars for straight women, etc.) There's a strong disinclination to face up to women's more usual role in the trade: raw, expendable material.

On the other hand, one could define the sex industry as a whole as corrupt, and unacceptable in a feminist vision of the world. This debate is entirely analogous to the debate over nuclear power: there are those who believe that incompetent and dishonest management, corrupt and complicit regulatory agencies, technological obstacles, and bad labour relations can all be cleaned up and replaced with good practice—and then the industry will work. There are others who believe that nuclear energy is a wrong technological path altogether, a mistake: an excessively risky and expensive technology with enormous hidden costs in human life and environmental damage, a silly and wasteful approach to matters that would be better addressed by a completely different philosophy.[20]

The alarmist rhetoric of scarcity is heard among both the capitalist investors in various polluting industries, and the friends of the sex trade. Nuclear developers characteristically predict the end of the world's oil and coal reserves (while the oil and coal companies are fervently denying the same); they cite the instability of the oil-rich

---

[20] These critics of the nuke business cite violation of Native American land rights treaties to get access to suddenly-precious uranium, abuse of Native American mining labour, long-term storage nightmares, uncomfortably close ties with the weapons trade, and a host of other byproducts of the nuclear-based power plan as indications of the industry's unsuitability, its unacceptability. They believe there is no place for it in a sustainable, healthy, reasonable world. Analogous objections exist in large quantities when we consider the sex industry.

Middle East as a motivation to achieve oil independence; they belittle and dismiss all alternative technologies, and assert that the nuclear industry offers the only alternative to a rapid breakdown of society under electrical famine.

Meanwhile the US oil industry, carefully avoiding the subject of dwindling reserves of a finite resource, cites repeated Middle Eastern crises as the rationale for opening up protected areas of the US to unrestricted drilling—the *only alternative* to a continuing sacrifice of "our boys" for foreign oil. Pro-porn activists predict that any restriction on the sale of any sexual media will lead us directly to Orwell's 1984, without passing Go and without (which I think is the real point) collecting $200. In each case, alarmist rhetoric is used to convince the public that the human or environmental costs of this particular capitalist enterprise are a tragic necessity—like the destruction of lab animals in unnecessary experiments, always sanctified as "sacrifice" in the published results. (We'll return later to First Amendment alarmism and its uses.)

In no case is a policy of moderation considered, a possibility of modifying our expectations or desires. In each case the citizen targeted by this rhetoric is encouraged to accept gluttonous overconsumption as a normal and necessary condition of life. The idea that we might reconsider our appetite for sexual entertainment in light of its costs, or alter our wasteful energy use patterns, is never mentioned. It's unthinkable, unspeakable. The US capitalist philosophy cannot come to grips with limitation: it's based on a model of boundless resource and infinite profit.

One concern of mine is the impact of the free-market "everything has a price" mentality on all of us, and its implications for feminists. The end result is that we no longer believe in anything *priceless*, anything whose value transcends the values of the marketplace. Most people would still agree that a human life is beyond price, that no one should be able to buy a license to shoot someone else. But those same people accept risk analyses by hazardous industries which assess the risk of fatal exposure, for example, at less than one in 100,000. If the exposed population is 200,000—and sometimes it is—then the implication is pretty clear: not necessarily, but very possibly, one particular person is being condemned to fatal exposure because 1/100,000 is an acceptable risk level and does not justify the expenditure of a couple of million dollars to redesign a facility or eliminate the use of a chemical or process. Which means that this unknown person's life is worth less than a couple of million dollars.

In some risk assessments, sums lower than $2,000,000 are at stake. My point is that we are already accepting the notion of *a reasonable price* for a human life—not my life or your life, of course, but the life of someone else whose name we don't know in advance. We are daily encouraged to accept widespread, possibly irreversible, possibly fatal environmental damage to our planet as *the cost of doing business*. The market economy and the market philosophy have prevailed; the lives and well-being of women and children are the cost of doing the sex business, and many women who still call themselves feminists are assessing this as an acceptable cost for a free market and "free speech."

It seems to me that we would be better off if we still acknowledged a category of things and qualities that are priceless, irreplaceable, not compensable. We would certainly be better off if one of those things was the health and integrity of every woman's body. We would be better off if we did not accept and believe that a man with enough money can pay a woman to submit to absolutely anything he wants to do to her, and *as long as he pays up afterwards it's all right.* We would be better off if we did not accept and endorse the ethic of prostitution, which is the free-market ethic, which is the basis of laissez-faire capitalism—which may turn out to be the most expensive and short-sighted ethic in history.

"And the party on the left, is now the party on the right..."

There is a consistent history of feminist criticism of prostitution, from the women's associations against "white slavery" to modern radical feminist critique. The salient points have been the appalling conditions of the lives of almost all the world's prostitutes, the well-known (if often-denied) connection between poverty, desperation, drugs, and entry into sexual service, and the brutal control and exploitation practised by pimps and power brokers in the sex trade.

Alongside this tradition there has always been a twin countercurrent. There is a Rightist argument that prostitutes are by definition degenerate and vicious criminals and not worth the sympathy or efforts of "good women" (loving wives or dutiful daughters). And there is the Leftist or libertarian argument that prostitutes are really fun-loving party gals with great senses of humour, who ought to be considered liberated and lucky compared to the "uptight bitches" who condemn the trade. The wife/whore dichotomy is very illustrative of the non-differences between traditional (male) Right and Left.

Both these positions are clearly born out of male self-interest: the Rightist elite does not want "its" women meddling about in the seamier side of capitalism and finding out just who is patronizing and profiting from those businesses; it wants to preserve a strong distinction between "well bred" women used for reproduction of eligible heirs, and "bad" expendable women kept for cheap entertainment. The Leftist elite simply wants to preserve its access to as many female bodies as possible, and tends to champion non-monogamy, birth control (for women), and the sex trade, more as preconditions for unlimited male sexual recreation than out of any sincere concern for women's liberty. One rhetoric produces the "Scarlet Woman," the terrifying seductress of conservative male myth; the other invents the "Happy Hooker" and the "Whore with the Heart of Gold." All of them are dealing in fantasy—the same kinds of fantasy which they all pay hookers to provide.

Rightist and authoritarian regimes have in fact only one morality, which is the preservation of power in the hands of those who now have it. This is the case whether we speak of the rule of the conservative rich over the working class and poor, or the rule of the adult male over the family (a Rightist regime which persists under many socialist governments). All other apparent moral codes are secondary.

The same Third Reich which scathingly condemned the loose morals of the Weimar Republic, particularly the widespread prostitution which "degraded German womanhood," made sure that the brothels of occupied France were among the first businesses to resume service after the conquest.[21] We should also note that this same Party operated

---

[21] "Yesterday ... the High Command ordered the opening af all houses of prostitution in the part of France occupied by German troops." (Shirer, p. 407.) There was certainly disagreement within the Party on this issue: rabid homophobe Himmler, for example, was strongly in favour of legal prostitution, which he claimed would "save" German youth from homosexuality.

official brothels *within* the concentration camps, which were used not only by camp guards and trusties, but (and this for me rates a place among the unthinkable horrors of camp life) by the male prisoners.

Let's take another example. There are highly organised commercial tour services which provide luxury hotel accommodation, guided tours, and local women to male tourists from the US, Germany, and Japan when they visit Third World countries—S.E. Asia, Africa, S. America, the Caribbean nations. The local governments, which often make a public show of deploring "immorality" and prostitution, grant favoured status to the big corporations who own the hotels and the restaurants and the sex services, who offer the bodies of Third World women as one more tourist attraction.[22]

In the US, the same doublespeak prevails. The Big Money Establishment is mostly Rightist in its policies and publicly defensive of decency, family life and the American Way; it sets itself up in opposition to the "alternative" or leftist community with its advocacy of "sexual liberation," its definition of prostitution as a "victimless crime," its open consumption and defence of pornography. Meanwhile, the Big Money and the Rightist government are setting up isolated R&R centers in remote countries for American oil workers, telecommunications crews, soldiers, airmen; and an inevitable result of the establishment of these "play zones" is the conscription of a large force of young local women to provide sexual and emotional service to the foreign workers.[23] And meanwhile, leftist critics of capital and exploitation are passionately defending major capital enterprises like *Playboy* and the porn video industry, which routinely realise their enormous profits by the exploitation of naïve, poor, or coerced labour.

So, though the pundits of contemporary American leftism proclaim that the authoritarian Right is threatened and undermined by loose living, sexuality, "free speech" (meaning unlimited publication of pornography) and so forth, I do not believe a word of it. The Right operates its whorehouses and blue movie mills privately and quietly, whereas the Left proclaims its right to sexual consumerism openly and loudly. I am not interested in these squabbles between bigger and smaller men over which of them is entitled to how much of what; my concern is for the lives and civil rights of women.

But lesbian sm is a product of gay culture, not corporate US culture. It was spawned in imitation of the prevailing gay male sm scene in the early eighties. Surely I have to admit that gay sex and gay porn are another matter—that homosexuality, at least, is deeply threatening to the patriarchal state. Surely I concede that the solidarity between lesbians and gay men is the natural foundation of "queer politics," whatever other side turnings it may take—or do I?

---

[22] On the other hand, there are the "alternative" tour guides oriented to the younger and less wealthy (but still male) tourist, which at one time used to admonish him to respect the people and leave the women in peace. That was a while ago: nowadays the "alternative" guide is more likely to advise him where the youngest and cheapest girls can be found. For the women, what is "alternative" about this? The only distinction is in the age and the income of the men who will expect and demand sexual service from them.

[23] For an overview of these issues see Mies, pp. 137-142.

Armed Camp: Gay Male Militarism

There is nothing about male homosexuality which inherently defies or contradicts male power and dominion. The real issue is not whether men screw boys or girls, but their cultural investment in the warrior ideal, the value which is placed on the "masculine" characteristics of aggression, toughness, ruthlessness, and violence. Where this ideal is paramount, you have what Eva Keuls calls *phallocracy*: ". . . the concept denotes a successful claim by a male elite to general power . . . . In sexual terms, phallocracy takes such forms as rape . . . and access to the bodies of prostitutes who are literally enslaved or allowed no other means of support. In the political sphere, it spells imperialism and patriarchal behavior in civic affairs."[24]

The Theban Greek tradition in which paired male warrior-lovers fought and slept together, and the Attic Greek tradition in which men's deepest and tenderest love was often reserved for teenage boys, were wholly consistent with imperialist expansion, militarist hero-worship, and the enslavement and imprisonment of women. So was their predisposition to public nudism. The men of ancient Athens "habitually displayed their genitals, and their city was studded with statues of gods with phalluses happily erect. The painted pottery of the Athenians, perhaps the most widespread of their arts, portrayed almost every imaginable form of sexual activity."[25] The public display of naked statues, phallus-images in stone and wood, and paintings depicting graphic sexual (and often violent) activities did not particularly improve women's position nor reduce military conquest.

Prostitution (both "straight" and "gay") was not only legal in ancient Athens, but completely institutionalised, with a portion of State income deriving from the brothel tax. A handful of exceptional women achieved wealth and pleasant notoriety in the trade; most remained sex peons, until old age rendered them worthless—at which point, without even the grudging support of a patriarchal clan, they died of starvation and illness. Since girl children were unwanted except for strategic marriages, the excess of daughters was disposed of by one of two methods: immediate infanticide or exposure (leaving the baby outdoors in either a remote or public place). The girl babies who were left on public streets were gathered up and raised by the brothel owners, so the system was as neatly self-perpetuating as our own. (In our system, the girls who run away from sexually abusive fathers and brothers are usually in their teens, so the whoremaster is saved the expense of raising them and can put them to work immediately.)

Amid the "glory that was Greece," the women of ancient Athens did not even rate individual names; their names (if they had any) were not recorded, and it was normal for a husband to address his wife as "woman." Prostitutes, however, were often referred to by professional nicknames derived from bodily characteristics or parts (like "Goldie" for a blonde woman), names roughly translatable as "Belly," "Gorgeous," etc.[26]

---

[24] Keuls, p. 2.

[25] Keuls, p. 2.

[26]"Such names as Choiris, Choirina, Choiridion translate roughly as Cunty, Cuntina, and Cuntlet." Keuls, p. 355.

So much for those who assert that violence and militarism can be attributed directly to sexual repression and State censorship; that public nudism, open prostitution, and free access to sexually explicit material, must inevitably pacify and civilise men. They would do well to study the ancient Greek city-states.[27]

But that was in the ancient world. Surely we all know that modern Fascism is puritanical, anti-sex, and ragingly homophobic? Perhaps.

The Nazis are the paradigm of 20th century fascism. Though they eventually got around to collecting and destroying male homosexuals along with the other "genetic undesirables" to be purged from the New Order (funny how Bush kept using that same phrase), earlier in the movement there was a strong homosexual faction in the Party. Modeling their aesthetic and philosophy very closely on that of ancient Greece, these Supermen romanticised military heroism as well as the beauty and vitality of young men. The most visible of these men, SA leader Ernst Röhm, was sufficiently active and powerful to challenge Hitler for power and party leadership, which led to the bloody putsch known as the Night of the Long Knives; soon thereafter, male homosexuality was officially forbidden in the Third Reich and the nightmare began for Germany's queers.

Although the Party's later diatribes about public decency and order, and the roundups of gay men, tend to make us assume that Röhm was purged only because of the sexual habits of himself and his officer friends, "how far SA leader Röhm's homosexuality . . . affected Hitler's decision is difficult to say. It seems plausible that it did, but the only evidence on this point comes from Schirach himself . . . one is left wondering how reliable Schirach is on this point."[28] (Baldur von Schirach was freed from the authority of the SA and put in complete command of the Hitler Youth organisations when Röhm was purged.)

We may indulge in a little speculation, however: suppose the Röhm faction had prevailed. The mere fact of homosexual activity among its officials and soldiery would not have impeded the military and social programs of the Third Reich. It might have been kept a Party secret, known only to initiates (like the details of the Final Solution) so as to spare the limited consciousness of the bourgeoisie—but it would have been in no way inherently contradictory to the general plan of conquest and empire.

It is sissiness that frightens, enrages and offends the men of the phallocracy, not queerness per se. "As in China, Byzantium, and medieval Persia, homosexuality . . . was mainly devoted to the expropriation of the bodies of people of inferior rank, which meant slaves and commoners of both sexes, by the powerful androcentric ruling classes of the ancient empires. Aristocratic men could indulge themselves with any form of hedonistic amusement that struck their passing fancy."[29]

---

[27] For a hard and scholarly look at the Golden Age of Athens (which we are all supposed to admire and revere as the foundation of Western Civilisation) I can only recommend that you read Eva Keuls' work in its entirety. I can't give a fair impression of the depth and excellence of her work in this casual overview, but I recommend it whole-heartedly.

[28] Koch, p. 89. See also George Mosse on the tension between the implied homoeroticism of the Männerbund, and the bourgeois respectability which the fascists sought to maintain both in Germany and Italy.

[29] Harris, p. 242.

Male homosexual activity of certain kinds is institutionalised into warrior culture, not only in ancient Greece, but among, for example, the Azande of the southern Sudan and the Sambia of Papua New Guinea. In each of these cultures young boys are the sexual partners and servants of young men, eventually themselves graduating to warrior status and acquiring boy-brides or servants of their own.

Among the Sambia, the boy apprentices are required to fellate as many young warriors as possible every day so as to assimilate into their bodies the semen which the Sambia believe to be the strength and courage of maleness. "Among the Sambia and similar Papua New Guinea societies, the solidarity forged in the men's house, the training for hardness and masculinity, the sharing of life-giving semen, have their payoff on the battlefield."[30] The fact that the men of the Sambia are careful in later life not to have intercourse too often with their wives, so as to avoid the polluting powers of women and the "wasting" of precious semen, gives some indication of the status of women in this warrior culture.

There are cultures, however, including our own, which do not permit the "insertee" in a gay male sexual bond to outgrow this status and become a "real man"—there are many men in America who believe that screwing another man only proves one's super-masculinity, but that permitting oneself to be screwed (as the colloquial uses of the word show) degrades one permanently to the status of a non-man: an object, or a woman. The infamous "Tail Gunner" Joseph McCarthy and his aide Roy Cohn, who so viciously and persistently persecuted America's gay men in the 1950's, were known to have had sex with men; but by their own standards that did not make them queers, it only proved that they could and did fuck queers as a means of asserting their maleness, contempt, and domination.[31]

The Nazi Party could, internally, have adopted any of these models to institutionalise male homosexuality within the context of its imperialist program for Europe. Their government was at no time constrained by mere bourgeois morality, whatever use they might make of it in their PR. For years the Party papers replicated reams of *Kinder, Kirche, Küche* [32] rhetoric about the sanctity of German womanhood and the German family. But later in the war, when the male population was diminished and the birth rate dropping, it was able without the least embarrassment to recommend the heroism of unwed motherhood. There was some bewildered opposition from the women of the Party, but its elite theorists were able to propose (seriously) the institution of state-funded brothels/baby-farms in which elite SS guards could pass on their excellent genes to selected Aryan damsels—and presumably, get a little R&R at the same time. The Nazis were busy trying to rewrite cultural tradition, philosophy, religion, law, and even biology; they had enormous ideological flexibility and imagination, and a place for male homosexuality in the New Order could have been engineered.

---

[30] Harris, p. 241.

[31] Here, in the patriarchal male's spite and contempt for anyone and anything fuckable, is a strong common ground on which women and gay men might build a joint critique of traditional masculinity.

[32] *Kinder* (children), *Kirche* (church), *Küche* (kitchen), the top priorities assigned to decent German womanhood at the turn of the century, to which was added a fourth K during WWI: Kaiser.

In summary: there is nothing automatically progressive about male homosexuality; it is perfectly compatible with male supremacy. The only truly subversive model of male gayness is one which rejects violence and the encoding of established power in the sexual relationship. Bonds of affection, tenderness and sex between males of approximately equal age and power are profoundly disturbing to the phallocracy; so are men who refuse to be "men." But the consumer model of sex, the master/slave, man/boy, top/bottom, john/hooker model of sex, has long been comfortable and familiar within male supremacist and warlike cultures, whether here and now or far away and long ago. Whether hetero- or homo-sexual, it has no power to challenge the phallocratic status quo.

One interesting side effect of the sex marketeers' efforts to open up the gay community as their new marketplace is the potential breakdown of "gay" and "straight" as political alignments. In Pat Califia's short story "The Surprise Party," for example, the lesbian protagonist is taunted and raped by men who the reader believes to be police officers, until they are revealed as her male friends in police uniforms. "Her own experience with straight sex had been . . . unsatisfying . . . But this act of penetration was firmly situated within a context of dominance and submission—the core of her eroticism."[33] In short, though Califia defines herself as a gay writer and the story is intended as lesbian pornography, the central sexual action is heterosexual.

The fact that the sexual action is sadomasochist, in Califia's story, is more important than whether or not it is lesbian. "Her eroticism" is not focussed on women, but on sadomasochism, and male friends who are willing to provide the scenario she prefers are acceptable sex partners. The definition of sexuality as a commodity leads to a market mentality, in which the gender of the whore and the client is almost irrelevant compared to the kind (or cost) of services required.

Bewilderingly, I now have more solidarity and sense of community with straight women who seek creative ways to redefine their relationships with male lovers (such as agreeing to forego standard heterosex entirely in favour of more egalitarian activities) than with lesbians devoted to sm, or gay apologists for pornography (though these are in theory "my people"). Their desire to derive entertainment from weary old racist and sexist clichés, from glamourised woman-hatred, from the "look and feel" of fascism—and their *pride* in this desire, their inconceivable arrogance in claiming it as an achievement and a liberation—anger me beyond words and beyond any sense of commonality.

At one point both the lesbian and gay men's movements emphasised the potential egalitarianism and tenderness of gay love, its radical potential for challenging heterosexual habits of dominance and hostility; now first the gay men and later the lesbians have proclaimed the sexy trendiness of dominance and hostility. The distinction between gays and straights is not so relevant as it was. In fact, I see the new dividing line not between straight and gay (what gender of whore do you prefer), so much as between two ethics for living. One is the "tough-guy" laissez-faire or consumer-oriented philosophy

---

[33]*Macho Sluts*, (Boston: Alyson Publications, 1988) story starts on p. 211, quote on p. 233; but this phenomenon dates from the beginning of the lesbian sm trend. I recall reading in 1980 or 1981 the words of a lesbian sm proponent who proudly said that she would rather be stranded on a desert island with a masochistic "boy" than a vanilla lesbian. Although several of my contacts also remember this statement, I was not able to attribute it before this book went to press. If you can supply the reference, please write to HerBooks.

which American industry would like us all to pursue; the other is the nascent, often inconsistent, "Green" outlook: an awkward mix of ecological and feminist concern, anti-racist intentions, and a striving away from excess and towards responsibility and moderation.

The gay communities are momentarily in the position of some Third World nations, divided in heart between those who believe success and liberation come from emulating faithfully all the methods and achievements of the First World, and those who believe that (as Audre Lorde memorably said) "the master's tools will never dismantle the master's house."[34]

Our Masters' Toys

If our masters' tools will not dismantle our masters' houses, can we hope to live in their houses ourselves? There is an argument current among gay men and some lesbians, that queers are now becoming entrepreneurs and consumers of the sex trade rather than its workers (or raw materials), thus changing their position in the free-market model.[35] The existence of lesbian strip shows, gay porn videos, sex clubs, and so forth, is cited as evidence of liberation. This is an error, and a common one.

It has often been claimed that the vulgarisation of privilege is the same thing as liberation—that is, the extension of the rights and privileges, tastes and habits of the very wealthy to the masses. Engels himself fell into this trap: "What is good for the ruling class should be good for the whole of the society with which the ruling class identifies itself."[36]

The oversimplification here should be immediately obvious. The goodness or badness of an activity, taste, or habit depends not on who usually gets to indulge in it, but on itself: what it is, what it costs, who pays for it. Many things available to rich people (like decent health care) are good and should be available to everyone. Some other things available to rich people (like snuff films) are bad and should not be available to anyone. Some things available to rich people (or nations) can only remain available so long as other people or nations are kept in want and misery, and therefore can never be extended to everyone.

The argument over pornography and prostitution tends to fall along these lines as well. At one time only the wealthy could regularly afford expensive and illicit items like

---

[34] Audre Lorde, "The Master's Tools Will Never Dismantle the Master's House," in *Sister Outsider: Essays and Speeches.* pp. 110-113 (Trumansburg, New York: Crossing Press, 1984).

[35] There's a traditional concentration of queers in certain lines of work, as there is of women and people of colour in their own "job ghettos." Queers (those who are not deeply closeted) have been marginalised into the sex and entertainment industry, into certain service trades, as producers, raw material, cheap labour. This has always struck me as similar to the forcing of Jews into merchandising and moneylending in mediaeval Europe; being prohibited from owning real estate, there were few other opportunities for them to make a living. Then, like queers, they became stereotypically associated with those businesses and stigmatised for it, just as modern Americans vaguely snicker at effeminate male hairdressers, interior decorators, dancers, movie directors—and butchy female cops, truck drivers, dog-handlers, etc.

[36] Engels, "Origin of the Family, Private Property, and the State," in *Marx/Engels Selected Works* (Moscow: Progress Publishers, 1976) Vol. 3.

drugs and pornography, and the use of prostitutes; only the independently wealthy could afford to support the reputation for "loose living" that would have ruined a common person socially and financially. The arguments we are hearing from "sexual liberation" spokespeople often imply that this imbalance should be redressed: we have the right to a *Playboy* under every bed and a whore in every garage.[37]

There is only one problem with this. The nature of pornography and of prostitution is the use of women and children for male sexual entertainment. This presupposes a population of women and children either willing to be so used, or sufficiently vulnerable to economic pressure or violence that they can be coerced into service. It also presupposes an outlook on the part of the consumer, that this service is his natural right and privilege. This outlook came very easily to the old-world aristocrat, who had servants to pour his wine, remove his boots, polish his silverware, run his bath, and so on. Sexual service was a logical extension of all the other personal services he required and received.

The modern bourgeois or proletarian, however, does not expect a valet, maid, cook, and butler (unless he expects his wife to be all this and more, which is less unusual than we might wish). He is still, however, encouraged in the fantasy that women (and children) are his naturally-decreed sexual servants. If he has enough spare cash, he can prove this theory by going out and renting one. [4]

What does it mean to extend this fantasy to gays, lesbians, women in general? For gay men it means little change; gay and straight men with money have had access to male prostitutes and paid companions, mostly younger men, for centuries. For women (both lesbian and straight) the situation is a bit different. Women are the infantry of the sex industry, not its customers. If women become customers, who will be their servants? The answer seems obvious: poorer women and men, probably mostly people of colour (a disproportionate number of prostitutes world-wide are women of colour).

Do we believe that a widening of the population which may expect to own or rent servants (sexual or otherwise) is a progressive or democratic trend? This is nothing but an illusion, and a mockery of democracy. It can only mean the substitution of class for caste. My personal ideal of feminism is not one in which women of the ruling class have equal power with men of the ruling class, while poor men and women go to hell together. This is, however, because my idea of feminism requires a general commitment to social justice and human dignity. A liberation which sets some women free to humiliate and exploit others is no liberation.

"Those Who Do Not Remember the Past . . ."

There is an old familiar slipstream in Western thought, of course, that personal liberation means *exactly* the freedom to injure others, that the ultimate experience of personal liberty is in the destruction or degradation of another. This doctrine, mystified and prettified, lies behind a great deal of what is called nihilism, libertinism, and so forth; this is the doctrine behind the appeal of sadistic fantasies (or realities): the defiance of all

---

[37] I should note here that though *Playboy* now means "a soft-core porn magazine," its original meaning was "a young, wealthy and idle man." The beginnings of what is perhaps the world's most popular sex magazine lie in the envy and imitation of the upper class lifestyle.

rules. It should not be associated at all with progressive or liberal politics; its genealogy is quite otherwise.

I find no prospect for liberation in an ersatz re-enactment of the excesses and privileges of an earlier aristocracy. Many of the members of the new sm social scene happily describe themselves and their hobby as "decadent," and references (symbolic, stylistic, artistic, literary) to the fall of the Weimar Republic are frequent and self-conscious. There are strong connections with the nihilistic Punk aesthetic, a convergence of style and manner, a shared fascination with violence, pain, and death.

There is also a peculiar reduction of privilege and oppression into a meaningless mess, manipulated whichever way is advantageous at the time. Sm lesbians frequently use the "politics of deviance" line to identify themselves as "a minority" within the lesbian community and to bewail their "oppression," "suppression" and "silencing" at the hands of an "intolerant," "normal" majority of "vanilla" lesbians. They identify themselves with the pioneers of Gay Liberation and heap indignant rage on those who are not delighted with them for "coming out" and "claiming" their sexuality.

At least some influential spokeswomen for sm identify the Marquis de Sade as a *victim* oppressed by a hypocritical and repressive society, an unfortunate and even a martyr for freedom of speech and sexual liberation. How women who call themselves feminists can manoeuvre themselves into this position is beyond me. The Marquis was, first, a man in a century in which men had even more legal and informal power over women than they now have. He was, secondly, a white man and a wealthy one in an age of imperialist expansion abroad and exploitation of a labouring peasantry at home, a beneficiary of others' labour and others' suffering. He was, thirdly, an aristocrat in a nation where the male aristocracy had for centuries enjoyed every form of self-indulgence and the unlimited abuse of powerless commoners. The women he abused were neither wealthy nor noble. He was no different from any rich white male today who can sexually harass his female employees, perhaps even beat or kill a whore in his hotel suite, with no questions asked. Yet to some lesbians today he has become a hero, and the libertinism he practised and advocated seems glamorous, desirable—and radical.

Libertinism, like "decadence," is the hobby of aristocrats and aesthetes. It is a concept rooted in the traditions of maleness and wealth, the idea that freedom means complete lack of social restraint and the right to do whatever one damn well pleases. It is the philosophically rationalised, highfalutin face of brute force. "Freedom" to the rest of the world's people means freedom from constraint, freedom from being forced to do other people's will, freedom to pursue one's own course unmolested; only to the violent, the wealthy, and the privileged does liberty mean license. The Marquis de Sade was silenced in the end only because he became too loud and offensive—effectively *letting down his team* by publicizing what his fellow-aristos would rather keep quiet: the degree and depth of their power and their appetite for its abuse. To describe him as a "human rights" martyr is the purest revisionism.

The libertinism of the age-old aristocracies evolved and was embodied in the Nietzschean "blond beast," the Superman whose physical vitality, mental acuity and innate aggression would give him the right to rule the world. "Might makes right," the ethic at the heart of male supremacy, had been given a new hairdo. The Aryan Superman into which Nietzsche's high-flying rhetoric was simplified and mass-produced was only the logical application of 20th century nation-state politics to centuries of the mysticism of kingship and male supremacy.[38] The aristocracy of Hitler's New Order would be a populist aristocracy, an aristocracy of all pure-bred Germans over everyone else. The arrogant and absolutist overlord of feudal times would be Everyman; the blond beast would be every foot soldier of the Reich, full of patriotism, youthful energy, and the glorious enthusiasm of licensed bullydom: the perfect vulgarisation of privilege.

The tragedy of the Third Reich has been so much exploited for its drama and for the private agendas of individuals, and is so little studied and known by the average person, that it has become to most people only a convenient symbol, a media event of sorts. As I've said before, the complexities of Hitler's grand plan for Europe get reduced to simplistic metaphors to suit almost any argument.

The extermination of gay men in the camps and the destruction of the Hirschfeld Institute are often cited to equate Nazis with homophobes, and vice versa. On the other hand, McCarthyites made a lot of mileage in the post-war years from the existence of the Röhm faction, and generated reams of scurrilous propaganda equating Nazis and "perverts." The public book-burnings conducted by the Hitlerjugend are used to associate the Nazis with censorship and repression. On the other hand, it was the embattled Weimar Republic which repeatedly jailed Hitler for inflammatory oratory, and Julius Streicher (the most effective propagandist of the early years) for his pornographic and anti-Semitic paper *Der Stürmer*; and both Hitler and Streicher described themselves as victims of State terrorism, censorship, and repression.

There are still those who equate the Nazis with Communists, because the Party built its initial appeals on the anger and unrest of Germany's imperiled working class and called itself "Socialist." On the other hand, Germany's Communists were the first and the most tenacious of her citizens to fight the Nazis, and they died for it in large numbers. There are those who associate the Nazis with attacks on Big Business and with nationalisation, because of the massive expropriation of Jewish business and State takeovers of the press and other essential concerns. On the other hand, Aryan Big Business in Germany was in league with the Nazis as soon as they proved themselves able to keep the power they had grabbed. German industrialists, some still living and in business, had no problem increasing their profit margins by the strategic use of slave labour from the camps.

Many associate the Nazis with any and all attacks on art, because of their ridiculous campaigns against modern art. The insane humourlessness and self-importance of their pseudo-scientists and philosophers are well remembered, and were even the subject of (whispered) jokes at the time. The Nazis are easily imagined as boring, regimented, fun-hating party-poopers who shut down the great friendly party that was Weimar. On the other hand, they showed a genius for spectacle and entertainment matched only by that of the modern American media industry. Leni Riefenstahl's film of the Berlin Olympics is

---

[38] It's worth mentioning Nietzsche, whose works did inspire some of the more intellectual Nazis, because he is still respected as a Great Thinker and still fashionable among young (mostly male) intellectual amoralists and nihilists. It's worth remembering that he himself was much inspired by those same Attic Greeks whose politics with regard to women we have briefly examined: "Among the visceral misogynists should be counted Friedrich Nietzsche, who began his career as a classical philologist. In his essay 'The Greek Woman,' he finds it inevitable that an advanced and creative culture should reduce its women to the status of vegetables." (Keuls, p.9)

127

splendid cinema. Their sense of symbolism and regalia, their knack for "accessorizing" their politics into fashion and style, their ability to provide glamour and show and pageantry, were phenomenal. They kept the public very well entertained, until the strain of the war years began to break down the PR machinery. There were secret societies to belong to, rituals to take part in, costumes to wear, grand rhetoric to repeat: many of those who were young during the Nazi climb to power remember it as a time of tremendous excitement and fun.

The Weimar Republic which was such an object of hatred and contempt for the young Nazis is now associated in the public mind with liberty and democracy, a brave era of liberation in which a women's movement and the beginnings of a gay rights movement briefly flourished. Packaged along with these things in many people's minds are the "decadence" of old Berlin, the sex clubs and strip shows, the "naughtiness" which drew tourists to Germany and upset churchmen and civic officials. On the other hand, the Weimar Republic was a government perpetually beset by economic disaster; unemployment was rampant, inflation repeatedly wiped out working people's savings, hunger was not uncommon. It was in this cold and hopeless economic climate that the club owners and madams of Berlin recruited their workers, and the tourists who came to a humiliated and bankrupt Germany to spend their valuable foreign currency were not unlike the wealthy who now throw their Eurodollars around in the hungry nations of the Third World. Berlin's notoriety as the bordello of Europe was not, at the time, a matter of great pride or achievement for Germans.

The same atmosphere of poverty, shame, unemployment, and foreign exploitation that produced the whores of the Alexanderplatz produced the Brown Shirts, just as similar (though less severe) conditions today have in the US produced both a burgeoning sex and drug trade, and the Skinheads. The poverty that makes an army of young, undereducated and hopeless women available for sexual exploitation makes an army of similar young men available for recruitment into whatever rowdiness and destruction is going around.

So it is hard for me to know exactly what to feel, when young women decked out in a close imitation of SS regalia call their lesbian sisters "Nazis" or "sex-fascists" for opposing pornography or prostitution—when both are traditional tools and institutions of 20th century fascism as well as ancient despotism.

Political Correctness

In accusing feminist social critics of being "fascists," the gay community is either setting or following the nationwide trend towards intellectual conservatism and away from progressivism. Doublespeak of this kind is echoing across college campuses throughout the land.[39]

---

[39] The charge of "censorship" has been hurled about in many contexts recently, usually with little regard for accuracy. The educated Right, for example, has discovered its new intellectual champion in Dinesh D'Souza, whose *Illiberal Education* is rapidly becoming both tract and handbook for the new academic conservatives. Mr. D'Souza and friends maintain that American academic freedom has been destroyed by the efforts of progressive activists. The revision of core reading lists to include works by women, people of colour, and gays is (in their eyes) no less than censorship. *(Footnote continued on next page)*

It appears that the American Right has learned something from its long surveillance of the feminist, gay, ethnic, and Green movements. It has learned the magical phrase "political correctness," so reliably effective in disarming and ridiculing any advocate of social conscience or personal responsibility. The Right has observed that even among self-styled liberals and progressives, it's relatively easy to redefine outspoken criticism as "censorship," efforts to redress injustice as "favouritism," and any exhortation to change one's habits as "P.C." The Right is not stupid. Neither are the pornographers.

Critics of the product or practices of the sex entertainment industry, whether at the corporate or the entrepreneurial level, draw an inevitable barrage of accusations: prudery, right-wing collaboration, Nazism, etc. It doesn't matter whether the feminist (or anti-racist) critic of the entertainment biz is questioning the social value of "Rambo II," "Clockwork Orange," or "Pretty Baby"—Norman Mailer or Larry Flynt—or more amateurish local thrill-vendors. In a reductionism worthy of Mr. D'Souza himself, she is transformed in the public mind into the all-powerful Agent of Repression. She is the advance-guard of an enormous conspiracy dedicated to stamping out art and literature, reducing us all to semiliterate peons permitted to read, watch, and sing only the drab and repetitive propaganda of Big Brother.

At one time sex-industry proponents argued their case (during the progressivist sixties and early seventies) in terms of social good. Free access to sex goods and services, they contended, would provide a cathartic outlet for male aggression, and all sex-related crimes (springing wholly from sexual frustration and repression) would vanish in a "free" society. However, during the decades of increased sexual license for men, limited social liberation for gays, and enormous growth in the sex trade, violence against American women has in fact escalated (or remained constant, depending on whose statistics you believe; but no one seriously asserts that violence in general, or violence against women in particular, is declining). The catharsis theory is dead, and a growing body of research indicates quite the reverse: that violent pornography intensifies hostility to women in male consumers.

So the apologists for the traffic in women have changed their tune, with the times and with the evidence. They now adhere to the libertarian line and entrench themselves firmly behind the First Amendment. The American Civil Liberties Union is their best friend, and their (highly profitable) business is the highest expression of their all-Americanism and dedication to "freedom." And the ACLU, which once distinguished itself by conspicuous courage and gallantry in the defence of persecuted unionists and peaceniks in the hard years of the twenties and thirties, has degenerated in our day into a pathetic defender of male privilege. Consider, for example, the ACLU's involvement in the case of Douglas Oakes. [5] One wonders whether the ACLU would exist at all, if it defended freedoms and rights other than those traditionally exercised by men at the expense of women and minors.

Increasingly, the ACLU and the general public can find no better meaning for "freedom of speech" than the license to lie, offend, and insult. I have been noticing lately the use of the phrase in advertising: a catalog of comic books came to me recently, with

According to D'Souza, freedom of thought and speech no longer exists on American campuses. Student confrontation of professors for sexist, racist, or anti-gay classroom remarks or actions is compared by the D'Souzites to Nazi thuggery.

an invitation to "those who love and exercise their First Amendment rights" to mail in money and a form so as to receive the company's "adult" catalog. A consumer book and audio catalog recently advertised a taped collection of the (in)famous "Amos 'n' Andy" shows as "finally available to you again, a triumph of First Amendment rights." The First Amendment, genuinely noble in concept, is now used as a marketing ploy: the consumer can feel righteous about buying racism and sexism.

A corporation, of course, can sue the daylights out of you for publishing allegations or assertions which might impair its business standing; an individual who is slandered or libeled has legal recourse. But the underdogs of American society: women, people of colour, queers—can be insulted in print, film, audio, and video as often and as nastily as will sell; and the First Amendment guarantees their inability to do anything about it, other than to publish whatever refutations or counterattacks they can afford to print.

This reduces the American intellectual scene indeed to a "marketplace of ideas" in which we are all hucksters—and the huckster who can afford the biggest and best PA system wins. This is Free Marketism applied to the world of art and politics: a naïve belief that some innate quality in human beings, or in truth, will guide the invisible hand of the market so that truth prevails. We might as well revert to trial by combat.

But, of course, many people will say, consumers of the media are not idiots, nor are they children (though children are routinely exposed to the same materials that I find objectionable even for adult consumption). It's common for porn apologists and First-Amendmen to caricature the feminist critique of pornography as a claim that "perfectly ordinary men" are transformed into Mr. Hyde after just one little peek at offensive materials. After reducing the feminist position to a cardboard cutout of this kind, they have little difficulty in ridiculing it. [6]

But what is a perfectly ordinary man? If exploiting, hating or abusing women is a perversion, then the average man is a predisposed pervert. The last twenty years of violent crime statistics and gender-psychology experiments can lead you to no other conclusion. No one, except a handful of embattled and increasingly dispirited radical feminists, wants to admit how much hatred of women there is in the perfectly ordinary man, how much it is a part of everyday life, how often ordinary men act it out, every day.

Which is odd; it should shock and surprise us no more than the efficacy of Mr. Bush's "Willie Horton" soundbite in arousing the latent racist fear and hatred in the white voting public's heart. Or, to put it another way, it should be equally shocking. The leftist press spent untold hours and uncounted reams of paper denouncing Bush's opportunistic exploitation of white racism to get a few cheap votes, repeatedly calling the Horton ad "outrageous" and "unacceptable" and so forth. *The Nation* was particularly eloquent on the subject.

In this case, apparently, the President's freedom of speech does not evoke their solicitous protection, as it surely would were he any ordinary pimp or panderer exploiting hostile male fantasies about women to make a buck. The essential difference is that the Horton ad was selling racism—something that leftist men don't want, or don't want to want, or have been forcibly taught that it is uncool to want—whereas for the sex industry they are still willing consumers. I personally find it rather gutless to take brave stances of principle against Bad Things when they don't appeal to you anyway; I would have more respect for the Left if there were more John Stoltenbergs among them, men who are capable of saying that the merchandise offered by the sex trade is as dirty as any of the other goods they faithfully boycott—no matter how it may appeal to them.[40]

It's about time the male left (New and Old) and the gay male subculture came to grips with, or were made to come to grips with, the one bastion of privilege all their rhetoric never challenges: male sexual consumerism. If that's too much to hope for, then at the very least it's time for the crowd of lesbian wannabes that follows them around to wake up and smell the coffee. A "free speech" that is merely a new name for age-old male libertinism carries no whiff or taste of freedom for women.

Furthermore, to meet serious social critics with threadbare reductionism and name-calling is a copout. We are all here, all in this together, and we are answerable to each other for what we do and say. Art is not magically excepted, sex is not magically excepted, any more than business or politics or the nuclear family or private property. The Censor is the Great Fear of the Nineties, exploited as was the Red Menace of the Fifties, in the best interests of business as usual. "Freedom of speech" has become the last refuge of hate-mongers and profiteers; we live in sad times.

But the Right seems very active in the cause of repression. Shouldn't we be very, very worried about them? Can we afford to permit any kind of State intervention in the media and arts, knowing what the agenda of the Right will be?

Keeping Our Priorities (too) Straight

The "threat to our civil liberties" posed by years of a right-wing regime in Washington is real, all right—no doubt. These men, not all of whom have departed with the Bush administration, definitely intend to reverse abortion rights decisions, persecute queers, bar the press from future military engagements, divert public funding to the military-industrialists and away from social services, the arts, and the schools. They are out to defend their corporate interests and the interests of their corporate friends. If they have lost this election, they will try hard to win the next one. I do worry about these guys; but there's more to this story.

People often talk about the abuses endured by women and children in the sex trade and pornography as "the price of a free society," implying that the lives of these people are a tragic but necessary sacrifice if we are to avoid totalitarianism, censorship and so on. My first reaction is always one of stunned outrage—it is so very evident that the people making the sad preachments about necessary sacrifices are never the ones who are being sacrificed, and the "freedom" about which they have such tender and righteous feelings does not extend to those who are enslaved to ensure it. Then comes a second

---

[40] Ironically, that same *Nation*, journal of the literate Left, which has published many a pointed and cogent criticism of racism and anti-Semitism in the arts and media, maintains its "testostophrenia" enough to crawl into bed with the Playboy Foundation. The two of them sponsored a major conference recently on the threat to "Commercial Free Speech." Nothing could illustrate more aptly the degeneration of the "free speech" ideal, from the defence of individuals risking unemployment and violence to assert their criticism of the Vietnam war, to the self-righteous protection of profits for the entertainment mega-businesses. The Left has somehow ended up hand in hand (or prick in hand?) with the big capitalists. It ought to be ashamed of itself.

reaction: What free society? For if the conditions under which the vast majority of prostitutes, and many unpaid sexual servants, live is not fascism, then what is?[41]

Further, I do not see that even the excesses of censorship and State control confidently predicted by diehard First Amendmentarians could make the lives of exploited women and children any worse than they are now. The supposed artistic and literary sufferings of a nation of consumers deprived of sexual content in their daily media do not impress me as half so severe as those of the women being coerced on a daily basis in the sex entertainment industry. If I had to make a choice between a highly censorious government which reduced the traffic in women and children, and a liberal and tolerant government which encouraged that traffic, I believe I might choose the former.[42] Basically, the health and happiness of women and children matter more to me than my "freedom" or "right" to read a dirty book. (Of course, this leads us immediately to the problem of defining what is pornographic; see p. 135)

It seems to me that what wins public regard as a crisis or an Essential Issue, even among progressives, is largely determined by male self-interest. Well, that's obvious; but take a slightly closer look. Everyone should recall the pompous pronouncements of sixties and seventies leftist leaders (male) who required that women working for social change not cause division and "waste effort" by "selfishly" focussing on "the woman question" when national and economic liberation (for men) was at stake. Many women around the world saw a point to this reasoning, and many of them have now found that in their post-revolutionary societies not much has changed; it was good of you to bear arms and risk your lives in overthrowing the capitalists, thank you, and now back to the kitchen. (In the US meanwhile, early feminists were getting fed up with the radical boys who preached world revolution while expecting the "chicks" to keep the coffee coming and run the mimeo machine.)

The popular progressive issues, the challenges to the regime which get money and press time, are going to be the ones that serve male interests. Abortion rights are definitely in the interests of men who want easier sexual access to more women. They don't have to feel any responsibility or take any, knowing that "she can always just get an abortion." Fear of pregnancy is one of the few arguments women can advance against sexual activity when men demand it; ready availability of abortion and the Pill (though women would be worse off without them) don't challenge men's sexual privileges. Only the Right, with its need to create ever-larger markets and its paranoia about being

---

[41] It strikes me that what we have here is a basic tenet of the American mythology: violence and exploitation done by the State (particularly against men) is Bad and Evil, but violence and exploitation done by individuals (particularly by men against women and kids) is all right, even Good—at least not on the same level of Badness. I have a serious problem with this. If one pimp, some hired muscle, and a couple of dealers can control the lives of twenty or a hundred people in a neighbourhood somewhere in a city near you, then how can you feel you live in freedom? When large numbers of fathers feel they have a right to impress their children into sexual service, how can we pretend that slavery is dead?

[42] Yes, I am all too aware that this is not a likely choice, and that the authoritarian and censorious government in the real world will be just as hypocritical as all those which went before; so exploitation and repression will in fact inevitably coexist. It isn't a real choice. But if it were . . .

"outbred" by the "coloured races," has a particular stake in forcing pregnancy on (middle-class, white) women.[43] Thus, the widespread co-ed support for Planned Parenthood.

Obviously a great deal of the energy behind the First Amendment, freedom-of-expression rhetoric, the ACLU and other related forces, comes from men who deeply fear and resent the possibility of being deprived of their sexual entertainment, and from men who are in the business of selling such materials and are afraid of a setback in the trade. In much the same way, as I've mentioned, those industrialists whose profits are most closely tied to wasteful and toxic resource use and/or abusive labour practices are the most passionately dedicated to free-market economics, and the most certain that government intervention in business practice will spell economic ruin for us all.

AIDS movement rhetoric in the US is relevant to my concerns about lesbians, gays and pornography; one of the newer arguments advanced by the pro-porn activists is that pornography is "safe sex"—and that opposing it is implicitly condemning people to die of AIDS by depriving them of this non-physical outlet for their (presumably) raging hormonal urges. Typical of this stance is the statement made by Earl Jackson, Jr. (gay male professor at UCSC and pro-porn advocate): "While I completely agree that certain pornographic materials and the industry behind them constitute violence against women . . . to restrict access to explicit sexual information, images, and forms of fantasy concretization is tantamount to manslaughter, if not homocide [sic]."[44]

In short, stripped of the fashionable rhetoric of academia and the liberal ambience of Gay Rights and Free Speech: women's lives are worth less than men's. Yes, we are free to consider pornography a menace to women's lives and freedom, a form of violence against women—but we dare not oppose or restrict it in case we might reduce the odds of survival for men. Men's lives are worth more than women's. But we knew that.[45] In fact, as the existence of snuff films and forced prostitution demonstrate, some men's sexual entertainment is worth more than many women's lives. Free Speech is therefore a noble political cause of overriding urgency, whereas public action to defend women's lives, dignity, and safety is a low, low priority.

I Know It When I See It

Critics of pornography, or more generally of hate-art, are often challenged by its defenders to define exactly what it is that they don't like about it; the difficulty and

---

[43] and in advocating forced sterilisation for poor women, especially poor women of colour.

[44] Earl Jackson, Jr. "The Politics of Ecstasy," *Lavender Reader* (June 1991), p. 31.

[45] Even when the media report the incidence of AIDS among women, the emphasis is often on the potential risk to men: "Japanese men are returning with the virus after visits to the brothels of Bangkok and other Asian cities . . . and many of the tens of thousands of prostitutes from Thailand and the Philippines working in Japan carry the virus." (The *Sidney Australian*, cited in *World Press Review*, (June 1992), p. 6.) Note that the reporter does not say that hundreds of thousands of women impressed into sexual service will die of AIDS in SE Asia, but that Japanese men are catching it there; not that poor foreign prostitutes will die of AIDS in Japan, but that they are *carrying* it—potentially to infect men. For a thorough treatment of the position of women in the AIDS epidemic see Gena Corea's *The Invisible Epidemic: The Story of Women and AIDS* (New York: HarperCollins, 1993).

subjectivity of this process is then cited as an insuperable obstacle to doing anything about it. After all, it is hard to write a statute against something you can't properly define.

I think it helps to look at pornography in its context, along with hate propaganda and advertising, as members of a broader family which I'll call "the manipulative arts." Roger Ebert has said that film is much less suited to the presentation of philosophical or intellectual positions than to the creation of emotional states in its audience.[46] He has a point, and he makes a useful distinction between the art that wants us to think about something and the art that wants to make us feel or do something.

Advertising is the ultimate refinement of the manipulative arts; political propaganda and campaign materials are just another kind of advertising. Pornography and propaganda have been intimately connected from the beginning (some of the first written pornography was intended by its author—an ancient Greek—not merely to titillate, but to cast slurs on a rival city-state). Demagoguery, hate literature, television ads, and X-rated videos have a lot in common. Their intention is absolutely not to induce thought in the consumer, but to produce an emotional state—and incidentally to get the consumer to do something useful because of this emotional state: buy more product.

We already noted the pornographic content of the first Nazi propaganda magazine, and a lot has been written about the prurient appeal of Klan-type propaganda accusing Black men of sexual crimes against white women. The people whose hatreds are inflamed by this material are getting off on it at the same time. My personal theory about this strong familial tie between porn and propaganda, from ancient Greece to the American White People's Party of our own century, is that sexual content helps to short-circuit the reader or viewer's critical or moral faculties. [7]

Certainly it helps to short-circuit the critical faculties of traditional leftists; we have seen them consistently defend materials and opportunists who relied on exploitative sexual themes and imagery, when they have often enthusiastically trashed similar materials trading on racism or class hostilities. Advertisers have long said that "sex sells," and it seems to sell disinformation, slander, and ideology just as well as it sells car tires, beer, and blue jeans.

A textual analysis of propaganda, advertising, and pornography will yield remarkable structural similarities: reliance on a limited lexicon of "buzz words" understood to have standardised and reliable effects on the consumer; discovery of a formula and endless repetition of that formula; appeal to fear, greed, hostility or sentiment rather than to reason; and always an implicit offer. In a sense, they are the drugs of art: they are all attempts to sell fantasy and sensation rather than fact. Factual analysis destroys their appeal immediately, "taking the fun out of it."

People are encouraged to believe and act on fantastical notions primarily by the manipulation of their emotions, not their knowledge; one mistake made by many a progressive movement is to assume that people with harmful or hateful attitudes are simply *misinformed,* and that exposure to sufficient facts will bring them around to a kindlier point of view. Nothing could be further from the truth.

---

[46] Ebert, p. 744, "Movies are not an appropriate medium for political and intellectual messages. The written word is best for those. Movies make you feel."

The big isms against which progressives wearily labour are *precious* to those who believe them: racism, sexism, classism, all those complex fabrics of lies and distortions are emotionally precious to their owners; in short, they are *fantasies*. The most insistent recitation of facts and statistics will not sway anyone who is deeply attached to a prejudice, a religion, or a lover. Fact and truth are unwelcome, destructive of fantasy, strenuously resisted, much as the "menstream"[47] of American society strenuously resists the realities of women's physical selves; ordinary facts like the natural growth of hair on women's bodies, or their natural fatness or skinniness or the natural graying of their hair with age, are perceived as abnormal, ugly, even unhealthy. They contradict the fantasy of what women are and should be; the hostility and even violence with which some men respond to nonconformant females can be explained only by the threat which fact poses to fantasy.

The entire sex industry is about selling fantasies; it is more about fantasy than it is about sex. After all, if the simple physical details of sex were all that counted, no more than twenty or thirty sexual scenarios would have to be described, once for all time, and could be xeroxed indefinitely for generations of satisfied readers. In fact, like propaganda and advertising, pornography sells people their personal and precious fantasies.[48]

The borders between advertising and pornography were eroded long ago, as were the borders between sensationalist literature and pornography: there is a continuum, one generic industry of the manipulative arts dedicated to pocketing the consumer's money in return for as little originality, quality, and effort as possible. Even when the manipulative arts set out to shock (as with mass-produced "slasher" films) they do so within well-established rules and conventions; anything truly shocking or surprising—suppose the screaming teenage girl took the chainsaw away from the maniac and cut him up with it!— would lower sales. The manipulative arts all have to walk a narrow path, titillating and interesting the consumer without once really challenging his (mostly *his*) preconceptions.

When anti-pornography activists are asked to define pornography, it is usually in contradistinction to "erotica," of which we are all confidently expected to approve. It has been said that erotica is pornography that costs more, and I tend to agree. Whether we call it porn or erotica, in either case we are dealing with a manipulative literature, a literature whose purpose is the arousal of the reader, a way of buying sex, an art whose purpose is perhaps to extend the readers' fantasies, but never to damage them with unwelcome facts.[49]

With all this in mind I would approach the definition of pornography in several ways, first (in the grand seventies feminist tradition) by examining the word: *porné + graphein,*

---

[47] I believe Sonia Johnson to be the inventor of this ingenious word.

[48] Note, however, that pornographers have often tried to hide behind the label of "educational" materials, much as the *Penthouse Forum* pretended to be an open exchange of sexual truths rather than a ghost-written grab bag of titillations. There is a strong parallel with the half-hearted attempts of the Nazis to redefine torture as "valuable medical research." And with the Whittle empire's introduction of mandatory "Channel One" advertising into classrooms as "educational TV."

[49] This is rather different from the appropriate place of sexual description or plot device in literature; whenever a writer includes sexual material in the course of telling the story, she takes the calculated risk that small minds will skim the book looking for "the dirty bits"—transforming her attempt at communication into manipulation, in fact.

"writings about, or images of, whores." Note that the *porné* was the lowest class of whore in ancient Athens, not the educated and occasionally wealthy *hetaera* (courtesan) but the run-of-the-mill "two-dollar" whore. (Although the first "porné+graphy" sometimes pretended to be the writings *of* whores, it was invariably written by men. Women of the *porné* class were not literate.)[50] Pornography is that which defines its subjects as whores and its viewers as customers: it is the art of pimps.

Secondly, there is the distinction between communication and manipulation. I would distinguish pornography from explicit sexual description which found its logical place in any work of fiction or film: the pornographic materials are the ones whose whole purpose is to manipulate me into a state of arousal, not to tell me anything, but to make me feel or do something. It is not an informative but a manipulative art.

Then thirdly there is the issue of truth: pornographic material is that which sells me my preconceptions, my prejudices, easily-digested cultural symbols and myths, my fantasies—not the complex and arduous texture of truth. The most blatant pornographic productions are simply, as one feminist slogan calls them, "lies about women"—big lies, too. The pornographers tell the sucker who pays them just what he wants to hear: that women are all young, beautiful, slender, and panting to have sex with him; that the purpose of women is to please him; that all women are for sale; that he can buy sexual satisfaction, happiness, virility, masculinity, romance, even love.

They tell him all kinds of other, very familiar lies, lies which in any other context we would recognise and abhor—about people of colour, about the rich and the poor, about the "sexiness" of children. When I find material which matches detail for detail *every one of these three criteria* except that the intended customer is a lesbian, I don't hesitate for a minute to recognise it as pornography.

Is nudity relevant in defining pornography? Anti-porn activists are often accused of being body haters of some kind.[51] There is nothing intrinsic about the naked human body which should offend any of us—after all, every one of us *is* a naked human body. But images of female nudity marketed, images of female nudity converted into voyeurism-objects, into product, into commodity, into symbol, is what I earlier called "objectification."[52] It's the conversion of woman into thing that is offensive—not to mention the images of outright pain and damage being inflicted on the female body.

Fourthly, pornography is that which entertains its consumer *by making him or her complicit in violence*, which converts violence into entertainment, which encourages us to

---

[50]Dworkin, *Pornography: Men Possessing Women,* pp. 199-202; Keuls, chapter 6 and 7.

[51] I detect a terrible reversal in the accusations of "body-negativism" which get casually tossed at women who object to porn. Surely anyone who truly loves and cherishes the physical human body *should* be appalled at the idea of buying and selling, imprisoning, humiliating, hurting, disfiguring, or destroying human bodies—all things which pornographers would have us accept as entertaining and titillating. Where is a deeper hostility being expressed than in this endless outpouring of sadistic imagery, directed primarily at the female body?

[52] Nikki Craft, on working with postal inspectors to intercept child porn: "The police always make, like, a frame with their hand, they look at the crotch, and they say, this we can prosecute, or no we can't. But to me, I look at the eyes, at the woman's face or at the child's face. It's in the expression, the pose, whether this person is being presented as just a sexually available thing." [private conversation, July 1992]

participate vicariously in the visceral satisfactions of bullying, brutality and terrorism. In this sense, the Persian Gulf War TV coverage was pornographic: state-of-the-art technology gleaming in the clear desert sun, the lovely and deadly planes in their formations, the video-game appeal of their taped bombing runs. It was a beautiful wrapper for the truths which did not appear on our TV screens: what bombs do to buildings and to bodies, what dead soldiers look like, what dead civilians look like, who pays the terrible cost of their rulers' war games.

This is the deep deception of pornography: the conversion of a truly frightening, painful, demeaning reality in the actual lives of women and children—their impression into sexual service to men—into a glossy, pretty, profitable product. Further, as with the Gulf War coverage, there is a subtext of satisfaction on the viewer's part, a secret knowledge that all this glitz and show *is* terribly expensive and that other people are paying for it dearly, but that *I* am not, a sense of aristocracy, of power.

It has been said of lesbian sadomasochism and of pornography in general that they are a way of transcending or transforming women's suffering under male rule: "victimisation turned into art." Well, that has been done before—but the last time I heard about it, it was lampshades they were making. This may seem a rather shocking reference, but I cannot better express the insane arrogance of those who presume to turn other people's pain and death into an art object, or (heaven help us) an entertainment.[53]

This is why I would say there is a pornography that contains no nudity or recognizable sex at all, the pornography of violence alone. There are films and novels in which graphic and frightening violence is described, and we feel the terror and shame of it in our guts as the artist carries us along; we understand what it is to be hunted, to be hurt, to be tortured and to die by violence. But there are other works in which the violence is the come-on, in which we are subtly or blatantly encouraged to experience it as the perpetrator does, to enjoy it and to be entertained by the imagined sufferings of "our" victims. The kind of literature that makes us members of the audience at the gladiatorial games is pornography: it invites us to watch human life and dignity sacrificed for our entertainment; it turns victimisation into art.

I won't speculate on *why* this should appeal to us, how empathy is defeated, how cruelty evolves, why some people are more subject to this temptation than others, why some lucky few of us are immune to it altogether. My point is that in a just world, which surely we desire, no one would be an expendable sacrifice to anyone's entertainment; if we desire a just world, then we should rightly be offended by those who repeatedly try to sell us the satisfactions (actual or imaginary) of an unjust and cruel one. We should, in fact, be wary of anyone who repeatedly tries to sell us *anything*; what are they getting out of it, and out of us?

The Pepsi Generation

One of my sorrows about the state of the world in my lifetime is the decline of the informative, and the triumph of the manipulative, media. It's common for the artsy and

---

[53] It's possible that some readers will not remember this: at Buchenwald concentration camp, lampshades were made from the skins of prisoners.

intellectual to grieve over the decline of US film and literature, the astounding stupidity of almost all of our television programming, the mediocre-to-inferior quality of many of our contemporary art forms. It's practically cliché by now to express one's concern over the barely functional semi-illiterates being mass-produced by what passes for our educational system.

But all these matters are related. A generation raised on moving pictures, and on the new advertising forms which grew up with them, has now raised its own new generation: one which, increasingly, finds reading unrewarding and too difficult, which expects to be passively entertained. This generation, I fear, which has grown up marinated in the manipulative media, now actively prefers them to anything requiring thought, the exercise of judgment and critical reasoning, or (god forbid) investigation, research, finding out one's own facts. Advertising is its definitive art form.

This generation of media-consumers, raised in the heyday of Madison Avenue, has developed a new tolerance for being lied to, even a cynical amusement at the untrustworthiness of the media which surround them. The modern US citizen *expects* advertising to be false, politicians to be dishonest, and everything on the screen to be doctored in the special effects lab. It is hard to stir a sense of outrage in people who are used to so many lies.

Pornography is the perfect entertainment medium for a semi-literate society: it requires little inventiveness, presents no challenges to vocabulary or reasoning power. It is a product; it's intended not to surprise us, but to do exactly what we expect. It's also completely self-involving: when we read erotica or pornography we are reading it not to discover something about anyone else, but to concentrate solely on the interesting effects it may have on ourselves.[54] The intellectuals of the new pseudo-feminism advise women to "pay attention to what turns them on," rather than what we are "too good at"—"telling what offends and is sexist."[55] In short, we are advised to stop thinking about the profound implications of race, sex, class, violence, and male-supremacy in the output of the sex industry, to withdraw our gaze from that larger world, and to retreat into our own heads to figure out how we may most successfully be manipulated by these materials.

This fits nicely with the capitalist agenda for the nineties—which is to reduce everyone who has any money to an uncritical consumer of as much product as possible. Other agendas may also be served; I don't think anyone with progressive leanings has completely escaped the suspicion that our government's loud wailings about the Drug Problem are more show than substance; in fact, it is entirely to the advantage of the ruling class if the poor are completely obsessed with internal drug wars and with the hunt for the next fix, rather than with the reasons for their poverty and unhappiness.

It would certainly be to the advantage of men who have been upset and threatened by the small successes of the feminist movement, if those pesky feminists would get out

---

[54] It has been pointed out to me (R. Harwood, private conversation) that young people do turn to pornography for *information* about sex, which is withheld from them in other contexts. Particularly, gay teenagers may have no confirmation at all of the existence of other gays except through the distorted offerings of pornographers. The tragedy is that youngsters, whether straight or gay, are thereby limited to learning from one consistent, capitalistic, abusive, misogynist tradition. We are often told that they would be worse off with no sexual information at all. This seems questionable.

[55] Wendy Chapkis, panel discussion at Kresge College, UCSC, Spring 1991.

of the streets and the law courts and start concentrating on something less disruptive, like what kind of porn video or sexual position suits them best. It would be a profound relief to men who have felt the slightest tremor in the deep foundations of their power, if women could be convinced that what we really need, after all, is just a good fuck. Particularly when that is something which they can convince us is in short supply—something they can sell us.

No Easy Way to be Free

In conversation with a long-time acquaintance a while back, I mentioned some of my concerns and reservations about lesbian sex shows, lesbian pornography, and so forth. My acquaintance responded, "But don't you think it's a mistake to restrict sexual expression? I mean, it seems like sex is in trouble these days generally, with the Right to Lifers and the gag rule and the Moral Majority."

Male sexuality is not now and has never been in trouble. No matter what the conditions or the risks, men have always found something or someone to fuck. For women, however, in the words of T. H. White, "everything not forbidden is compulsory."[56] In eras when women are supposed to be virginal they are called insane if they masturbate; in eras when they are supposed to be whores, they are pressured to think themselves defective or insane if they don't have sex all the time.

Neither of these scenarios removes from women the obligation to service male sexual demands. The nature of those demands, and the attitude required of the woman, vary over time; but the essential fact remains—the fundamental things apply. This is why I believe that the only possible sexual liberation for women has to begin with freedom *from* sex as we know it, freedom from the obligation to please and serve others sexually, freedom from sexual awareness and abuse forced on women from the earliest age.

Who knows what women would choose or do in an atmosphere of real freedom? How many would choose women, how many would choose celibacy, how many would be bisexual, how many monogamous, how many would bear children? Most of us have never had enough freedom to know what it means to choose.

The "sexual liberation" rhetoric of the sixties, and its latest incarnation today, offer women only menu choices: we can be "into" this or that kind of trendy sex, we can prefer this or that position or practise, we can buy this or that porn video, but we still have to shop at Daddy's store and we still have to accept the idea (the capitalist idea, the patriarchal idea) that sex is something we buy or something we sell, a consumer choice. Real freedom of choice would mean freedom to tear up the menu, not merely to select from it.

A couple of years ago I heard the story of a writer friend who submitted a manuscript for publication by a lesbian press. It was considered, but the editor told her she would have to write in a couple of explicit sex scenes before they would accept it. She refused,

---

[56] T. H. White, *The Book of Merlin,* (New York: Berkley Medallion, 1978), p. 66: "Over the entrance to each tunnel there was a notice which said EVERYTHING NOT FORBIDDEN IS COMPULSORY BY NEW ORDER." He was writing about a nest of ants, which he used as a heavy-handed satire on Fascism. The reference to the New Order (Hitler's *Neue Ordnung)* is deliberate.

and it was not published. (I have been asked not to identify the women involved, and so am unable to provide more details.)

Is "sexual expression" in trouble, when you can't get a piece of lesbian fiction published without it? We have a word, "censorship," which describes the suppression or alteration of the artist's work by governmental edict intended to prohibit the expression of certain ideas. We have no word for what happened to the writer who refused to splice gratuitous sex scenes into her work. We have no word for the mandatory inclusion of the predictable, invariant Sweaty Sex Scene in nearly every contemporary film intended for adults, nor for the daily, unavoidable overload of sexual images used to sell other kinds of products. It is a sort of reverse censorship, imposed by market analysts who don't believe anything will sell unless coated with sex. Liberation it is not.

Sexual liberation rhetoric fails here, in its bland refusal to look at the motives of the amateur barristers who argue in its arena. The fact that sexual content is *imposed on* authors, readers, and viewers by marketing considerations is conveniently ignored when we discuss artistic freedom. The fact that porn sells, and that fortunes are made in it, is somehow irrelevant to the noble arguments for First Amendment rights in which pornographers and their customers excel. The fact that men get off on purchasing demeaning images of women, which cater to hostile and bigoted notions of woman's place and nature, is somehow irrelevant to the impassioned pleas of those same men for artistic freedom and sexual liberty for all. The self-interest which catches our eye immediately when we discuss the tax-exempt status of TV evangelists becomes invisible as soon as we talk about the sex trade.

Why do many feminists oppose pornography and prostitution? Not because they stand to make millions from selling a competing product (they can't even get air time), not because they get a secret delight from interfering in other people's private business—but because of basic concerns about who benefits, who is used, who loses, who is hurt. These are the same reasons which any progressive would use to justify boycotting or confronting any other major corporate endeavour. They are not the reasons of the radical right (God disapproves, it's un-American). In examining the rights and wrongs of the debate about commercialised sex, pornography and sadomasochism among lesbians, we have to look hard at the motives of the debaters.

Is sex in trouble? Justice and fairness are in trouble, and feminism is in trouble, and women are in trouble. When these issues are on the table, can we afford to say that sex (whatever that means) is the only real issue, can we mark it Sacred and take a simple stance to oppose all interference with it? Will that ensure our freedom?

What will that do for women and children? Suppose we took a different stance, and called the bodies and dignity of women and children Sacred, and opposed all exploitation of and interference with them? Why is it that women, women who call themselves feminists, lesbians who of all people should have the least faith in Big Daddy, are more anxious and willing to stand up and defend *sex* than to stand up and defend *women*? Why does the freedom to choose from a familiar menu of sexual alternatives mean more to us than the freedom of all women to live our lives in safety and security?

How did we get here? Where on earth can we go *from* here?

I see some hope in the emerging international "Green" movement. It provides a moral, and possibly a political, choice far more meaningful than the choice between, say, Republicans and Democrats in the US. Though almost as disorganised as the "Peace" movement of a previous generation, it does encompass an encouraging mixture of ecological, economic, and feminist concerns.

The eco-movement, dominated as it is by male organisers and achievers, has its dubious moments. Nevertheless, there is a strong female and feminist presence among the Greens; women have led many and many a grassroots campaign against major ecological criminals. For good and bad, there is a persistent tendency to associate and compare male sexual greed and abuse of women with capitalist greed and abuse of people and resources. Sometimes this leads to sickening oversimplification (help us defend poor, helpless Mother Earth from the vicious rapists) but at other times it leads to a healthy re-examination of male prerogatives and assumptions and of *all* forms of capitalist consumerism.

For example, the slick PR materials distributed by Big Industry ("How Exxon is Saving the Caribou," "DuPont Preserves this Beautiful Land for America's Future," etc.) are known among the Greens as "eco-porn"—which implies a very sharp awareness of the capitalist nature of pornography and also of its essential dishonesty.[57] Two kinds of slick lies purveyed by exploiters in their own self-interest are here recognised for what they are, and I find that hopeful. It's a radical step away from the traditional Left, at least, with its knee-jerk defense of pornographers as trailblazers of liberation and free speech.

One of the best byproducts of the Green movement, and even of Green hype, is the introduction in the public mind of a skepticism about the worth of packaging. We are drowning in packaging, one way and another: overpackaged products are sold on their attractive wrappers rather than on the contents, and all that packaging—plastic, foil, cardboard, paper—gets thrown away as soon as it's bought.

The beginnings of a distaste for overpackaging, its inefficiency and foolishness, may (if we are lucky) lead to a cultural swing away from the *concept* of packaging, a mood of doubt, a demand to know essential facts rather than to be entertained by surface appearances. A public in this mood would not be distracted by pretty air manoeuvres over Iraq, but would be asking hard questions about the cost of our involvement and the real reasons for it; a public in this mood would question the wisdom of farming ever more photogenic and perfect fruits and vegetables with less and less guarantee of real taste or nutritional value or even of safety.

A public in this mood would think a woman more beautiful as she really looks than as the product of high technology, artifice, diet, and surgery. A nation in this mood would shrug at cosmetics and squint closely at commercials, detecting fakery and disliking it. A person in this mood would not be drawn to the hollow confections of pornographers or the simulated thrills of prostitution, but to some kind of reality. A preference for the natural

---

[57] One reader of the first draft of this paper commented, "Yes, but are they as good at recognizing porn-porn?"

over the artificial, the substance over the packaging, and reality over fantasy, is at the heart of both Green and feminist thinking.

Radical feminist objections to the "commodification" of women and of sexuality are well-aligned with Green critique of capitalist rapacity and the commodification of just about everything.[58] Both share a radical critique of the meaning and appropriate use of property and of profit, and are deeply opposed to the prevailing free-market ethic. The presence or absence of this critique may be the essential distinction between the "mainstream" feminism of middle-class America (with its emphasis on integrating selected women into the existing machineries of state) and radical feminism (which aims to redesign those machineries from the ground up).

The Old Left succeeds when it demands a material (factual) analysis of people's working and living conditions instead of jingoism, rhetoric, sentiment or tradition. But it has failed, over and over again, when it cannot give up the tradition of female service to male fantasy, the jingoism of sex, the rhetoric of masculinity, the sentimentalisation of female sexual labour for male profit. The New Left, the Greens, the defenders of the natural world against the brutal greed of capitalism, might be able to cross that last bridge and declare that the consumption of people as product is just as unacceptable to them as the complete conversion of planet into product.

The Greens fail when they fail to consider the power that is specifically men's, as well as the power that is exercised by all humans over the natural world. They fail when they neglect to read and learn from the legacy of feminist research and thinking on male aggression and male hatred of women, the human body, and the natural world. They fail when they ascribe all evils to high technology and capital, without looking at the patriarchies which have thrived without either one. They fail when they romanticise all historical periods or cultures less technologically sophisticated than our own, disregarding the use of women and/or children as the slave labour which enabled "the simple life." They fail when they forget what the technological revolution has meant to twentieth-century women in terms of personal freedom, survival of pregnancy, access to paid work, literacy, education. (They fail in the same way when they fail to imagine what technology and industry can mean to the poor of the world, when they prescribe that unindustrialised nations should remain so and be thankful.)

They fail when their rhetoric makes use of the tired old stereotype of the spoiled rich *woman* to personify capitalist greed and decadence, when they describe environmental devastation as the result of female demands on men. They fail when they appeal to women only as mothers and wives, when they describe environmental recovery as women's natural work and responsibility (cleaning up after the boys again?), when they suggest that we need to save the world "for our children." They fail when they lump lesbians and gays together with the "unnatural" features of the industrialised world, when

---

[58] I sometimes wonder, in my more desolate and paranoid moments, whether the accelerating pace of ecological destruction, the strip-mining and paving of the planet, is after all *not* merely a byproduct of stupidity and buccaneering, but right in line with someone's agenda. Is it entirely ridiculous to suppose that it might be in certain parties' interest to destroy and despoil every last shred of natural beauty in this world, so that there was no longer any pleasure at all available *for free*? So that we would have nothing real left to amuse or please us, nothing but the fantasies they offer for sale?

their attachment to a narrow conception of what is "natural" leads them to prescribe heterosexuality and childbearing as the Green way of life for women.

They certainly do have a long way to go. But the philosophy at the heart of Green politics is extremely compatible with the radical feminist tradition, and that feminist tradition, taken internally in large doses, will enrich and further radicalise Green thinking. Objections to the "disposable" society apply with particular force to the use of "disposable" women and children by the sex industry. Objections to rapacious consumerism, and luxuries achieved at the expense of others less privileged, apply with particular force to the traditional male sexual consumption of women and children. Objections to the reduction of whole species and ecotomes to their "commercial potential" apply with particular force to the reduction of female human beings to salable sexual commodities. One could say, in fact, that Green thinking is really the application of radical feminist ethics to the entire natural world. As such, it has tremendous potential.

It may yet fail to realise this potential. Green activists can afford to sidestep or betray feminist interests, in their search for ever-wider popular support. But feminists cannot afford to ignore the effects of free-marketeering, the new multinational economy, and environmental devastation, on women's lives. Although I look forward hopefully to a feminist radicalisation of the Green movement, my more realistic hope is for the interpolation of Green concepts and values into radical feminism.

An Army of Lovers . . . ?

Radical lesbian feminists have long felt that there is some peculiarly powerful potential in the combination of lesbian life and feminist values; some have gone so far as to say that a lesbian life is the only way to live one's feminist principles. This argument has sometimes been transformed into the untrue proposition that anything lesbian (lesbian sex, in particular) is necessarily feminist, radical, and destructive to patriarchy.

What I observe is that lesbianism ceases to be threatening as soon as it's put in a context where it serves men.[59] "Lesbian" sex shows have for years been a staple of commercial sex entertainment. While male homosexuality is completely absent from porn videos available at your average video store, 57% of females are shown in heterosexual situations, 35% in bisexual situations, and 8% in homosexual ones.[60]

Female sexuality itself is not threatening: 95% of masturbation done or simulated in these videos is by women. So long as men can watch, so long as men have imaginary or real access, visual or physical, to the women, sexual activity *of any kind* on the part of women is not in the least threatening to male power or privilege. The simple fact of two women having sex is, to the average man, merely titillating. In virtually every commercial porn scenario involving lesbian sex, the action is either observed by a male voyeur

---

[59] A real cynic might perceive recent trends in the lesbian community—close alliances with pornographers, romanticisation of motherhood and increasing incidence of lesbian motherhood, increasing bisexuality, astonishing heroics in the cause of AIDS research and education—as unconscious propitiatory gestures to a threatening world. In other words: we are useful, we're not all that different, we serve you too in our own way, we won't challenge your privileges, please don't kill us, we could be the mothers of your sons.

[60] Weiss, p. 163.

(besides the consumer, that is) or a male character eventually appears to provide a "climax" by fucking both women.

What current theorists confidently describe as "radically deviant" sex is in fact perfectly acceptable and always has been, so long as it is rationalised into the realm of capitalist exchange and entertainment, so long as it has no intrinsic value but is a performance for a (usually but not always male) observer, as long as someone is paying for it and someone else needs the money. And, like "foreplay," as long as it is merely the overture to the main event, which is male sexual satisfaction.

The increasing emphasis on fantasy as the dominant (you should pardon the expression) operating mode for sex among trendy lesbians and gays is likewise hardly a radical experiment in gender, or a manipulation and disassembly of prevailing power structures. It seems to me more like a public reassurance to the watching and hostile world that lesbian and gay sex *is* just make-believe, play-acting, and performance after all. And the welcome extended by the lesbian community, or certain of its members, to the various aspects of the sex industry, is the same kind of assimilation. If we are a market for product, we are less likely to be disposed of; someone has an interest in our continued existence.

Many lesbians sincerely believe that the consumption of pornography makes them more radical; like the belief that using drugs instantly makes you a revolutionary, it's a tragedy, a farce, a splendid triumph of market forces over good sense and the soul of the individual. Alas, we can't buy radicalism, any more than we can buy romance or adventure or good looks or luck—though all the finest minds of Madison Avenue are dedicated to convincing us that we can. We cannot buy a better world, either; in fact, most of the time, we can only *buy* a worse one.

Having sex is not enough. Simply being a lesbian is not enough. So where on Earth does it make sense for lesbian-feminists to make a stand?

The liberation of women from sexual servitude should be of primary interest to lesbians. Lesbians are women—meaning that even though we may screen men and male influence from our private lives, we walk the same streets and do business with the same men as every other woman. It is in our best interest not to have to deal daily with a male population raised from boyhood on hostile and exploitative imagery of women and accustomed to sexual placation and service from women.

Lesbians have relationships with other lesbians, and those relationships are conditioned by the atmosphere of the surrounding culture, especially in this climate of assimilation. If we would rather not be exploited and objectified by other lesbians, it is in our interest to challenge and attack the objectification of women everywhere.

We cannot afford to let the Right monopolise such essential words and concepts as *decency, safety, morality, respect.* We cannot fall into the trap of adopting indecency, danger, amorality, and contempt as the banners of our revolution. To be fooled by the deeply amoral demagogues of the Right into rejecting wholesale the ideals of civic responsibility, of lawfulness and social justice, of peace and an orderly and secure existence, is to be fools indeed.

For women, *including lesbians*, have absolutely nothing to gain from nihilism, fascist chic, self-conscious decadence, and a romanticisation of the crimes of dead privileged men. That is not the way to legitimise our lives and lovers. When life is valued cheaply and pain is in vogue, it is women's and children's lives which will be valued cheapest of all, and women's and children's pain that will be the raw material for entertainment. When fantasy is valued over truth, it is the truths about *our* lives and deaths which will be hidden, and the fantasies of others which we will be made to serve. When brute force is admired and bullies are cultural heroes, the vast majority of women and children will be the losers.

It is therefore in our simple self-interest, if we want a world where women and kids might live secure and happy lives, to be steadfastly opposed to exploitation, to arrogance, ruthlessness, violence, hyper-masculinism, war, sadism, objectification, slavery, and all those forces of which we are traditionally the victims and targets and of which we do not, in our right minds, ever want to become the perpetrators. It was Dr. Einstein who said that you cannot simultaneously prevent and prepare for war; I firmly believe that you cannot simultaneously oppose and worship violence. People who find whips exciting and bruises alluring, Nazi regalia attractive and slavery titillating, will have a hard time suspending their love affair with evil for long enough to oppose it.

And it is in our self interest, as human beings in a tottering economy on a ravaged planet, to challenge the commodification of all things—sex, women, the natural world— and to oppose objectification and the raw free-market ethic. In opposing these things we cannot very long avoid confronting them among ourselves, in the form of lesbian sex capitalists and lesbian apologists for sadomasochism.

Epilogue: A Kinder, Gentler, More Civilised World?

Here I use the word "civilised" not in its literal sense of "citified, urbanised" but in the other common sense of "respectful of others, having a sense of politeness and control over one's greedy and violent whims." In this sense, as has often been pointed out, the !Kung of the Kalahari—without metallurgy, roads, the wheel, agriculture, writing, or much in the way of law—are far more civilised than industrialised Westerners: murder and rape are foreign to them, and they walk where they please without fear of each other.

I write in the assumption that we wish we were civilised (you and I)—that we wish to live without fear of violence or insult, that we try to avoid hurting or insulting other people, that we would rather not live among cheats, liars and bullies, no matter what pretty costumes they may wear for us or what pretty words they may find for their aggression and greed. I write in the tradition of those who would rather see well-fed children than waving flags, clean air and water than a falsely inflated GNP.

We are engaged, here at *fin de siècle*,[61] in a radical alteration of the concept of social contract. The raw terms and conditions of laissez-faire capitalism and libertarianism, based exclusively on property rights and direct interpersonal harm, are obsolete (though many cling to them desperately out of self-interest). The idea that burger-consuming Americans are in some way answerable to South American indios for the devastation of their forests and villages is new, strange, and unpalatable. We are used to defining our responsibilities only at arm's (or fist's) length.

The idea that corporate CEO's are answerable to the public for the environmental damage they do is new, strange, and threatening. The idea that the producers and

---

[61] "The end of the century," or by implication the end of an era or of a world.

consumers of art that demeans and insults women or gays or people of colour are answerable to those people for that insult, is very new and still a minority viewpoint. The idea that producers and consumers of art that glamorises and eroticises slavery, rape, or other brutality are answerable in some way to the victims of real abuse—*that* idea is very uncomfortable, new and strange. It offends deeply against the comforting libertarian principle, "I have a right to consume whatever I can afford to buy." In our world, the right to own and consume (and be entertained) is primary, like the right to drive.

The struggle we are engaged in is about the nature of individual rights and social accountability. This entails a bitter warfare over the boundaries between "private" action (nobody's business but my own) and ethical obligation to others ("It wasn't his driving that sank the Exxon Valdez. It was yours."—Greenpeace) Increasing numbers of people are questioning what they and others eat, drink, wear, watch, read, buy, and sell, trying to track down the hidden costs of the way we live. But America has a strong, even mythical, individualist tradition: advocates of social responsibility have chosen an uphill fight.

The conflict of values can be represented as a struggle between ethics of excess and moderation. The US (and most of the industrialised world) enjoyed an unprecedented expansion in the years since the Industrial Revolution: massive exploitation of resources at home and colonies abroad made possible a tremendous wave of growth in technological expertise, manufacturing and agricultural potential, and economic well-being. By various methods, some innocent and some less so, the economies of the West were able to *overproduce* on a scale never before imagined.

Large numbers of ordinary people, whether or not they managed to win for themselves the benefits they saw accruing to others all around them, had their expectations and desires expanded. Resources and pleasures which were only accessible to the aristocracy a short time before were suddenly within the reach of—if not everyone—very large numbers of people. The Engelian idea that the privileges of the wealthy should be extended to everyone seemed to be coming true.

In the long term, though, it turns out that this brave new world of prosperity and democracy-through-consumption was built on a shaky foundation: hidden costs and deferred payments. The cheap oil that fueled the boom economies of the forties through the sixties is running out, and its producers are taking control over its consumers. The improved health care that has made us live longer and raise more healthy children has increased our numbers, and they are increasing alarmingly fast still. The improved and streamlined agribusiness that manufactured mountains of food to feed us all is running out of petrochemical resources, being forced to admit the unwanted side-effects of its miracle pesticides and fertilisers; the debts incurred by third world nations trying to buy into that big agribusiness are turning bad and threatening the economies of the lenders. The aging nuclear power plants of the sixties and seventies, and the tons of hot waste that we have no idea how to deal with, are a fitting metaphor for the boom years as a whole: we dreamed big and we built big, but we didn't look ahead, and we bought more than we could pay for.

To many people of my generation it is as if we had found ourselves living in the dreary tail end of an enormous frat house party: the house is a mess, there are people throwing up in the front yard, two car accidents to resolve, and the landlord is on the phone—but the guys who threw the party are still staggering about in drunken bonhomie, telling everyone to go ahead and have a good time. They don't seem to have realised what the rest of us are waking up to find: the bills are coming due.

But to say these things marks me in many people's eyes as some kind of Puritan, not just another humourless bitch of a feminist but worse: a religious nut or a Communist or something. Would I deny that the majority of people are better off now than they were at the turn of the last century, that we live longer and work fewer hours, that women's lives in particular are infinitely improved in terms of freedom and opportunity? Don't I believe in Progress? I would not deny these things, particularly if we remember to restrict our commentary to the industrialised nations. But these improvements were not the result of loving-kindness and a sharing of resources. They were the accidental byproduct of an era of general excess and abundance, and that era is now closing.

We have two ways to proceed from here. One is to follow the traditional path of failing empires: diminished prosperity, increasing disparity between rich and poor, a tendency for the nation and the world to fragment into warring cliques defined by race, culture, or religion. This path brings us to the dystopian futures of many of our best science fiction writers, the world not of Luke Skywalker and his lovable droids but of *Soylent Green, Mad Max, Blade Runner:* the Depression years, but with niftier technology.

Another is to practise moderation, and search soon and desperately for sustainable ways to live: and here I will return to specifically feminist concerns, hoping you will pardon this last long digression. The model of conspicuous consumption, of ruthless capitalism, of waste and excess, cannot be overturned without a major change in more than our shopping habits.

To accept that the costs borne by strangers in far-off lands make our way of life unaffordable implies that we learn to respect those people and that we become ashamed of living at their expense; to accept that we are responsible for the damage that we do to our soil, water, and air means that we learn to clean up after ourselves; to accept that resources are precious and should not be wasted is to learn that the world is not a consumable, an expendable—and neither are its people. To accept that our way of life is costing too much means accepting less: giving up excess, resolving to live within our means. Shoving off the costs of your behaviour onto others, expecting someone else to clean up your mess, blowing away the household economy with irresponsible spending, treating other people as objects to be used and discarded: are these not some of the traits for which feminists have persistently criticised and confronted men, the habits of privilege and arrogance?

Grabbing all you can while you can get it is an expensive way to live. It may turn out to be an expensive way to die. A generation which took this lesson to heart would be less likely to use up, despise, abuse and discard women and children as sexual toys.

Unfortunately, the lesbian and gay community today is subscribing whole-heartedly to the frat-party ethic: live it up and get what you can while the getting's good. Excess, self-indulgence, obsession with fashion and sexual entertainment and with Self are by no means limited to the two-income Yuppie families caricatured by our cartoonists. I think many of us have an uneasy feeling that the Titanic is sinking; the sensible and responsible thing to do might be to bail like hell, or throw a few things overboard to lighten the load, or take a crash course in small-craft navigation. But most of us just have a couple more drinks and ask the band to play louder.

147

Emulating and adoring the behaviours that have brought us to this pass will not get us out of it. The symbols, language and style of lesbian sm chic are the symbols and language and style of male supremacy: violation, ruthlessness, intimidation, humiliation, force, mockery, consumerism. Words like *respect, tenderness, gentleness*, are boring and passé, according to our new fashion leaders. What we want is excess, and lots of it: extreme experiences of every kind, a great bazaar of fantasy for our shopping pleasure.

And this is why I have lost my faith in "gay liberation" and in "gay community," and why I am unmoved at this point by "Gay Pride." What seemed to me twelve years ago to be the most exciting challenge imaginable to male power, female subservience, and the foundations of the capitalist state has now been fitted into the machinery of the marketplace and is standing in line with VISA cards in hand, patiently awaiting admission to the Theatre of Dreams.

Ruthlessness, hardness, force and intimidation have characterised the successful businessman, soldier, gangster, politician and pimp from the very beginning. If we admire those qualities, we implicitly endorse the world these men have created—perhaps we subscribe to the fantasy that women can become hard enough and mean enough to compete with men on their own turf. Suppose we do so, and suppose some of us win: will a world that contains a token handful of lesbian aristocrats among its ruling class be a better world?

Now suppose for a moment that an ethic of mutual respect or common decency might gain popular support, that slogans like "Nice guys finish last," and "Never give a sucker an even break," might become anachronisms of a barbarous past, like the Iron Maidens and chastity belts in our museums. Suspend your disbelief for one moment and suppose: women and children would fare better in a world that despised arrogant exploitation, a world which idealised thoughtfulness, truthfulness, moderation and gentleness. In essence, the less aggressively and traditionally masculine, warlike, and brutally market-based we can make our public and private ethics, aesthetics, practises and beliefs, the better off we will all be.

We might begin modestly, as we do with recycling and phasing toxic products out of our homes. We might begin by refusing to play-act in other people's fantasies, or to ask others to play-act for us. We might begin by refusing to buy or sell sex, by boycotting those businesses which buy, sell, or rent women or sexualised images of women, by phasing toxic media out of our homes. We might begin by refusing to defend pornographers and pimps, and by confronting—regardless of their gender or sexual affinity—those who do. The challenge to pornography, prostitution and sadomasochism is like the challenge to the nuclear plant, the bomb factory, and the styrofoam cup: a necessary first step, if we are ever to achieve a livable world.

End Notes

[1]
    For argument's sake, we might imagine a kind of prostitution in which there is not this element of catering and serving, in which the whore's expertise at physical manipulation, like that of a

trained masseuse, is the only service expected or provided. In this model it would not matter what she looked like or what she wore, nor would she be despised by other kinds of workers.

Masseuses and masseurs are not generally considered a subhuman servant class, nor are doctors, who must often touch their patients in intimate and sometimes distasteful (for either party) ways. In these cases, the commodity being offered and paid for is a technical expertise. The model can be applied only to a limited extent, however: the mechanics of sexual stimulation are so basic and uncomplex, particularly in the male, that no enormous lore or expertise is required. If that were all the customer required, he could in 99 cases out of 100 do it for himself.

But most men despise or are least embarrassed by masturbation: it's the behaviour of callow youth and pathetic losers, those who "can't get any." I have a feeling that it embarrasses them in the same way that it would have embarrassed and humiliated an 18th century Marquis to dig his own potatoes or clean his own shoes: this is a service to be performed by a servant, damn it, not something he should have to do for himself. He wants more than orgasm: he wants his fantasy, and one essential element of his fantasy is power over a woman, power of force or power of cash, to make her (even temporarily) a servant. If she was a plain, muscular, heavy-set matron of 40 in baggy overalls with the no-nonsense manner of a senior nurse, no matter what extraordinary manipulative skills or physiological expertise she might have, only one man in half a million would choose her over a frightened, angel-faced teenager in spike heels—or a woman who manages somehow, in a dim light, to look a little like one. (In fact, take note of the long and strong tradition of male hatred of "matron" types, older females with professional competence who have temporary authority over males.)

[2]

The Reynolds Co. pushed the same myths and fancies that the pornographers push today: smoking is glamorous, unconventional, disobedient—will express your rebellious and unique personality—is practised by "fast," sophisticated, wealthy people in urban settings—and establishes your adulthood. Now that a few generations of Americans have died of lung cancer, the acceptability of smoking is barely beginning to be questioned, and the old Reynolds ads seem mostly ludicrous, vaguely sinister.

Both the sex industry and the smoking industry share a characteristic requirement for women: to play a dual role. The bourgeoises and their sisters of the upper class must be made to consume products; women of the working class and in the Third World must be made to labour as cheaply as possible to produce those products in quantities and at costs which will ensure large and profitable sales. The two types of woman are not intended to know each other, any more than respectable women are supposed to socialise with prostitutes, or a mistress to introduce herself to a wife.

For every glamorous flapper who flourished her elegant cigarette-holder in a Reynolds ad there were tens of illiterate "girls" rolling cigarettes for slave wages in the factory. For every "liberated" woman who expresses her daring by bringing home an X-rated video, there are tens of women (hungry, coerced, cynically cooperative, or infatuated with the men who exploit them) working to make thousands of videos for her to choose from.

I don't know how many generations of women will have to be recruited, broken, used up and spat out by the sex trade before the gloss and glamour of the business wears off and its current PR efforts begin to look dated and silly—and sinister.

[3]

The more intelligent variety of Libertarian often has a store of entertaining anecdotal evidence of governmental idiocy: cases where blundering, heavy-handed, incompetent State intervention has prevented individuals from exercising initiative, self-sufficiency, industry and other Libertarian virtues. They will often assert that it is only the welfare state that keeps people poor, and that without it there would be room—in a free market and a land of opportunity—for everyone.

Although these arguments fit a number of modern facts, and have a surface appeal, they are historically shallow. There is more than ample documentation of the hideous suffering of the poor and disenfranchised under pre-welfare-state conditions, from the ancient world through feudalism to the nascence of industrialism. Any ascription of human poverty and misery to the top-heavy public sector economy of America in the second half of this century is naïve in the same sense as a feminist analysis of male violence which simply blames television. The effect of TV on modern citizens (pernicious though it is beyond a shadow of doubt) can hardly explain the drinking bowls of ancient Athens, decorated for the pleasure of carousing males with vivid scenes of men raping, beating, and killing women. (Keuls, Introduction, Chapters 2 and 6). The modern welfare state, however unwieldy it is, whatever niches it offers to petty and spiteful people, cannot explain the workhouses and whorehouses of Dickens' London.

[4]

For example, at one time aristocratic and wealthy men could rape women of lower classes, and sometimes of their own, with impunity. They could commit murder (called duellng) without arrest or imprisonment. The argument that these privileges should be extended to ordinary men of all classes, in the name of freedom and democracy, ought to make us laugh. Similarly, at one time the wealthy members of the ante-bellum Southern culture owned large numbers of slaves. A governmental edict redistributing slaves more equally, so that even the poorest white could own one or two black slaves, would not have contributed much to social justice.

Subtler and more interesting examples abound in our post-industrialist age. At one time only kings and queens could enjoy peaches and strawberries in December, fresh fish in inland cities. Nowadays the average consumer can have almost any food product at almost any time of the year—a great advance for society. Or is it? We are only now beginning to assess the hidden costs of the long-distance trucking and shipping network that transports our out-of-season treats, the preservatives and pesticides that make them perfect to look at, the economic wreckage of the countries where the cash crops are grown that end up on our tables.

At one time, only the very rich could own and run an automobile. The ingenuity and determination of one Henry Ford and his competitors ensured that by the late 20th century, almost every American could own independent transportation. It was a great advance for society. Or was it? Now we are facing the sobering fact that our vast fleet of automobiles may be costing us far more than we thought they were worth, and wondering how we might reconstruct the rail and trolley systems that were destroyed to make way for them.

On the other hand, there have been times when only the well-off could afford expert medical care, an education, decent nutrition, housing, or even a bath. No one would argue that these things should have remained limited to a small segment of the population; their extension to as many people as possible practically defines most progressive concepts of "the public good."

[5]

Douglas Oakes had photographed his 14-year-old stepdaughter posing topless on a bar, in the fashion of a Playboy model; this was kept secret from the girl's mother, and the girl herself tore up and buried the prints when she saw them. Oakes forced her to dig them up again; she informed her mother, who filed for divorce and initiated charges against Oakes under a Massachusetts child pornography law. Oakes was convicted and received a ten-year sentence, but the Massachusetts Supreme Judicial Court overturned the sentence and it went to the US Supreme Court. The ACLU was involved in Oakes' defense, and invited the American Sunbathing Association and the Naturist Society to file an amicus brief in hope of overturning the Massachusetts child pornography law . . . in defence of free speech, of course.

Feminist Nikki Craft was involved in a naturist test case at the time, filing suit against the Cape Cod National Seashore for prohibiting nude sunbathing. She and fellow female plaintiffs in *Craft vs Hodel* withdrew from the case after the ASA committed $15,000 to Oakes' defence (Letter to the *ASA Bulletin*, signed by Nikki Craft, Steve Paskey, Jon McCreight). Their lengthy statement concluded that "The naturist movement can no longer have it both ways. It cannot support and shelter pornographers (both child pornographers and those who exploit adult women) and expect the support of feminists. It cannot merchandise women in its publications, nor can it discount, attack, ridicule, snub . . . and oust women who express valid feminist concerns. (Nikki Craft, personal correspondence 1991-2)

I have ventured into so much detail here because the incident is remarkably illustrative of everything I have said so far and have yet to say. Nudism, commonly associated with liberalism and libertarianism, enjoys a progressive or positive aura. Certainly it is ridiculed and opposed by the Right. Yet, in a case where a man deceived a woman and exploited her daughter, the ASA was willing to commit thousands of dollars (an amount hardly available to the average woman or women's political group) to defend him.

And the ACLU, which at one time was the champion of the underdog, supported and encouraged his defence. The child's right to privacy, her mother's right to know what her husband is up to with her teenage daughter, the violation of these rights was of no interest to this "pro-freedom" association. The man's "freedom of speech"—his right to enjoy and possibly to market to other men (this kind of amateur pornography finds its way into the commercial mainstream in large quantity) the photographs he had taken by means of deception and the exploitation of his power as a man and an adult—those rights were worthy of the ACLU's high principles and purposes.

[6]

Colin Watson does this argument justice, in his excellent book *Snobbery with Violence*, when he contends that exposure to a literature of violence does not lead to instant emulation: "During long and lively discussion of the influence of 'undesirable' literature upon behaviour, there has come to light not a single case in which a formerly normal person has been induced by his reading to commit a violent crime."

But being an honest writer, he goes on to make the very relevant point that "The influence of books is of a more subtle and involved nature. The most lasting, and therefore the most serious, harm they can do is to confirm—to lend authority to, as it were—an existing prejudice or misconception. Lies fully grown have been sent as strangers into the world of books, but these have seldom survived for long. The prospect is much better for the lies already present in embryo in the mind—the 'feeling' that this or that is so—the 'fact' that 'everybody knows to be right' . . ."

Watson's primary concerns are racism and classism; like most authors regularly published in the leftist press, he does not care to tackle the Woman Question, save perhaps in a token chapter or paragraph. What we need to consider, though, is that large numbers of men, probably a clear majority, do harbour pre-existing hostility to and prejudice against women, and fall into his category of readers who may well be influenced and confirmed in their undesirable beliefs by literature which reinforces them.

[7]

When a woman reporter filed a story on the official practice of showing pilots pornographic films before their runs (during the Persian Gulf war), the US military made a half-hearted effort to suppress the story. She and other journalists made some noise about the censorship of various pieces of their Gulf war reporting; the story made a local paper and caught my attention. The first thing which struck me was that the military knows very well how male aggression is heightened by exposure to pornographic stimulus, and that they employ it intelligently (just like advertisers) to short-circuit sensible emotions like fear, doubt, or guilt—which might impair the performance of fighter pilots, or of bombardiers as they destroy the human lives below them.

The military doesn't want its fighting men in a state of happy, mellow loving-kindness as they go into action. They want their troops alert, aggressive, self-absorbed and devoid of compassion, as "manly" as can be. They would not be stupid enough to treat them to entertainments which made them kinder, gentler, more civilised people. There is, and will be as long as patriarchy endures, this inseparable tangle of masculinity, militarism, violence, pornography, and commercialised sex.

[This matter was covered in the *Washington Post* during January 1991, and then cited in the Fall 1991 *Media and Values Quarterly* (#56). Pilots aboard the USS *John F. Kennedy* watched pornographic films before flying their missions.]

References

Dworkin, Andrea. *Pornography: Men Possessing Women.* New York: Perigee Books, 1987.

Blumberg, Paul. *The Predatory Society: Deception in the American Marketplace.* New York: Oxford University Press, 1989.

Ebert, Roger. *Roger Ebert's Movie Home Companion.* Kansas City: Andrews, McMeel, and Parke, 1991.

Gubar, Susan and Joan Hoff, eds. *For Adult Users Only: The Dilemma of Violent Pornography.* Bloomington: Indiana University Press, 1989.

Harris, Marvin. *Our Kind: Who We Are, Where We Came From, Where We Are Going.* New York: Harper Perennial, 1989.

Keuls, Eva C. *The Reign of the Phallus: Sexual Politics in Ancient Athens.* New York: Harper & Row, 1985.

Koch, H. W. *The Hitler Youth: Origins and Development 1922-45.* New York: Dorset Press, 1975.

Koonz, Claudia. *Mothers in the Fatherland: Women, the Family and Nazi Politics.* New York: St. Martin's Press, 1987.

Mies, Maria. *Patriarchy and Accumulation on a World Scale.* New York: Zed Books, 1986.

Mosse, George. *Nationalism and Sexuality: Respectablilty and Abnormal Sexuality in Modern Europe.* New York: H. Fertig, 1985.

Shirer, William. *Berlin Diary: The Journal of a Foreign Correspondent, 1934-41.* New York: Alfred A. Knopf, 1941.

Weiss, Daniel Evan. *The Great Divide: How Females and Males Really Differ.* New York: Simon and Schuster, 1991.

Watson, Colin. *Snobbery with Violence: Crime Stories and Their Audience.* London: Eyre and Spottiswoode, 1979.

Acknowledgements:

I've been trying to write this essay for at least eight years, or perhaps trying not to write it. It has not been fun. I'd like to thank the acquaintances, friends, and lovers who during all that time tolerated my obsessive monologues and the depressing nature of my favourite topic of conversation. Thanks to those who agreed *and* disagreed with me while I tried to figure out what I really thought. Special thanks to the readers who suffered through the early, awful drafts: particularly D'vora T., whose thorough and incisive comments really helped in the very beginning, but also Nikki C., Lyn G., Kathy M., Melissa F. and Rachel H. each of whom corrected my follies or led me to a wider perspective. Extra special thanks to Julia, and as always to Irene: for her integrity as editor and friend. All of these women convinced me that "the paper from hell" was worth writing; without them it would never have been more than a pile of notes. And lastly, thanks to Andrea Dworkin, whose clarity, passion and sheer stubborn courage continue to amaze me. I dedicate the piece to her.

Contributors' Notes

D.A. Clarke: I became a feminist and came out as a lesbian at the very end of the seventies, into the "second wave" of the lesbian/feminist culture described here by K. Miriam. I soon became involved in political work against antiwoman violence and pornography; I believed that lesbianism was going to save the world, and that the revolution would take place not much later than next Thursday. When lesbian sadomasochism first began to manifest itself as a sociopolitical phenomenon, that was the end of my naive political idealism; it was the beginning of many years of disillusionment, confrontation, and intellectual struggle as an anti-porn and anti-sm thinker and writer. I was able to write this paper only because I still harbour an irrational hope: that we will one day build human societies in which bullying, greed, and contempt for others will be discouraged and devalued, rather than rewarded and admired as they usually are. I don't know how we are going to do this; I no longer expect it in my lifetime; I have to admit that it's unlikely (in the light of our history as a species so far) to happen at all. In fact, it's probably hopeless. Nevertheless, I intend to go on trying to make it happen. I hope this paper will be of some use or help to someone, somewhere, engaged in the same struggle.

Jamie Lee Evans: is a Feminist-Activist Mixed-Blood Asian "lesbian of color." She works for Women against Rape and the Aunt Lute Foundation in San Francisco. She likes orgasms, but as her friend Michelle Anderson says, she wouldn't sell her brain for one. She'd rather be destroying pornographers.

Sharon Lim-Hing was born in Jamaica in 1962. Her writings have appeared in *Piece of My Heart: An Anthology of Lesbians of Colour* and *Sinister Wisdom*. She is editing an anthology of writing and artwork by Asian Pacific lesbians and bisexual women to be published by Sister Vision Press.

Anna Livia: is the author of four novels and two collections of short stories and a translation of the work of Natalie Clifford Barney. Her new novel, *Bruised Fruit*, tells the story of a lesbian, a hermaphrodite and a bisexual serial killer. She is currently working on a PhD in French linguistics at UC Berkeley.

Kathy Miriam, a graduate student in the History of Consciousness program at UC Santa Cruz, is a radical lesbian feminist and an unabashed theory head.

Pat Parker, Black lesbian-feminist, health activist, and writer of five books of poetry, *Jonestown and other madness, Child of Myself, Pit Stop, Womanslaughter,* and *Movement in Black* died of cancer in June 1989. Her courage and passion are greatly missed.

Irene Reti: My parents are both child surivors of the Holocaust and I was the first person in my family born in the US. My writing has been published in *Ghosts of the Holocaust, Word of Mouth*, and many HerBooks titles. I am currently working on a novel about children of Holocaust survivors and an essay on feminist ethics and gardening.

HerBooks Titles
P.O. Box 7467 Santa Cruz, CA 95061

Mail orders welcome. Please include $1.50 postage for the first book, .25 for each additional book. (Bookstores 40% discount. Write for our catalog or order from Inland or Bookpeople.)

Childless by Choice: A Feminist Anthology
edited by Irene Reti / $8.95

Cats (and their Dykes): an anthology
edited by
Irene Reti and Shoney Sien / $10.00

Bubbe Meisehs by Shayneh Maidelehs:
an anthology of Poetry by Jewish Granddaughters
about Our Grandmothers
edited by
Lesléa Newman / $8.00

Lizards/Los Padres
lesbian-feminist stories
Bettianne Shoney Sien / $7.00

Sweet Dark Places
poems by
Lesléa Newman / $8.95

Love, Politics and "Rescue" in Lesbian Relationships
an essay by
Diana Rabenold / $3.50

To Live With The Weeds,
poems by D.A. Clarke / $7.00

messages: music for lesbians, cassette
D.A. Clarke / $6.00